UNHOOKED GENERATION

UNHOOKED GENERATION

The Truth About Why We're Still Single

JILLIAN STRAUS

New York

THEY CAN'T TAKE THAT AWAY FROM ME
Music and Lyrics by GEORGE GERSHWIN and
IRA GERSHWIN
© 1936, 1937 (Renewed 1963, 1964) GEORGE GERSHWIN
MUSIC and IRA GERSHWIN MUSIC
All Rights Administered by WB MUSIC CORP.
All Rights Reserved

Dialogue on pp. 89–90 from *Everybody Loves Raymond* appears
courtesy of HBO Independent Productions, Inc. Used with
permission. All rights reserved.

Library of Congress Cataloging-in-Publication Data

Straus, Jillian.
Unhooked generation : the truth about why we're still single /
Jillian Straus.—1st ed.
p.   cm.
ISBN 1-4013-0132-0
1. Single persons—Psychology.   2. Interpersonal relations.
3. Man-woman relationships.   4. Commitment (Psychology).
I. Title.
HQ800.S78 2006
306.81'5'0973—dc22   2005052508

Hyperion books are available for special promotions and premiums.
For details contact Michael Rentas, Assistant Director, Inventory
Operations, Hyperion, 77 West 66th Street, 11th floor, New York,
New York 10023, or call 212-456-0133.

FIRST EDITION

1   3   5   7   9   10   8   6   4   2

For my parents,
Joe and Jody Straus,
for teaching me to love
and to dream

CONTENTS

UNHOOKED
GENERATION

1

Introduction

Unhooked Generation

*First comes love, then comes marriage,
then comes the baby in the baby carriage.*

—CHILDREN'S RHYME

It was half past eight on Friday night in New York City. Here I was, on yet another first date with an "interesting" thirtysomething accountant named Jeremy. He had a square jaw and a mane of black hair. We were sitting in a candlelit restaurant in Tribeca packed with hipsters, drinking a bottle of white wine and talking politely about our jobs. I was thinking to myself, tiredly, could this be the man I spend the rest of my life with? But even though the conversation was engaging and clever, I found I could not help checking my watch. I knew already that chances were it was just another evening, in what felt by then like a lifetime of first dates. It had been three years since my last relationship. I wondered how many more dates I had to go on before I found "the one."

My thirty-four-year-old friend Drew, a newspaper reporter in Chicago and a serial monogamist, has a string of failed relationships behind him. Blessed with a striking visage and charm, Drew has no trouble finding dates. He dated Audrey, a petite blonde, for two years before she moved in with him. Prior to Audrey, it had been Suzanne for two years, and before her it had been Terry, on and off for four years. Women fall hard for Drew, and in turn he falls in love easily; but ultimately his relationships break up because—even though he says he desperately loves each of these women at the time he is with her—he can't get to the next level with any of them.

My friend Michelle, twenty-eight, an Atlanta elementary school teacher with offbeat good looks, is afraid to give love another chance after having been dumped countless times. She often calls me crying, asking: "What is wrong with me? Or is something wrong with the guys I am choosing?" When her friends meet somebody new, she waits for the axe to drop on them, too. This once easy-going woman has become quite cynical.

Ian, thirty-one, a Los Angeles lawyer, is also having trouble in his romantic life. He was engaged at twenty-five, but his fiancée called off the wedding. She said she wasn't sure she wanted to get married; her parents had had a "bad marriage" that had made her too suspicious of marriage in general to take the ultimate step. It took Ian six years to get serious with someone again. About a year into his new relationship, he and his girlfriend Clara discussed living together and getting engaged. But when they started to look at apartments, things became tense between them; Clara had gotten a new job and was becoming more independent in the relationship, and Ian was anxious. With every fight, he questioned whether the relationship was right. Before a lease was signed, the two had broken up. Clara says now, "It just wasn't perfect enough for him."

By the time I myself had turned thirty, I was realizing that I had spent hours on the phone with both my male and female friends all over the country discussing their relationship troubles. The conversations with men were anguished, and the conversations with women were tearful. These people have full lives—busy jobs, close friends, and passionate interests. Yet I couldn't help noticing that the topic of our failing relationships dominated almost every conversation. Though they lived in different parts of the country, came from different kinds of families, and worked in different professions, so many of my friends were echoing the same sentiment: they were frustrated, confused, and even depressed about their romantic lives. Some had turned to their parents for guidance. But the older generation, no matter how sympathetic, didn't seem to truly understand our plight or to have advice that was really applicable to us. It was as if the two generations were speaking a different language.

These conversations made me wonder what was going on with my peers. I started to ask myself: Do we just talk more about our unhappiness with relationships than other generations tended to do? Or could it be that our generation is indeed having a particularly difficult time in the search for love and commitment?

When I began to ask that question out loud, my life changed completely. Men and women both would practically pin me to a wall to talk to me about this issue: they spoke of lonely years between serial relationships, painful breakups, and bad dates.

At the time, I didn't have any of the answers they so clearly craved. I didn't have a clue about how to find love and commitment myself, despite the fact that my own parents had seemed happily married for forty-two years. But I began to understand that something unusual was going on with us; this issue seemed to resonate so widely and deeply. What was happening? How hard could it be, after all, to court and pair up? Generations had done it since time immemorial. Were we immature, or just unlucky? Misguided, or just appropriately picky? Were there pressures on us, perhaps, that were a greater hindrance than the pressures that had borne down on other generations before us?

I decided I would have to try to find out, if I could, what was going on with our generation—and whether there were any answers out there for us when it came to our search for love. This book explores why so many of us face a rocky, detained, or pit-fallen road to long-term commitment. Why is the search for love so difficult for us, and what can we do about it?

First I will take you through my own story as a typical thirtysomething single, urban professional. Then I will examine the cultural factors uniquely affecting this generation, what I call "The Seven Evil Influences," that undermine our relationships every day. Through the stories of single men and women I will explore how these influences make us look at potential partners, how they confuse the dance by which we court each other, change how we perceive commitment, and pose real obstacles on the path to romantic fulfillment. Throughout this book you will see particular terms highlighted, many of these terms Gen-Xers will recognize and laugh at, other terms I have coined to give a name to modern dating approaches and scripts that are also unique to this generation. (See the dictionary at the end of the book for a complete list of terms.) Finally, I will take you through the stories I discovered of actual, real-life, happy couples. I will tease out the lessons they learned and show you how we can all, ideally, share in the joy of these insights about long-term love.

To get a fuller picture of our dilemma, I decided to interview one hundred single people living in various cities throughout the United States. I focused on Generation X—the first generation after the baby boom—because no other generation has faced the same set of choices and concerns. Some generations are defined by war or depression; absent these events, generational identities are arbitrarily defined. I decided to look at men and women between the ages of twenty-five and thirty-nine because it is the cohort that at its oldest was born just after the boomer era, and at its youngest is now old enough to date seriously.

This book is not a broad sociological study. I did not seek to pin down a breadth of data, but rather to identify a generational atmosphere and attitude. I started asking questions of my own network, which is mostly composed of people who are younger, urban, and educated. Word spread; networks alerted other networks; responses started to pour in—and I made a concerted effort to widen my reach. I decided to interview people in six cities in different geographic regions of the country: San Francisco, Los Angeles, Chicago, Minneapolis, Dallas, and New York. I put the word out in these cities through Internet postings, ads in local newspapers, Web sites such as Craigslist (which connects people in urban areas to jobs, apartments, and dates). The queries I sent out varied but essentially asked for respondents who were looking for a partner. I also randomly scouted men and women in places in which single people congregate. I interviewed one hundred singles, ranging from middle to upper middle class, most of whom had some college education or had completed their BAs. About one quarter had some graduate education. Thirty percent were people of color. Why did I focus on these younger, mostly urban, educated singles? Because these were the people who had the same questions I did.

The identities of everyone in this book have been disguised. I have changed names and altered personal features and locations to gain the most candid accounts possible. However, the experiences and the words that appear in the pages that follow are rendered just as these men and women spoke them.

Throughout this book, I examine the issue of commitment between men and women of this generation. For some Gen-Xers, commitment is defined by marriage; for others, it is defined in other ways. I decided to limit my subjects to heterosexuals, because the emotions and current politics surrounding gay courtship and gay marriage deserve to be the subject of another book.

In every city to which I traveled, singles abounded. I encountered scores of singles in bars in New York, packs of singles at street fairs in Chicago, throngs of singles at crawfish boils in Dallas. The singles I met in all of these cities all over the country seemed to have much in common with one another: similar interests, values, and educational levels. Over and over again, single people in each of these cities told me it was hard to meet other singles because of where they lived. In other words, I saw crowds of people all looking for someone special— all unable to find what they were looking for, and all convinced the problem was where they lived. It was clear to me that geography was not the problem, however—the problem had something to do with the seeker's approach.

My subjects each gave me over two hours, some in the middle of their workday, to tell their stories. They were all hoping for some magical answer to the question of why they haven't been able to find love or, having found it, what the key is to making it last. Many told me they hadn't shared any of these intimate details about their love and sex lives with anyone: not lovers, therapists, or best friends. I listened to men and women who had never been married, people who had been divorced, and those who were in less than fully committed relationships. Though the individuals varied, many common themes emerged. They all seemed to share an attitude. This attitude makes them part of what I call the "Unhooked Generation."

Some articulated their longings for a relationship in a way that struck a powerful chord with me. Laura, a thirty-four-year-old physical therapist in Minneapolis, with freckles and a raspy voice, expressed herself with poignancy as we sat in a run-down pancake house in downtown Minneapolis. "For three years," she told me, "I woke up miserable every day [because] I didn't have someone in my life. It wasn't societal pressure, it wasn't my family, it wasn't my biological clock. I just wanted someone. It was a constant source of sadness, every single day."

I heard many variations on this theme from my interviews with one hundred singles. Although most rarely stated feelings of emptiness this directly, I saw the pain in their faces, heard it in their voices, and sensed it in their body language. My stereotypical assumptions about commitment as it relates to gender began to fade. Men and women expressed similar longings. Some of the people I spoke to had been struggling in bad relationships for years. Others dove deep into a commitment until they found a flaw and then moved on to the next partner. Still others had a series of superficial short-term unions—all in a failed quest for that ultimate bond. It became clear that my generation craved connection and longed for intimacy—just like every generation that has walked the earth—but many of us didn't know the path to get there. We wanted to share our family frustrations, career dilemmas, dreams, and fears. Yet hundreds of thousands of intelligent, successful, emotionally stable, attractive twenty- and thirtysomething men and women remained single despite their longing.

Numbers bear out our frustrations: According to the Census Bureau, one third of men and nearly one quarter of women between the ages of thirty and thirty-four have never been married, nearly four times the rates in 1970.

Part of the reason for the growing single population is the high rate at which men and women are delaying marriage. According to the Census Bureau, the average age of first marriage for women is now twenty-five, and for men twenty-seven. This is the first time in U.S. history both sexes are choosing to marry so late. In other words, our generation is living a historic extreme of having multiple committed partners prior to marriage—and therefore we are experiencing historic levels of heartache and disappointment. It is not that we don't marry; eventually, most of us will. But many who do get there do so with a lot of angst—which leads to self-doubt, as well as skepticism about the lasting bonds of commitment. From broken engagements to multiple breakups and angry ultimatums, making a lifetime commitment for this generation has become a new kind of challenge. The common denominator in your story and mine is not that we are individually incapable of relationships, or that our partners are. The problem is much deeper.

This book does not mean to idealize any other era. There are many benefits of being a member of this generation but, as with most treasures, each has a downside. Other generations have documented their particular struggles with relationships and marital life—from the suppressed housewife and distant husband of the '50s to the broken homes of the '70s. There is nothing new about the struggle for intimacy and commitment. But the old struggle has a particularly new guise.

On my journey of listening, I realized that everything I learned in the culture about how to find and sustain a relationship was wrong. In fact, I discovered that the people who seemed to have the secret were doing the very thing my peers and I had been advised to overlook or scorn. I will take you through the voices of these people who are looking for love in ways we will all recognize but are counterproductive. You will see the obstacles, pitfalls, and challenges that threaten people our age in their search for love. But remember, at the end of this journey there is hope. I will also introduce you to people who have found lasting love by using an approach that is the opposite of what we are taught to believe. My hope is that my experience and this book will help you learn faster than I did. Don't lose heart—it's only by looking at these obstacles that we can see differently.

Let's start with my own story. In the comfortable, leafy suburb of Los Angeles where I grew up in the 1970s, most of the families were intact and most of the homes had three or more bedrooms. My mother and father had, for the most part, a good, solid marriage. My father ran a small business and my mother was a substitute teacher. In spite of being long married, they indeed seemed to have passion in their daily lives: amidst visits to pediatricians, parent-teacher conferences, and busy work schedules, their love affair kept simmering. Every morning when my father left for work, he would bring my mother the newspaper in bed and kiss her good-bye. One morning, I found him watching her sleep; he said to me, "Look how beautiful your mother is" as the sunlight flooded their bedroom.

Their attachment seemed to bloom more openly when my sister and I went away to college. When I returned home over Christmas break as a freshman, my father was away on business. My mother and I were watching our favorite TV show: it was, I am embarrassed now to report, *Knots Landing*. We were lying on the couch and my mother dozed off, but when she heard the sound of the key turning in the door she suddenly sprang awake. "Dad is home," she said, with a lilt to her voice. When he walked in, she smiled at him with her chin lowered; her eyes looked up at him like a high-school girl with a crush. Although he had only been away since that morning, they acted as though they'd been separated for a week.

I remember teasing my mother by asking her whom she loved more, my sister and me or my father. Quiet and pensive for a moment, my mother hesitated and then looked up at me and said delicately, "You are my child. I could never love anyone more, but your father is my life." At the time I was shocked by her response and, as I recall, a little hurt. But her honesty helped me to better understand their union. Their relationship was based on friendship and deep mutual respect—and they shared the feelings of adoration that I could not wait to share with someone of my own.

Love happened for me for the first time in my sophomore year of college. I fell in love with a dark-eyed senior named Alessandro who was half Korean and half Italian. He was the first man to give me the feeling of what lust felt like when it was mixed with love. In his Bob Marley–filled flat, with its dead joints in the ashtray, I would gaze at him while he slept after our lovemaking. We had a typical college romance: studying side by side in the library, attending formals, and going to football games together. We loved to stay up late and discuss politics and philosophy. The mere sight of him across the grassy quad excited me. After a year, I wanted to get more serious—but Alessandro wanted to play poker, hang out with his friends, and find a job. Though we were seriously in love, I never dared to utter the "M" word, for that was not a part of the college vernacular when I was becoming a young adult. And Alessandro himself was a child of divorce; marriage was the last thing on his mind. I found that reality too painful to endure; we broke up in my junior year. Instead of a purely romantic reverie, which in past generations of lust-dazed men and women may well have led to the altar, we went our separate ways. That was my first experience with heartbreak, but certainly not my last.

Aside from the pain, that experience had one more side effect: I started to question whether love could indeed last a lifetime. I heard Alessandro talk about his childhood and his parents' vitriolic divorce and now I had experienced firsthand with Alessandro that love didn't necessarily mean "happily ever after."

The fact that someone like me—whose parents were actually well matched—had already absorbed a seed of doubt about lifelong commitment attests to the fact that the marriage ideal was no longer intact as I became an adult. As I mentioned earlier, my generation faces a host of cultural factors that, somewhere along the way, make us look at commitment and marriage in a different way than our parents did. After all, we have more options, more skepticism, and more heartbreak born of experience. For the women of my generation, marriage is no longer the singular feminine goal. And for the guys—well, you can imagine. They don't have to look at divorce to question marriage and commitment; all they have to do is open the latest issue of *Maxim* magazine.

So I, from an intact home, went into the world—and into a typical postcollege experience of dating and serial monogamy.

Certain commentators have made the point that an early adult experience of serial monogamy leads to a lot of heartbreak and cynicism, and that it can actually undermine faith in marriage and commitment. One of these is Rabbi Shmuley Boteach, author of *Kosher Sex*. Rabbi Boteach argues that, by the time you have seriously dated a couple of people, slept with them, and left them or been left by them—that is, before you ever make it to the altar—there is "scar tissue" on your heart. Maggie Gallagher, who wrote *The Abolition of Marriage,* makes a similar case. These books defy the conventional wisdom of our generation—handed down to us by the boomers—

that a series of intimate relationships prior to marriage can strengthen the marital bond, much like training wheels strengthen the skill of bike-riding. The problem is—as I began to feel after listening to my own heart and hearing the feelings of my male and female friends—when you painfully experience your training wheels falling off a couple of times, it is hard to trust your bike.

After graduation, I fell in love twice more, experienced my share of heartbreak, broke a few hearts (in retaliation?), went on dates, and submerged myself, over the course of my twenties, as did many of my peers, in a handful of long-term relationships. They all ended miserably, and they made me question what it was that I was searching for and how I would find it. My peers had their own relationship angst. Even those who were certain they wanted marriage had lost some faith as their own relationships failed.

In spite of intermittent years as part of a couple, for most of my adult life I have been a single woman. I spent my twenties at a high-powered job I had long aspired to: working in television production for *The Oprah Winfrey Show*. I was passionate about my work; I earned a good salary and got promotions over the years; I lived alone in a nice apartment; I ate out; I shopped; and I traveled when I could. I embraced the sexy identity of the independent single girl—and I wore it with enjoyment and pride.

I had what was in many ways an enviable life—rewarding work, plenty of male and female friends to share free time when I had it, evenings out, movies and dinner. I went on lots of dates, sometimes so many that I felt as though I was on an assembly line, and sometimes so few that I felt like a spinster. Unlike many of my friends, I never hated dating; I enjoyed the unexpected conversations and the mystery of meeting someone new.

But the chaos of my career in television kept me moving so fast that sometimes I didn't even notice what was missing in my life; often I was so busy with my job that I hardly noticed how lonely I was. But when things calmed down, when the pace slowed, when the noise quieted, something happened: after the production was over, and all the videotape had been edited and the voice mails returned, I felt a silence stir inside me. In these darker moments, I felt that swelling loneliness that I did not have someone with whom I could share a life.

My busy career and active social life entertained me for long periods, but I slowly realized they were not going to fill the void when those empty feelings came up. These were emotions I was actually ashamed of; the girls on *Sex and the City* would sneer at me if they knew. The feminist in me did not want to let myself fall prey to the specious belief that I couldn't be happy without a man in my life. But I had to face that fact: The woman in me wanted a man. The need to "connect" intimately with someone was indeed powerful.

This term **"connection"** is a popular buzz word for my generation. It means a deep emotional intimacy—an intense bond. My single friends and subjects expressed the same longing. It seemed ironic that a generation that was so eager for connection seemed so terribly disconnected.

This exploration for me was a life-changing one. Wisdom indeed came from some unexpected places. I saw myself in so many of my subjects, and realized these themes were indeed universal. I was touched by my subjects, every one of them. As I wrote the pages of this book, I literally heard their voices and they became my guides. I knew from our hours together that something had to change.

Ironically, a few months into my research, I met a wonderful man, whom I started to date. It was time to put theory into practice. At first I resisted this relationship, as I thought it would interfere with my role as a student of single life. But I fell in love as my perspective grew broader. For the first half of the year that I was writing this book, I was a single woman whose romantic life seemed as though it had been stalled for a decade. For the second half, I was a woman becoming more and more deeply involved with a mate. So I write with both the skepticism of an independent woman with a string of failed relationships, and with the optimism of a slowly opening heart. As I went on this journey, I dropped my own self-defeating expectations and began to overcome my own fears of commitment. I want to thank the people who shared their heartbreak and happiness with me because it helped me discover what I was doing wrong. I hope that what I learned from all those who spoke to me about love will help me find my true love this time—just as I hope that the disappointments and fulfillment they shared will help you find yours.

2

How Did We Get Here?

*"It is so hard these days to connect with someone.
You've got all these factors. It is like aligning the moon, the sun, and the
stars. I can't believe it ever happens.
It seems like a miracle."*

—LAURA, 34

Stephanie was calling at nine p.m. on a weeknight—upset again. She was asking rhetorically, "Why is it so hard? My mother fell in love and got married. . . ." Even as I tried to calm her, I felt myself asking the same question.

Why was it so damn hard?

After all, we as humans should innately be drawn to certain people and fall in love. But my generation seemed to be having a particularly difficult time.

I wanted to be able to answer Stephanie's question—and my own. So I did what I was trained to do: I looked at the research and started asking questions about love and commitment.

Here is what I found: The cultural influences specific to this generation together have created obstacles in our search for true love. I found that almost all of the Gen-Xers I spoke with were affected by at least one—if not all—of these factors, what I call **"The Seven Evil Influences." These are external influences that bring about in** us internal inclinations that, in turn, stand in the way of our finding the love we are seeking.

Evil Influence #1: The Cult of I

We are all familiar with the ultimate boomer I.D., "the Me Generation." Boomers focused on their own needs, wants, and goals in a way that was unprecedented at that point in history. We broke their record: circumstances surrounding Generation X took that self-oriented heritage to an extreme new level. Members of our generation, according to a recent study by the General Social Survey, now prioritize marriage below the pursuit of educational and career goals and achieving financial independence. The problem is that people of my generation, after years spent accomplishing these goals, realize in retrospect that they were achieved at great cost to their personal relationships.

Sean, a thirty-two-year-old software salesman living in Los Angeles, said that graduate school took him away from the love of his life. Now he longed desperately for a relationship like the one he let go. He explained: "I was in love, but I left (my girlfriend) and went back to school. I thought I was too young to have found 'the one' and I needed to focus on my career. I would probably be married to her now if I hadn't. She is the only girl I have ever thought about marrying. I feel like I am paying for it now. I haven't found another woman I loved this way. She is the stick I measure every other girl by." Sean's regrets were profound, but at the time, he could not imagine passing up the chance to have his exact dream—on his time line, with no modifications.

Women, too, in this postfeminist generation, talked about putting their career goals first—sometimes to the detriment of their love lives: Robin, a thirty-four-year-old doctor from San Francisco, said: "I spent the first twenty-seven years of my life focusing on career, and pushed guys aside in college and throughout my residency. I got everything I wanted: a job I love, in the city I love. I accomplished every professional goal. Then I began to ask: "What else do I want?" Now that she is established professionally, she can't seem to find the man she wants to be close to personally. What she wants now is a relationship—something, until recently, she never took the time to seek out or develop.

It isn't only the autonomy brought on by specific career goals that force relationships to the back burner: it is also the autonomy of an obsessive sense that one's independent lifestyle must not be curtailed in any way. A number of the people I interviewed found themselves unhappily single long after they experienced all the things on their to-do lists. The men and women I spoke to often—consciously or unconsciously—resisted relationships, said they gave up their one-time "soul mate," or couldn't make their relationships work because in one way or another a deep commitment might impair their self-oriented, carefree lifestyles or cause them simply to make compromises. Many of my unhooked singles wanted to "do their own thing" and expected love and relationships to be on their schedule, on their terms, and to come without too much personal sacrifice. This is fine if you are happy to remain single, but if you want intimacy, this won't work.

Where did this intense independent streak in this generation come from? The majority of Gen-Xers had two parents who worked outside the home, often leaving the children with more autonomy than they had had themselves. Learned independence is one outcome. In fact, the characteristic of "being independent" is so revered by this generation that many of the men and women I spoke to said it was the quality they most valued in another person (and in themselves). They feared giving up these independent identities. Mia, a thirty-four-year-old Chicago district attorney who was born in Colombia, explained: "I think part of me and my life has to die for a relationship—my identity as single girl, being so busy. That is counter to being in harmony in a relationship."

This is a sharp contrast to the 1950s when a majority thought that single individuals were "too selfish or too neurotic." In the Kelly Longitudinal Study, which consisted of several surveys of six hundred randomly selected white middle-class men and women who formed families during 1935–1955, a housewife described her independence as if it were a chronic disease or an allergy that flared up now and then to bother her. The removal of the stigma associated with single-hood that has occurred since then is certainly a positive development, but in many ways it has been taken to an extreme. In contrast, in to-day's independence-obsessed culture, it is embarrassing to admit that you want a relationship. My unhooked singles often were reluctant to admit their desire for a partner: "I don't need a man in my life. I don't need or want a relationship because I am lacking anything. I only want it to add or enrich," said Alyssa, a twenty-six-year-old New York advertising account executive from a traditional Chinese-American family. Similarly, Brandon, a thirty-one-year-old writer from Dallas, said, "I am pretty good at being alone. I would be fine if I was single forever but sometimes I do feel like it would be great if it 'happened' with someone."

This external "Evil Influence" can lead Gen-Xers to develop the inner inclination to believe that we will be able to schedule love for whenever we are ready for it, and that it shouldn't involve much personal sacrifice. It can also result in a "What have you done for me lately?" attitude in relationships.

Evil Influence #2: Multiple Choice Culture

Our consumer culture has always offered individuals choice, but to-day the number of choices consumers have has grown exponentially. New developments in our fast-paced lifestyles, driven by the Internet and electronic media, have multiplied choices and made more options just a click away. We are the first generation to grow up computer literate, as well as being plugged into TV, cell phones, instant messages, and cash machines. New technologies are the signature of this generation, distinguishing it, for better or worse, from those that came before.

"The best choice without commitment" says an ad for GoPhone. These kinds of messages surround us. How does consumer culture magnified by this technology affect our love lives? First, online dating sites offer access to more potential partners, and create a sense that countless options exist, options that make it difficult to commit to one person. From the choice of dozens of different kinds of toothpaste to hundreds, if not thousands, of channels on television, in a consumer culture we are told that having more choice is always better. But all these choices can contribute to indecision, anxiety, dissatisfaction, and, in some cases, even clinical depression, as many recent studies have pointed out. For example, when making a big purchase such as a computer, the dozens of models, brands, and countless technical options can become so overwhelming that you may actually be tempted to avoid making a decision. When you finally do make a purchase, you may in fact feel dissatisfied by the choice you made, always wondering if you should have made a different choice.

Just as you go on the Internet to find a car that fits your exact specifications, you now can do the same thing when choosing a partner. This has created a new framework for looking at relationships: A generation of men and women is now looking widely, but perhaps not deeply. No longer hoping to meet someone by chance at church or a dinner party, the creation of an online community suggests that our true soul mate might be just one more click away. These communities of singles in urban areas, artificially created by the Internet, have resulted in a vast dating marketplace. In a marketplace with so many choices, the notion of finding your soul mate can seem daunting at best. Yet the promise always exists that if one relationship doesn't work out or gets old, you can log on for something better. With a glut of choices, it is easy to see why so many men and women remain single, despite their search for their "one and only."

The multitude of choices can lead Gen-Xers to develop an inclination to commodify our partners. We do this by creating detailed "checklists" so we can theoretically design our own ideal mate. In the process we may begin to constantly compare our partner to what else is out there, making us perpetually dissatisfied with our choice.

Secondly, technology messes up communication. People used to talk to each other in courtship, whether it was in poems, or the whispering of sweet nothings or seductive words over the telephone. Now, the same lover trying to reach his beloved on e-mail or IM risks miscommunication. While these capabilities may offer convenience and immediacy, when it comes to romantic communication they can create emotional distance and are prone to misinterpretation. For example, a friend of mine who had been dating her boyfriend for two months was confused when he did not call over a three-day period. He instead e-mailed her. She took his curt and impersonal one-liners to mean he was losing interest. But when she finally saw him she realized his feelings hadn't changed at all. He said, "I've been swamped at work. I thought it would just be more efficient to e-mail." Ironically, the more connected this generation is by technology, the more distant we are from each other personally. Cultural rules have not caught up with our technology. **This can lead Gen-Xers to develop an inclination to rely on technology for intimate communication, so that we often become noncommittal and inexpressive about our true feelings. This communication is then prone to misinterpretation.**

Thirdly, Gen-Xers' ability to commit is weakened by the fast-paced nature of technology—which replaces and outdates itself continually—as well as by the short-term nature of consumer commitments. In the fifties, a partner—like a pair of classic earrings, or a job—could be for life. Today, we want to connect with and discard or alter our information and our consumer styles at a moment's notice; it is not surprising that as we acculturate to this fast and disposable view of our surroundings, love would be seen as fast and disposable as well. Why would you chuck the wallpaper and keep the same old girlfriend?

But technology is just one factor that contributes to our multiple-choice society. When it comes to staying the course, in consumer and job terms, our view is: Why? Why not switch to a better brand or a better career? From short-term leases to month-to-month memberships, this generation doesn't have to lock into many long-term commitments in its everyday life. Because of our surrounding culture, we tend to expect our connections to be immediate—but our investments not necessarily long term.

But what does this do to our romantic lives? In our one-click culture, this generation's impatience, and obsession with novelty, finds the finality of marriage more difficult. Claudia, thirty-two, who designs a line of jewelry in Chicago, expressed her frustration with marriage's permanence—not surprisingly, comparing the relationships of today to shopping: "Marriage is very final; it is like the most expensive thing in the world, and it is not returnable." **This mentality can lead Gen-Xers to develop an inclination to be impatient with potential partners, refusing to give them and the relationship a chance. Finally, it can make us hesitant to stick with one person.**

Evil Influence #3: The Divorce Effect

This is not a new point, but it bears repeating in this context: more than any previous generation, Gen-Xers are the products of divorced parents. This legacy leaves many of us conflicted about marriage and at a greater statistical risk of divorce ourselves. This experience of growing up in a divorce culture, perhaps more than any other single factor, influences this generation's own romantic relationships. It is well documented that children of divorce are often relationship- and marriage-challenged. According to E. Maris Hetherington, author of

For Better or for Worse, "Children of divorce are often reluctant to commit wholeheartedly to marriage, have few relationship skills . . ." But for those who grew up in the eighties, divorce was on every corner, every block, in every classroom. It is hard for us to even imagine a time when marriage truly meant "till death do us part." Whether your parents stayed together or split up, if you are in my generation, this wave affected you. Even if you are from a happy home, chances are many of the people you grew up with or date aren't. Widespread divorce has put a permanent dent in the idea of "happily ever after" and created a generation of men and women highly skeptical of marriage.

Growing up in an age of divorce not only leads to the inclination to be skeptical of marriage, but it also inflates our expectations. As a thirty-two-year-old Dallas woman in human resources named Roslyn put it, "That person has to be so amazing for me to get married. I have to be so sure so that I will never get divorced."

Evil Influence #4: The Inadvertent Effects of Feminism

Let me be clear: I consider feminism a spectacular influence. Nothing that my generation of women values could have been achieved without the feminist movement. Yet there is no question that it has had a dramatic impact on our romantic relationships, for better and for worse. In the 1950s, as I noted, most women, with few options for a fulfilling life outside of marriage, agreed that a less-than-ideal marriage was much better than no marriage at all. They also felt that marriage itself offered benefits that compensated for their husbands' shortcomings. Marriage provided "peace," the promise of a "comfortable life," "status," and "stability."

But the sixties, of course, presented another side of marriage. It was in 1963 that Betty Friedan changed the course of history with her groundbreaking work, *The Feminine Mystique,* which declared that middle- and upper-class women in suburban America had "a problem that has no name." The problem, she said, was their boredom: the result of an identity that revolved solely around the needs of others. She wrote: "In the feminine mystique, there is no other way for a woman to dream of creation or of the future. There is no way she can even dream about herself, except as her children's mother, her husband's wife."

Friedan's work thankfully opened many doors for women, but it also helped uncover the cracks in the foundation of marriage. One effect of her exposé of domesticity was the spotlight it cast on the dark side of certain aspects of domestic life. With the groundswell of discussion that followed, the experience of marriage, once generally viewed as peaceful, stable, and comfortable—although not without its shortcomings—now was also seen by many as being oppressive, laborious, and unfulfilling, for women in particular. In addition, as women gained ground in the workforce and supported themselves, of course their dependence on marriage faded.

While Friedan's "problem that has no name" stemmed from virtually a one-option life as homemaker for the middle- and upper-class women of our mothers' generation, many women of our generation suffer from a different problem. We have multiple choices, but not multiple lives, and the message is that in one life we can't do it all. Those of my peers who focus assertively on career often find love elusive, and those who make marriage the first priority but don't find a partner or grow disappointed with their unions worry that they have passed up a career. While only one road—in my mother's day—was too few, a map with no clear directions, the postfeminist map, seems daunting. Our relationships can suffer as a result. **In addition, men and women in a postfeminist world often have contradictory expectations of each other and inflated expectations for marriage itself.**

Moreover, while the clearly defined dating script of the past that was based on traditional gender roles is outdated, there is no new dating script to replace it that accounts for changing gender roles. **This can often result in courtships that are fraught with confusion and mixed messages.**

Evil Influence #5: The "Why Suffer?" Mentality

My generation sees little value in suffering. Many generations are asked to sacrifice, but for this generation, whose biggest sacrifice is giving up carbs, the nobility of suffering seems outdated. Many men and women of this generation have no sense that working through pain may ultimately make us and our relationships stronger.

Victor, a thirty-nine-year-old health care consultant from New York who is in a long-term committed relationship, said: "If I am suffering, whether or not I am married, I'm leaving." It is difficult for many of this generation to accept that commitment involves good days as well as bad ones. It is not that this generation is lazy; we are working longer hours than did many previous generations. But when it comes to love, we have a sense of entitlement. We feel that all should be easy—and if it isn't, one should get out of the relationship.

This "Why suffer?" generation is the first to live in a culture in which therapy carries no stigma. While therapy certainly has merits, the patient-therapist relationship can set the tone for one's expectations of relationships outside the shrink's office, too: We can become acclimated to the notion that an ideal union is one in which the other person exists to attend to all our emotional needs—just as our shrinks do. Many of us have a sense that simply because a need is felt, that need should be met.

In addition, many members of this generation have become accustomed to the notion that it is healthy to analyze, focus on, and talk about their discontentment continually—just as they do with their therapists. And when complaints are validated—as they often are in therapy—the once-valued ability to overlook flaws and difficulties has been dismissed as denial or, worse yet, victimization. A friend of mine told me that although her boyfriend brings her many wonderful joys, she can't talk to him the way she talks to her girlfriends. She wonders, despite all his good qualities, if she should break up with him because he can't fill the need she has to communicate with him in that same way.

In addition, when therapy doesn't offer relief fast enough for patients of this generation, many are encouraged to turn to medication. And while medication certainly is necessary for people with many various mental and emotional conditions, the mainstreaming of anti-depressants and anti-anxiety medication for immediate relief for normal, everyday Gen-X pain reiterates for my generation that we should not have to be uncomfortable even temporarily. According to Keith Valone, PhD, a psychologist in Pasadena, California, this impatient generation seeks shortcuts to everything, including happiness. Valone notes that about 40 percent of his patients are on psychotropic medication, something he attributes to "an unwillingness to tough it out and go with uncomfortable feelings . . . you miss a whole channel of information that could help you lead a better life. Growing and changing require suffering a little bit. I'm not saying suffering is good. But learning to put up with moderate levels of discomfort is important."

The assumption that any amount of suffering is unnecessary has taken hold in romantic relationships. This generation often seeks immediate relief from temporary emotional pain that may ultimately short-circuit them out of long-term relationships.

The inclination resulting from this "Evil Influence" is for many Gen-Xers to feel entitled to a relationship that is always fun and easy; when the relationship has challenges and requires work, we often believe it is time to move on to the next one.

Evil Influence #6: The Celebrity Standard

Our culture's preoccupation with celebrity life also hinders our perceptions when it comes to relationships. Celebrities indeed have become this generation's icons—icons that stand for luxury, youth, and the single life. The 24-7 news cycle and proliferation of thousands of channels has created a "media monster." Entertainment magazines like *People* and *Entertainment Weekly* were of course also born in our generation, making the lives and relationships of superstars daily fodder. Gen-Xers grew up on an unprecedented diet of tabloids and celebrity gossip. Ordinary people become hypnotized by the deluge and crave an identification with these celebrities.

Media images send the message that making money has far greater value than nurturing a relationship or starting a family. It is well documented that this generation aspires to a higher standard of living than previous generations. The average Gen-Xer spends more on luxury goods than the average baby boomer, according to marketers. And although Gen-Xers inherited harsher economic conditions than their parents, according to Karen Ritchie, author of *Marketing to Generation X*, many Gen-Xers view marriage as a compromise to their financial independence. I found this to be true of many of my unhooked subjects. It is easy to see how the attainable 1950s fantasy of having a family and owning a home with a white picket fence could, for some of this generation, be replaced with an unreachable fantasy of an extravagant, fast-paced lifestyle. The glamorous picture of a life of material excess, constant change, and excitement dwarfs the image of the simplicity of domestic family life.

In addition, celebrities themselves have seemingly disposable relationships, sending the message that mates need not be mates forever. These stars seem to wear their romantic partners like accessories, changing lovers as quickly as their latest albums hit the top of the charts. Images of these celebrities, single or not, often show them globe-trotting around the world without partners, surrounded by people of the opposite sex and attending fabulous parties until dawn. Even those famous people in "committed" relationships fail to serve as role models because tabloids never cover the celebrities that have been long married and are happy; rather, they focus on the more dramatic aspects of these unions such as weddings, breakups, and divorces.

The standard set by celebrities can potentially lead Gen-Xers to the inclination to get caught up in fantasy images of luxury and the single life that are often at odds with real commitment.

Evil Influence #7: The Fallout from the Marriage Delay

As I mentioned earlier, the average marrying age today for men is twenty-seven and for women is twenty-five. This is the first time in U.S. history both sexes are choosing to marry so late. While the delay gives men and women of this generation time to focus on their careers and personal goals, as well as to mature, the delay can also become a major contributing factor to our difficulty in finding a partner and committing to a relationship. The marriage delay has become both a cause and an effect of a noncommitment culture. Falling in love for the first time is easy: expectations are few, cynicism is minimal. Once you've done it more than once, though, skepticism can set in and baggage accumulates. **The inclination of Gen-Xers who delay marriage can be to become more protective and less open to love and again have inflated expectations. In addition, after many years of prolonged single life, compromise can become more difficult.**

The marriage delay also raises the stakes of a relationship. Obviously, women facing the pressure of their biological clocks are at a disadvantage in a culture in which potential male partners face fewer physical pressures to commit. And unfortunately, as a woman ages, she may become less desirable because of both her decrease in fertility and the scrutiny of a youth-obsessed culture. She may face aging out of the dating market. **This can lead to men's and women's conflicting timetables and "agendas."**

All of these factors affect our generation every day, creating obstacles to the attainment of permanent love and commitment. These influences contribute to this generation's struggle for relationships, raising our expectations to Everest-like heights.

3

Outrageous Expectations

The Search for "The Checklist,"
"The Upgrade," "The Soul Mate"

1. Loves children
2. Hard working
3. Has the ability to listen and communicate
4. Poised
5. A team player
6. Looks good/sexy
7. Balance—the ability to keep things in perspective
8. Enthusiastic/love of life
9. Shows initiative
10. Knows how to be a friend
11. Patience
12. Has religious conviction
13. Determined and persistent
14. Considerate of others
15. Has self-control
16. Has faith that things work out
17. Loyal

18. Ambitious
19. Loves sports
20. Loves music
21. Loves to travel
22. Good mental, physical, emotional condition
23. Sense of humor
24. Alert
25. The ability to be herself

The above is a list of the twenty-five things Derek, a thirty-seven-year-old pharmaceutical sales representative living in a suburb outside San Francisco, wants in a wife. He is not alone in having a long and detailed set of expectations.

The majority of my unhooked informants had such high expectations for their potential partners that their **"checklists"** would be just about impossible for any mortal to fill. I found that many men and women of this generation treat dating as they would a trip to the supermarket: they enter the store with a carefully-thought-out list of all the things they have to have in a partner before they consider buying.

I was recently at an apartment party in the Bay Area, where I met Derek. Twenty- and thirtysomethings crowded into the small apartment with vaulted ceilings, crimson walls, and coffee-colored wood floors. The women wore low-slung jeans and lace tops that looked like lingerie. The men were dressed in collared shirts and wore their hair greased back. U2 was playing on the CD player and two women sandwiched one man, dancing provocatively close. A man donning a backward baseball cap acted as bartender, mixing up Ketel One and cranberry juice in the kitchen while passing bottles of beer to his buddies. The conversation among one group of women ranged from tales of a recent ex-boyfriend sighting to the cancelled engagement of a roommate. There I met Derek, a soft-spoken man with an upbeat countenance and smoky grayish eyes that offset his chocolate brown skin. He agreed to sit down with me a few days later for an interview.

When we sat down to talk, he wore a long-sleeved Gap T-shirt that flattered his slight but toned frame. Although timid at first, he was eager to speak. He immediately told me about his own smorgasbord of needs, his "checklist"—which he had actually written down on a piece of paper thirteen years ago and has kept ever since. "I believe in making a list and sticking to it. Don't deviate." The list hadn't helped Derek find true love; though it dates from when he was twenty-four, he has never married.

Whitney, a twenty-five-year-old Los Angeles Web developer with a sardonic sense of humor, has her own list. She has kept what she calls her "dream list" carefully tucked away in a special box in her closet for years:

Open-minded
Cultured
Handsome
Comfortable with self
Well traveled
Into the same things I am
Can teach me new things
Gregarious
Generous
Emotionally available
Traditional
Sensitive
Communicative
Motivated
Independent
Charming

Derek and Whitney were among many who looked to a checklist to help guide them on the search for "the perfect mate." Of course not everyone had actually written down such a list, but many Gen-

Xers had much more than a vague notion of what they were looking for in a partner. Tina, in public relations, who is still alone at thirty, told me, "The older I get, the more conscious I am of my checklist."

"So, what are you looking for?" I asked.

"Someone tall, educated, well-traveled, ambitious but down to earth, and compassionate. Someone who can teach me things but would also allow me to have my own experiences. And someone who has lived but is not too old," she said.

The "checklist" mentality plays such a prevalent role in our current culture that some therapists even advise their lovelorn patients to create one. New York psychotherapist Marilyn Graman, author of *There Is No Prince,* who has led workshops on relationships for the past twenty years, urges her patients to make a list of "must haves" and "can't stands" to prioritize what singles are looking for in a relationship.

Of course, a checklist can be extremely helpful as a guide—as a way for one to become more self-aware and to clarify one's own values. But the checklist, as it is being used today, has morphed from being a general guide—used with the understanding that no one person is likely to embody everything—into a rigid can't-live-without list that serves in practice to exclude wonderful potential mates and to set the bar too high for any one person to reach.

A friend of mine, newly single, has put out plenty of inquiries to acquaintances and coworkers that she is looking to meet someone. The question she almost always gets in return is: "What are you looking for?" The cultural script of a checklist is so entrenched that her friends assume that she must have a specific set of requirements that she is looking for in a mate, even though she has never mentioned a checklist to any of them.

The idea of a checklist is, of course, hardly unique to this generation. Obviously, men and women have always had some kind of list of requirements for a spouse. A hundred years ago, the higher you were in a social hierarchy, the more choices you had—except, of course, the choice to marry outside of your social class. But even most people of the peasant class had a very basic "checklist," one that might have looked something like this, very broadly speaking:

For both: *Is this person from an appropriate background and religion?*

For him:	**For her:**
Can she bear children?	*Is he sober?*
Can she keep house?	*Can he support a family?*

A friend's great-grandmother, for instance, who married in Russia in 1905, was looking for a Jewish man from her village whose family was respectable, who was not known to drink, and who was himself able to provide food and shelter for her and her children. Issues such as personal attraction, social compatibility, similar senses of humor, shared politics, or shared interest in leisure activities were completely beyond consideration.

Today our requirements are much more specific. One man, a twenty-eight-year-old magazine editor from New York, told me he had to be with someone who "took his breath away" when she walked into a room. He is still alone and waiting to be breathless. A thirty-year-old artist from Minneapolis said she wanted to find someone who "could enjoy a beer and a hotdog at a ball game, but also could appreciate a nice dinner over a great bottle of wine." The most notable element of the various checklists I heard were how few of the points had anything substantive to do with the meat-and-potatoes of long-term commitment, such as shared values, kindness, and dependability. Rather, my unhooked singles seemed more concerned with shared hobbies than shared values.

Checklist requirements often focused on finances and age. Some men made comments such as: "She can't be too high-maintenance." "High-maintenance" is a term used by many Gen-Xers to describe someone who expects the finer things in life and could be expensive to "maintain" (even if she theoretically could maintain herself). Similarly, a few women noted: He has to be "successful." Other people I talked to had specific age requirements or "cutoffs." Men often wanted younger women. Women, on the other hand, sometimes opted for older men whom they believed would be more mature and established in their careers.

Many Gen-Xers have a highly detailed mental picture of what they want and they have created a list so that they can, theoretically, locate this person. This is a result of a blend of Evil Influence #2 (Multiple Choice Culture) and Evil Influence #7 (The Fallout from the Marriage Delay). The glut of choices when combined with years of dating experience often results in singles with extremely particular specifications for a mate. Nick, thirty, a stocky, olive-skinned legal recruiter from a large Italian family, had a fairly specific checklist. We sat down at his home in a suburb of Chicago with hardwood floors, Pottery Barn furniture, and stacks of tattered, dusty books. To start, he wanted someone fun, professional, outgoing, and passionate about work, but not too aggressive. He stressed that someone physically attractive was a high priority; preferably someone petite, since he was only 5'9"; in addition, he had a fondness for brunettes. It was also very important to Nick to find a woman who could "hold her own" at a party, so that he would be free to socialize. Finally, he stressed that she could not be a lawyer. Even though Nick was a legal recruiter who spent most of his time around lawyers, and the women he was most likely to meet were lawyers, he had at one time been an attorney and found them to be "too opinionated." Nick had had a lot of girlfriends throughout his life, but not one of them met all of his criteria. He, like others I interviewed, took a practical approach to the challenging, seemingly never-ending, process of finding the right partner by relying on the checklist. Nick is still unmarried.

Why do Gen-Xers need a checklist? Perhaps more to the point, why would such a thing appeal to them? The "checklist" mentality appears to offer a skeptical generation, with a lack of role models and guideposts, some practical assistance by making one's requirements in a romantic relationship concrete.

Second, it seems to offer something more tangible to rely upon than chance. The idea of meeting someone across a crowded room and falling in love, the way my parents did, seems unlikely to many in our cynical, overscheduled generation. So, rather than rely on the power of chemistry or happenstance to lead him to a romantic relationship, Nick preferred to use a checklist as a guide on his search.

Time pressure is also a factor for busy Gen-Xers. Many of Nick's peers see the checklist as an efficient dating strategy: If someone has the qualities on their list, then the relationship warrants pursuing. But if something is missing, they just move on. My friend Marcy, a twenty-nine-year-old psychologist from Denver, met a man online who told her on a first date: "When you are meeting people online, if there is no immediate chemistry, you have to move on." After that comment, she did just that. The mind-set among many Gen-Xers is: Don't invest time and emotion with someone who doesn't meet all of your requirements. And as singles grow older and their time to find a mate grows shorter, many seekers feel they do not wish to waste time on an intriguing or lovable partner who does not have the requirements they believe they need in a potential lifetime mate. The checklist lulls them into thinking they are on track in the search.

Frequently, my respondents' expectations for potential partners were not only excessive, but some were actually internally contradictory, making satisfaction in a relationship truly difficult, if not impossible, to achieve. For example Ariel, a twenty-eight-year-old esthetician from Dallas, described wanting to find an "alpha male" but she said it was important to her that he was also sensitive. Nick, too, was conflicted. No one ever seemed quite right to him, even if she met most of his qualifications "on paper." Nick gazed pensively out the window and told me that his last relationship of three years had ended, but he couldn't say why, since the woman seemed to fulfill most of the qualities on his list. Nick himself offered a glimpse of self-awareness that suggested that perhaps the list was, for him, a defense against intimacy and commitment: "Maybe I just haven't met the right person—or maybe I have all these impossible expectations because I am not capable of true intimacy, and I've let some quality people go because in one way or another they didn't meet my requirements." Nick is not alone. Impossible expectations were an obvious way to shirk commitment for many Gen-Xers. After all, if the list of requirements is specific enough, it will be difficult for anyone ever to satisfy the seeker. Nick, like so many with "a list," harbored a skepticism about marriage brought on by a blend of many of the Evil Influences.

The Gen-X continual quest for personal happiness is informed by the consumer world around us. The definition of domestic fulfillment has changed; it is more like catalog shopping for something fabulous than rocking gently on the front porch. Since marriage is no longer a sole source of economic security for women, nor a prerequisite for having sex or children, our motive for marriage today is to boost that happiness quotient. But this kind of "happiness standard" is hard to achieve and by definition very challenging to sustain.

A former coworker of mine, Felicia, now a thirty-two-year-old publicist from Boston with a two-year-old daughter, is contemplating divorce after only three years of marriage. She describes her husband as "an incredible husband and father" and as being her best friend—but she feels they should have more passion in their lives together. She said: "For me it is all about choices. Nowadays, if you are not totally happy, there is no incentive to make it work." Her attitude was clearly affected by Evil Influence #2 (Multiple Choice Culture) and Evil Influence #5 (The "Why Suffer?" Mentality). She explained: "In the old days, if you were a single mom on your own, there was the threat of being ostracized. Demi Moore is a single mom. So are Calista Flockhart and Angelina Jolie. There is no threat of being stigmatized. And my ex won't have to take care of me. I can provide for myself. We marry for more of the right reasons today because you don't have to marry to be taken care of. But it is also easier to walk away if it is not everything you want."

Felicia's awareness of the contrast in her situation to marriage in "the old days" shows how "happiness" in marriage has evolved in a way that makes it almost impossible to sustain for those of our generation. In 1950s studies of marriage, the same themes echo among the women interviewed: women reported that their marriages were "happy" if they were stable and provided security; they were pleased that they were part of a family, that they had a provider for the family, and that they had "companionship"—a word that came up regularly then, as the great positive in the married state. But companionship scarcely figures today as something that we might be grateful for; it is a low-key, everyday kind of thing—not "hot," not exciting, not hyperstimulating. Indeed, male companionship can be had easily enough for all of us with male friends—and without the price of commitment. So the one thing that marriage can most reliably deliver—companionship—just doesn't rate very high on the desire scale anymore.

The prospect today of living a lifetime with someone who gives you only stability, a family, and companionship? Grounds for Valium—or divorce.

In contrast, for men and women in the 1950s, an independent life outside of marriage carried enormous risks. Single men who did not marry were seen as unstable and immature by their colleagues and employers; single women with children, of course, were ostracized, and those without children often lived at home and were considered "old maids."

One would assume that this enforced expectation of marriage would drive my unhooked informants crazy. However, it would seem that the opposite was often true: marrying because one had little choice paradoxically led to higher levels of contentment within marriage. Indeed, women in particular reported high levels of satisfaction in their marriage despite what we would call real sources of discontentment. In the Kelly Longitudinal Study, over 80 percent of both the husbands and wives in a random sample of three hundred white middle-class couples who formed families from 1935–1955 rated their marriages as being "above average," and nearly two out of three rated themselves as being "extraordinarily happy" or "decidedly happier than average." And yet, when many of the middle-class homemakers in the study who reported that they were satisfied with their marriages were asked whether they would marry the same person again, they responded that they might not. Elaine Tyler May, author of *Homeward Bound,* concludes from this not that marriages in the fifties were qualitatively better; rather, she attributes the greater marital satisfaction in the 1950s to a willingness to compromise—and even to accept and make the best of more realistic expectations. In other words, she holds, the married people reported that they were happy because, in effect, they were determined to see the best aspects of their situation.

That certainly does not appear to be the case today. In fact, over the past three decades, people have become less satisfied with marriage, according to the research of divorce expert and psychology professor E. Mavis Hetherington, PhD and author of *For Better or for Worse: Divorce Reconsidered.* About her longitudinal study of two generations of couples, she writes: "Over half our couples in the parents' generation who were in their first seven years of marriage reported themselves to be 'very happy,' versus one third of the counterparts in their children's generation. Twenty percent of the parents reported themselves to have had a serious marital problem in the past year, at the seven-year mark, versus 38 percent of their young children during the same period of their marriages." Hetherington writes, "Conflict, inability to resolve disagreements and lack of mutual supportiveness were more common in our contemporary couples. Some of the difficulties in these couples were associated with trying to juggle family life and two careers. They complained about the lack of time spent together—especially time without children—and this new generation of better-educated, more economically self-sufficient young women were very vocal and resentful about inequities in the division of labor in the household." These studies, when put side by side, shouldn't suggest that we should lower our expectations for a partner in a way that is unnatural to us; but they may suggest that learning to appreciate what we have, in a consumer culture that stresses what we don't have, is an urgent skill to make love deepen and grow over time.

Expectations in fact determine happiness, according to new research. *Mind Wide Open* by science writer Steven Johnson discusses the new "science of happiness." He looks at recent research about dopamine, a chemical that acts as a "reward accountant" in your brain.

It turns out that the dopamine level—the happiness level—one's brain receives depends less on the experience itself than on one's expectations regarding the experience. If you expected a date to be great and it's just fine, you might feel let down afterward. However, if you expected to sit home alone, you might feel happy after the just-fine date—because you are glad to be out at all. You only get a pleasurable "dopamine cocktail" if something happens that is better than what you expected. In other words, inflated expectations of our lovers lead to low dopamine in our brains—resulting in unhappiness. More realistic expectations for a partner give us a better chance of regular dopamine injections—in other words, regular bursts of happiness.

New York psychotherapist Florence Falk, PhD, who has treated hundreds of patients over the course of twenty years, counsels many relationship-troubled men and women of this generation. She told me, "It is about expectations. They have very false expectations. People think that [a relationship] should be perfect and when parts of the [partner's real] self start to emerge, and the idealism shatters, it is exceedingly painful, disappointing, and enraging [for my clients]." Behind these expectations, she feels, lurks a real fear of intimacy:

"Patients of this age whom I see are more noncommittal, or very romantic—which can be another form of being noncommittal. If you are overly romantic, then no one is quite right," she explained.

A man I was once dating said to me: "I think your expectations are the only thing that are keeping you from truly being happy in this relationship." He had a point. Although his observation was astute, he, too, was trapped in his own expectations. On more than one occasion he half-jokingly compared me to ex-girlfriends who were more athletic, more domestic, and more light-hearted—all qualities he secretly hoped his future wife would possess.

While high expectations can contribute to delayed marriage and commitment, the delay itself also raises expectations. Many of this generation feel that since they have waited this long for the right person, they are not going to settle now. Years of life on your own may make you much less willing to compromise and at the same time "the checklist" may actually continue to grow. As a generation in which both sexes are choosing to marry so late, by the time most of us are ready to tie the knot, we have already experienced a number of permutations in partners and have grown picky. As my friend Beth, a thirty-one-year-old IT specialist who recently moved from Los Angeles to New York after a breakup, put it: "The longer you hold out, the more perfect you want it to be." Anthropologist Helen Fisher, PhD, author of *Why We Love,* makes the case that the longing for romantic love is hardwired in our brains. She writes that we each have individual "love maps," molded by a combination of childhood experiences and biology, that guide us to fall in love with one person or another. As we enter school and make new friends, we engage in infatuations that mold our likes and dislikes: "As we develop more durable love affairs as teenagers, we continue to expand this personal psychological chart," she writes. "And as we ride the waves of life—and experience a few romantic disasters—we trim and enrich this mental template." In other words, with each failed relationship, the checklist or set of prerequisites becomes even more defined. And so the more partners one has, the narrower the search becomes. So, in a vicious cycle, just as time increases our desire for a mate, it also makes finding someone who meets all of our expectations far more difficult. Evil Influence #7 (The Fallout from the Marriage Delay) in this sense can have a negative effect, particularly when it is combined with Evil Influence #2 (Multiple Choice Culture).

To further complicate matters, consider that these "checklist" requirements don't even address the common desire of a Catholic to marry a Catholic or someone of a Korean heritage to find someone else with that same heritage. When race or religion are added to the checklist, the chance of someone finding "the one" may become even more daunting.

Take, for example, the desire of an African-American woman who wants to be with an African-American man. It is well documented that African-American women in particular have a tougher time finding mates and marrying. Forty-nine percent of black women in the 30-to-34 age range have never married, compared with 20 percent of white women, according to estimates of the U.S. Census Bureau. Why? Experts attribute this largely to the dramatically decreased pool of marriageable African-American men. African-American women reach higher levels of education than their male counterparts; therefore, their checklists tend to be even harder to fulfill, since fewer mates share both their race and educational level.

Deborah, an attractive thirty-six-year-old African-American woman with high cheekbones, who exudes confidence, is an assistant advertising executive in Oakland, California. Full-figured and sensuous, on the day I spoke with her she was wearing a maroon-and-white flowered dress that hugged her hips. We met on a Saturday afternoon in the staid conference room of her office building. She told me she broke up with her last boyfriend because he wasn't on a professional career track. He was a manager at Kinko's. "He wanted to marry me. We were together for nine years. I paid for everything and took care of everything," she declared. "A black man needs a degree, a job, and a normal schedule. You want someone to be your equal."

Black women, of course, have a legacy, descending from the family upheavals brought on by slavery, of having to take on the role of being heads of their households. So they are in a cycle of having to accomplish—which then further narrows the pool of equal-status partners for them.

Deborah and some of the other African-American women with whom I spoke also complained that the pool of desirable black men is actually shrinking as more black men choose to date white women. A study of residents of twenty-one cities performed by M. Belinda Tucker, PhD, a psychologist at UCLA and coeditor of *Decline in Marriage Among African Americans,* found that 78 percent of black men had dated interracially at least once, as had only 53 percent of black women. Deborah, who is still holding out to date a man of her own race who is also successful, explained that many of these men aren't so eager to tie the knot. "The successful black man is either married, or he knows he is a hot commodity so he doesn't want to settle down," she said with an imperious tone. Of course men and women of other races also have their own particular set of dynamics that can make their search for a mate equally challenging.

Deborah and I had talked for about an hour and a half when her friend Kevin, thirty-four, a broad-shouldered African-American man wearing a blue golf shirt and khaki shorts, joined our conversation. They had been friends for years but never dated. Apparently they weren't each other's "types." He was a business consultant from the Bay Area. He agreed with Deborah. As a successful black man with an advanced degree, he spoke from experience when he said: "If you're a black man with a good job, you've got a lot of options and chances are you are in no rush to marry."

A frustrated Deborah, still maintaining a strong tone of voice, talked about yet another dilemma that kept African-American women from finding men: "As a black woman, if you do have it all together it is scary to a black man. I wonder if men aren't asking me out because I am the typical strong black woman. What do you think, Kevin?" She looked squarely at him.

Kevin replied, "It is a challenge for a strong black woman not to break her man down. She needs to carry her strength without saying it. My mother did it. She made the decisions in our house, but made my father feel like he was the one making them. If a black man doesn't feel he is making the decisions and that he is the protector, he wonders what his role is. He needs to feel needed. Black women have to empower their men," he said. "I am sorry to say it, Deborah, but that is the way it is."

Not only does Deborah have a checklist that is very hard to fill, she is also led to feeling ambivalent about the qualifications in her own bio. Indeed, yet another dating conundrum.

Internet Profiles and Endless Possibilities

Whitney, the one who kept her checklist in a box in the closet for years, found that her checklist had not helped her to meet anyone, so, like many Gen-Xers, she went online looking for a relationship.

While an extensive checklist is almost a guarantee that our search will be never-ending, at the same time, consumer culture and technology, both part of Evil Influence #2 (Multiple Choice Culture), reinforce this way of dating. Because this generation has checklists, we go on the Internet to date, and because we have the Internet, it enables us to have checklists. The Internet gives Whitney and the rest of us hope that we can indeed find a partner with all our specifications. Some Internet dating profiles are literally set up like a checklist, so that the user can check off desired qualities for a potential mate.

On Match.com, for instance, the user can select the specific physical characteristics he or she wants in a mate, such as body type, height, hair, and even eye color. Beyond the physical requirements, the site also allows users to select what profession and salary one requires in one's date.

The Match.com site actually encourages the user to be as selective as possible, by offering "personality" and "physical attraction tests." The idea is that the tests will help you determine even more specifically the requirements that you have, even teasing out subconscious ones, so that the site can find you a mate tailor-made to your specifications.

I decided to take these tests to see how they actually worked. When I took the "physical attraction test," I was asked to pick out a man who "wowed" me from about a dozen pictures. I was also given a set of drawings so I could select the type of nose, facial structure, and body type that I found most appealing. Technology that allows you to handpick a partner by a specific physical description is one effect of Evil Influence #2 (Multiple Choice Culture). This kind of Internet dating is designed to allow the user to look at all the choices and types of people so that he or she can then narrow down the pool. I was then asked to identify, through a show of pictures, what kind of chin, what shape lips, and what shape and size breasts I have. I had no idea my search for a date on a Web site would make me feel like a mail-order sex worker!

After being subjected to this humiliating test, I was a little disappointed to find that I didn't get to choose the penis size of my potential date. It seemed only fair.

While I was surprised at how detailed the test was when it came to appearances, it was no different from the physical expectations of some of my friends and informants. Among my female friends, I heard over and over again the need for a tall man, or a full head of hair, or a certain body type. Men, on the other hand, said they had such requirements as the need for buoyant breasts, a toned body, or a certain color of hair. Some of the men admitted to me that "looks" were the "number one" requirement on their checklists. I asked a friend, a thirty-three-year-old dentist named Garrett from New York, exactly how important physical appearance was to him. He replied, "Looks [if unattractive] are the terminator." In other words, if a woman didn't meet his exact physical standard, she was immediately terminated from a potential relationship with him. A handful of men told me it was not enough for their potential partner to fit their attractiveness quotient now, they also were concerned about how their mate would age. One of my unhooked males called it "looks retention." He wanted to find someone whom he suspected would maintain her good looks judging by her current body type and skin.

The personality test on Match.com was less intrusive than the "physical attraction test," perhaps, but just as specific. I was actually able to select my preference for a man with very particular characteristics, such as how he handles stress or whether he is punctual.

Many online dating sites offer "compatibility tests" or "personality profiles" that are advertised as "scientific"; that is, they promise to screen all potential partners for mutual compatibility. This "scientific" approach to compatibility, of course, is self-centered: It involves finding someone who meets *your* ideal preconceived picture of a mate. It effectively screens out anyone who might open you to the possibility of falling in love with someone who may not conform to all your advance specifications. The process appeals to "the checklist mentality," of course, but ignores the very real element of chemistry and connection—which, by definition, cannot be predicted or quantified. Furthermore, this approach can be misleading, because it operates with the presumption that the person taking the test is telling the truth, which is not necessarily the case.

"The Upgrade"

Despite the handful of much-talked-about success stories in which couples have met on the Internet and married, I have found from my interviews that the checklist approach to relationships in an online, consumer culture is often potentially dangerous in the search for a partner. It lures you into believing that you can customize a partner to your specifications the way you can a car. Many online dating sites send this very message to users, sometimes in the most unsubtle way: "Today you can find anything online, why not love?" reads the Date.com website, acknowledging potential dates as yet another acquisition. This kind of commodification is clearly a result of Evil Influence #2 (Multiple Choice Culture). It is not surprising that many Gen-Xers actually use the phrase **"the total package"** to describe what they are looking for in a mate. "The total package" refers to a combination of good looks, personality, and brains. To Gen-Xers, this dream man or woman is a "package," just like every other acquired commodity.

Internet dating also creates a multiple-choice dating atmosphere that helps the user go on lots of dates, but doesn't necessarily set that user up to form a deep connection with any of the people on these dates. A friend of mine recently e-mailed a man on Matchmaker with whom she seemed to have a lot in common. However, she never got a chance to know him. He e-mailed back: "I'm flattered that you like my profile but I am dating like seven people right now." A woman I met at a party described a new man she met online as "like a kid in a candy store." She said since he discovered Internet dating, he went from having few dates to having so many. He confessed to her that with so much opportunity, he was hesitant to commit to her.

These Web sites reinforce the belief that there are countless people out there who may meet all of your specifications. Many young people begin to wonder: Why settle for someone who doesn't meet all of my requirements when the Internet provides easy access to millions of other singles who might? Internet technology, as it appears on many dating Web sites, fuels the consumer's constant desire for something better. If one date doesn't work out perfectly, trade up for something better: hop on JDate.com, Lavalife, or Match.com and shop for an **upgrade**. My criticism is not of Internet dating itself, but of how the technology is being used and shaped by Gen-Xers and the culture.

This attitude, of course, is not limited to the computer screen. Preston, a thirty-four-year-old sales manager from Dallas, says he has ten qualities on his checklist. His current girlfriend only meets about six of those requirements. He admits that when he is out, he is in **"upgrade mode."** Even when his girlfriend is standing by his side, he says, he constantly compares her to what is out there: "You start saying to yourself, 'Am I getting everything I want?'" He explained that he looks around and in about ten seconds he can size up other women and decide if there is someone that he is tempted to "try." He asks himself if it is worth risking his relationship with his girlfriend to try to get to know these other women he sees from afar. Although he may sound crass, his insecurity exemplifies the **"disposable love"** mentality that has become common among my generation.

Fear of Settling

Preston, like many singles, will tell you that he is trying to ensure that he is committing to "the best" woman possible because he desperately fears "settling." "You wonder if you are 'settling,' by taking six out of the ten qualities. When I was younger, I always thought I could get all ten. Now I don't know. My options are becoming more limited. The singles pool gets more shallow the older you get." "Fear of **settling**," a phrase I'd often heard from both the men and the women with whom I spoke, is just about the worst fate a Gen-Xer can imagine. The intense phobia that you might settle for someone who doesn't meet all your expectations keeps many in our generation from making a real commitment. "I think people date a lot and are waiting for the fairy tale, but it doesn't come, so they settle just because they want to be married," said Reed, a thirty-five-year-old engineer living in Naperville, a suburb of Chicago, who has vowed never to settle. Everyone in my peer group seems to know—and discuss—someone whom they think has 'settled'—taken whatever he or she could get.

Where does this almost morbid fear arise from? It's the friend whose husband has untrimmed nose hairs and horrible table manners; perhaps it's the guy at the gym whose wife refuses to let him play poker. Whomever it is, that person's alarming relationship takes up an unusual amount of space in our mental landscape. One half of the couple, one thinks, lost the coin toss, while the other partner clearly scored.

In my psychological map, a friend of mine from high school, whom I'll call Angela, is the one who carries for me the specter of what it would mean to have "settled." Angela, who works in a nebulous position at a talent agency, is an adorable brunette with Shirley Temple curls and eyes the color of sherry. She is considerably smarter, more attractive, more personable, and much more sophisticated than her husband, David, who always strikes me as pretentious and grating with almost no personal appeal. (Of course, *she* is my friend so I may be a little biased.) David is an accountant who has specks of silver in his hair and an uptight dimple on his chin—John Travolta meets Dustin Hoffman. David pretends to be an expert on every topic and relishes an opportunity to share his knowledge. Angela, on the other hand, is humble and kind: there is nothing she wouldn't do for a friend. She is modest, yet also extremely well read and can talk sagaciously about any number of subjects. Angela's union is for me a kind of dreaded signpost of what could lie ahead if I "settle": Angela had dated quite a bit—from handsome actors to successful doctors—but no one had ever proposed. At thirty-three, Angela was ready to get married. She met David on a blind date—he was thirty-eight and also "ready." He took her to see *Tony n' Tina's Wedding* and prattled the entire time. I don't remember hearing about any fireworks or enthusiasm after the date, but before I knew what happened, the wedding was being planned. Five months later, Angela was Mrs. David James. Angela rarely expresses more than a passing complaint, the kind that most women might express about their husbands. What scares me, though, and reinforces Angela's marriage as my personal romantic horror film, isn't what she *does* say; it's what she *doesn't* say—or do. Angela doesn't gaze at David lovingly; she doesn't talk about him with veneration; and she rarely expresses overt affection toward him. Nothing about their union makes the still-single girl-friends around her say, "I want that." Now, this could be a very judgmental attitude—you can never know what is inside two people's marriage, and perhaps there is something between Angela and David that I can't see. But it is telling that so many of my friends and un-hooked respondents have an Angela of their own to warn them away from some—perhaps self-imagined—fearful abyss of a permanent union with the absolute wrong person.

For many Gen-Xers, any commitment may feel like settling because they don't really want to commit to one person. Many of the people I interviewed would describe it otherwise. They were emphatic that they would rather stay single than settle. "I want marriage, but not so badly [that] I would settle. I enjoy my life. I live in the city and have tons of friends. It wouldn't be devastating to be alone for the rest of my life. I would rather that, than be with the wrong person," said Lynn, a sanguine twenty-six-year-old nurse in Minneapolis.

Does this phobia about "settling" simply mask our generation's fear of commitment? Perhaps it is by raising our expectations so high that we are able to keep ourselves from facing that ultimate fear. After all, in order to enter into a long-term commitment, we all must "settle" to some extent. We grow up with a fantasy of what the person we choose to be with forever will be like—what he or she will look like, sound like, smell like. For some, the requirements are as specific as what the person would do for a living, and what kinds of tastes, likes, and dislikes they would have. But ultimately, we all must choose a real person and not an idealized image. What person can live up to a patchwork dream? It is easy to see how a fear of settling keeps us disconnected. If men and women of this generation found their perfect mates, they would be forced to commit fully to a relationship. Many aren't ready to take the leap.

Waiting for Mr./Mrs. Right

On a sunny March day in downtown Chicago, Peter, a spindly, 6'6",
thirty-two-year-old man with a clean-shaven head, wearing the red-
and-black sweats of his college alma mater, met me at a coffee shop. I
arrived early and grabbed a table in a quiet area of this psychedelic
place with pumpkin-colored walls and beads hanging in the doorway
that reminded me of Greg Brady's room. New age music played in
the background as billows of smoke lingered overhead.

When Peter walked over to me, I had to tilt my neck to meet his
eyes. We exchanged hellos and he shook my hand nervously. His
befuddled countenance and fretful body language gave way to an emotional floodgate. We sat down and he divulged that he had become
overwhelmed by his quest for the right partner. He was currently in
a relationship with a woman named Molly whom he loved dearly.
She happened to be sleeping in his bed at the time of our conversation.
He had lied to her in order to meet me, I was startled to learn:
he had told her he was going to the gym because he didn't want her
to know he was meeting me to talk about his relationships angst.
Molly loved Peter and, a year into their relationship, she had started
talking about marriage. Peter loved her in return, but he was not sure
he was ready to take the plunge. This wasn't the first time Peter had
faced this dilemma. His relationship before this one had been with a
woman named Katy. He talked about Katy with even more fondness
than he did about the trustfully sleeping Molly. The first time he uttered Katy's name, the sides of his mouth curled up with delight.
Katy also loved him, he said, and it was obvious by his adulatory description of her that he cared deeply for her. Katy had also made it
clear to Peter that she had wanted to get married. But the situation
had been identical: he was not completely "sure" with her either.
Katy grew tired of waiting and eventually assumed he was never going

to propose; she finally left him. "When I realized what I was letting go, I campaigned to get her back. It didn't work and I regret it," he explained with a vexed expression. Katy was now with someone else and it pained Peter. When he told me about Katy's new boyfriend, he looked down at the table and fingered the chrome sugar bowl.

Peter thought that something was wrong with him because he had been unable to commit not only with these two women but also with others: "I've had five serious relationships and I could have been married to four of the women. They were all amazing. Two of them were my best friends. All of them wanted the commitment and I didn't. It wasn't that they weren't right. I never took a chance." So after Katy, Peter did what many Gen-Xers do in a state of confusion—he went to therapy. The first thing he asked the therapist was, "Does this mean I am not in love?" After a couple of sessions, he came to the realization that a lack of love was not the reason why he couldn't commit. He also learned it wasn't that he wasn't ready for marriage: He wanted marriage and a family. He couldn't wait to be a father: "I don't know many things in life for certain, but what I do know is that I was meant to be a dad," he said as his face softened. And it wasn't that he wanted to play the field before he embraced family life: he didn't long for the bar scene, hookups, or the responsibility-free life of a single man.

Rather, after hours of analysis, he discerned that he was truly afraid that something better was always around the corner—and it was paralyzing him. At that moment, I could see his anxiety mounting as his thin shoulders crept up to his chin. He lamented, "I've met so many great women. I feel like they were missed opportunities in my life. But, at the same time, I don't want to feel like the door is closing, I want an escape hatch. I love Molly to death, but sometimes I think: who else is out there?" he said with frustration. "What if I am supposed to be with someone else?"

Peter articulated what I heard from so many of my unhooked

subjects and friends: "Until you fully commit, you want to **keep your options open**. . . . Is there a perfect mate? I probably have this ideal in my head and I am the first to admit she doesn't exist. But I hold out the thought—maybe."

This commonly spoken phrase, "keep your options open," stayed with me. "Keeping their options open" is a way many of my generation think they may avoid settling. The limitless choices this generation faces in all areas of life, including in their potential partners, play a powerful role in many young people's high expectations and inability to commit. The more choices men and women have for potential mates, the higher this raises their expectations; but the higher the expectations, the fewer the people that will meet that standard. In the back of Peter's mind was always the question: "Is there an upgrade out there? What if I settle for version 2.0 and 3.0 comes out ten times better?"

Barry Schwartz, PhD, author of *The Paradox of Choice,* contends that an overload of choice carries a cost. The cost, he says, is that choices can make you question the decisions you make before you even make them and can foster unrealistically high expectations. In a study titled "When Choice Is Demotivating," business professor Sheena Iyengar examined the issue of too much choice. She and social psychologist Mark Lepper, PhD, set up a display of exotic jams in a high-end grocery store. In one control of the study, six varieties of jams were available for tasting. In another, twenty-four varieties were available. The larger array of jams attracted more tasters than the smaller array, but when it came to buying, fewer choices actually meant larger numbers of purchasers. In fact, the difference was remarkable: *ten times* more people bought jam from the smaller display than from the larger. Iyengar speculates that a large array of options might actually discourage consumers because it forces an increase in the effort that goes into making a decision. Alternatively, they reason that the effort the decision-making requires can detract from the pleasure of making the decision. And finally, they suggest that too many options may diminish the attractiveness of what people see.

Peter just could not choose his jam. What he learned through his therapy sessions and own self-analysis was that his resistance to making a commitment stemmed from his many choices and consequently high expectations. He feared that if he picked the wrong person, he might repeat the mistakes of his parents who, in his eyes, did not have a good relationship: "As a result I have very high expectations for my spouse and what I want in a relationship. I want to go into it with total confidence that it is the right person," he explained with an intense tone.

I understood the obsessive focus on making the right choice. My high expectations had also paralyzed me in many of my past relationships. I remember, still with a tinge of pain, the time my first love sat on the bed of my college dorm room and said to me: "I just don't know if I will ever be able to meet all your expectations." He was the first man to say this to me—but certainly not the last. I had related to many of my single informants but, oddly, I related the most strongly to Peter—though the source of our problems seemed exactly opposite. My parents were happy, so I was scared of making the wrong choice; his were unhappy, so he was scared. We both narrated our problems as if they derived from our personal life circumstances, but obviously they came from something much bigger and common to our whole generation.

Peter, like many of the people I interviewed, became exasperated by his own indecisiveness: he didn't trust himself—or love. Falling in love had become an angst-ridden journey of second-guessing, constant indecision, and perpetual confusion. He felt he might never know if he made the right choice: "I hate it when people say they met the person and 'I just knew,'" he said. "My biggest fear in life is never knowing. That feeling may never come."

Does the "Right" Person Equal
an Eternally Happy Relationship?

Many of the singles I spoke to were clearly affected by Evil Influence #2 (Multiple Choice Culture) and focused obsessively on making "the right choice" in a partner, as if that alone would guarantee that the relationship would work. At the first sign of trouble, or with each argument, some of these men and women would conclude that it wasn't the right person. A friend of mine, a thirty-three-year-old New York musician named Hillary, with diminutive features and sultry style, said to me before she got married: "Everyone talks about how hard marriage is. Marriage shouldn't be hard if you chose the right person; it should be wonderful." After a three-year marriage, she is filing for divorce. It is difficult, even for her, to separate out all the different factors that contributed to her decision to leave her husband. Still, I can't help but think entering into the union with Evil Influence #5 (The "Why Suffer?" Mentality) and counting on having made the "right choice" played a role.

Many men and women of my generation seem to think of marriage as being like an Expedia vacation. They believe if they only select the right destination, all will be well. No one talks to them about the journey, or that it is sensible to be prepared for rain in paradise.

While earlier generations may have had unrealistic expectations when it came to the *institution* of marriage—for example, see the 1950s image of domestic bliss—this institution-skeptical generation instead seems to pin all its hopes and dreams on another *individual*. At least as important, but rarely discussed in our generation, are the choices that you make every day in a relationship that determine the success or failure of the romance.

At the end of our conversation, a frustrated Peter said, "I wish someone would hit me over the head and make it clear that I should marry them." I replied, "Maybe they already have." He sighed. I hoped that my conversation with Peter had as big an impact on him as it did on me. Seeing his profound angst opened my eyes to my own pattern of setting impossible expectations and second-guessing my relationships.

The Cynical Generation's Quest For Romantic Love

Despite the skepticism of Gen-Xers, their expectations for relationships often still include intensely romantic notions about love. Jim, a thirty-five-year-old banker with pale skin and dark, horn-rimmed glasses, refers to his quest for a mate as "the battle between **'the résumé'** and **'the buzz'**." For him, "the résumé"—his private term for what I have called "the checklist"—always seems to be in conflict with the indescribable romantic connection, what he calls "the buzz." He has dated scores of women that had either the résumé or the buzz; but he wants both in one package. In his last long-term relationship, his need for the buzz won out over the résumé. Jim ended a seven-year relationship with a woman whom he describes as "an amazing, quality person," because in that union, the kind of connection that makes your heart flutter was missing. To Jim, heart-fluttering was important enough that he ended this otherwise stable, satisfying relationship to try to find it elsewhere.

Some Gen-Xers are so afraid of having their romantic notions let down that it can keep them from forming real relationships from the start. For example, Brandon, the thirty-one-year-old writer from Dallas mentioned earlier, told me that he recently met a woman for whom he fell instantly: "We had an electric conversation that was probably induced by vodka and Red Bull. I am really into that kind of energy connection, like the kind you had when you were in high school. I haven't called her, though. What if the next date doesn't live up to it and I am disappointed?" Brandon would risk never seeing this woman again rather than find out that she doesn't live up to his romantic fantasy.

Romantic love looms larger than ever in otherwise cynical Gen-Xers' minds precisely because they no longer have to marry for practical reasons. Melissa, a twenty-nine-year-old blonde with a turned-up nose, recently opened her own stationery store in San Francisco. She said, "I don't need someone to take care of me. I can take care of myself. I'd have to be really crazy about someone to want to get married." Melissa is looking for romantic, erotic love first; stability and economic partnership are way down on the list. I had to wonder if Evil Influence #4 (The Inadvertent Effects of Feminism) had left Melissa with expectations that were not necessarily sustainable in a long-term relationship

The idea of romantic love, of course, is nothing new. Romantic love is also cross-cultural: in a survey of 166 varied cultures, anthropologists found ideals of romantic love in 147. But throughout history, almost no culture married for notions of romantic love; it was usually seen as a stage or a form of madness, not a basis for a lifelong partnership. Of course, troubadours in twelfth- and thirteenth-century France celebrated the idea of romantic love that we inherited—but they never meant it to refer to a spouse. It was not until quite recently, in historical terms—the mid eighteenth century—that the possibility of marrying for "romantic love" became a reality for some middle-class young people in Europe and America. By the nineteenth century, romantic love had become embedded in the Western ideal of marriage—and while all the other bases for marriage—social status, economic partnership, the need to raise children—have weakened for Gen-Xers, the legacy of romantic love has strengthened.

Unfortunately, Gen-Xers inherited an impossible notion. In the nineteenth century—read any Jane Austen novel—romantic love was, ideally, supposed to draw a young couple together initially; more mature emotions would follow and seal the union over time. But today's young people expect that first rush of erotic and romantic feeling to be not the enticement to the union, but the glue that holds it together forever.

They could not, apparently, have a more deliberate recipe for frustration. Anthropologist Helen Fisher, PhD, writes in *Why We Love* that falling in love is a basic biological human drive and cites what are by now multiple studies that early courtship releases chemicals in the brain that cause feelings of elation, a "biochemical high." But a team of neuroscientists recently concluded that such a feeling on average only lasts between eighteen months to three years before it subsides.

What a conundrum for Gen-Xers, who have mostly not heard this news. Consumer culture tells our generation to expect that an endorphin high—from running, luxury goods, or love—can be renewed at will. And if that high subsides, it is natural, given our context, to conclude that we are in the wrong relationship and we should find another mate.

Holly, a thirty-six-year-old freelance photographer living in New York, clearly got that message from the culture around her, and it affected her marriage for the worse. Holly, a coquettish and cool blonde with soft laugh lines, fell madly in love with her husband, Stuart, a quirky character with a goatee who is always cracking jokes. They dated for two years before they married. Holly thought she had landed the man of her dreams: during their courtship the couple enjoyed long walks on the beach and romantic rendezvous out of town.

But when marriage actually happened, and real life—alarm clocks and late nights working—took the place of bed-and-breakfasts and candlelit dinners, Holly started to complain to her single friends that she no longer felt attracted to Stuart. The butterflies of the first year were gone, she said. Though Stuart still wanted her, Holly gradually stopped having sex with her husband. "I love him as my friend," she cried to her friends on a daily basis, "but I don't feel anything anymore when I kiss him."

Holly started to avoid her young husband. She even began to

spend a couple of nights a week at a girlfriend's apartment. Stuart was crushed, but tried to understand by giving her space. After only a year and a half of marriage, Holly had started to tell herself that she had made a mistake and thought she should get a divorce. Holly, like so many of her generation, had expected to sustain the euphoria of the courtship stage throughout her marriage.

To her credit, Holly didn't want to give up without a concerted effort to make it work. Her parents were divorced and she didn't want to follow in their footsteps. She decided to go to a counselor, who suggested that she and her husband try to create more time and romance with each other. She and her husband worked on their sex life. They communicated more and tried to get away on the weekends when they could. Holly started to realize that she had to work on romance and their sex life just like everything else. Their marriage is now flourishing—although it was almost destroyed because the power of the romantic fantasy in Holly's mind was so much stronger than the message she should have received—that even romantic love takes work. This may sound obvious to people of our parents' generation, but to many Gen-Xers, it isn't quite as apparent. My generation knows what it is like to work hard: we don't expect to get in shape without going to the gym or to get a promotion without putting in long hours. But when it comes to love, many of us think that all we should have to do is show up.

The Search for a Soul Mate

This generation has put a high premium on the belief that certain matches are destined. A 2001 Gallup survey commissioned by Rutgers University's "National Marriage Project" of men and women ages twenty to twenty-nine confirms this generation's desire for that perfect match, what is commonly referred to as a **"soul mate."** An overwhelming majority (94 percent) of never-married singles agreed with the statement, "When you marry you want your spouse to be your soul mate, first and foremost." Similarly high proportions of men and women agree that they want to marry a soul mate. And 87 percent believe they will find that "soul mate" when they are ready to get married. Furthermore, a "National Marriage Project" study of singles in their twenties reported that, even in the face of the divorce epidemic, the sexual revolution, and the women's movement, young people have not cynically rejected the ideal of love and friendship in marriage. "If anything, they've raised the standard to a higher level," the study said. "Finding your soul mate" seemed to my singles like an inoculation to relationship failure in this divorce-prone culture.

So where did this notion of the soul mate come from and what does it really mean? The Greek philosopher Plato is most often credited with the idea. According to Plato's story in the *Symposium,* in the beginning there was only a single human, who had all the necessary male and female parts. But this human was tragically split apart, and since then, the two halves have been searching for each other to be made whole again. A "soul mate" today obviously means different things to different people, but from my interviews, the best Gen-X definition of a soul mate is your perfect match: someone you are deeply in love with and with whom you share a friendship and a physical and spiritual bond—from whom you will never part.

Stacy, a thirty-five-year-old working mother, said she not only found her soul mate, she married him. After having listened to a number of my unhooked subjects tell me about their longing for a soul mate, I couldn't wait to hear what she had to say. She greeted me on a street corner in Pacific Heights on an overcast San Francisco day, wearing a stylish pale pink raincoat and a radiant smile. She had auburn hair and big blue eyes that softened her short, boyish haircut. She exuded confidence and warmth. She had recently founded her own interior design firm and business was booming. On her lunch break, we went to one of the neighborhood's coolest spots, the Grove, a hippie hangout overflowing with men and women wearing anything from Birkenstocks to the latest Banana Republic items. The first thing Stacy said to me was that she had thought she was immune to marital problems, having married someone whom she felt was her "soul mate." But as I kept listening, it seemed that there was a serpent in the soul mates' garden.

Tragically, but almost understandably, given how unrealistic the soul mate fantasy can be, the serpent in the garden was the responsibilities of family life. Stacy explained that she was currently in the midst of a separation from her erstwhile soul mate.

She had met her husband, Jake, when she was twenty-four and he was twenty-six; they married two years later. They had been together for ten years and had what she described as a "happy marriage." "It was a wonderful relationship. We could have been an ad for happy marriage," she recalled as her voice began to tremble. She explained that she and her "soul mate" shared an intense spiritual connection.

But everything changed when her son was born. She said that her husband wasn't a hands-on father. He was irresponsible, she claimed, and didn't help around the house with daily chores. While she was working and tending to their son, Jake would go surfing, just as he did when they were young and carefree. "I realized just because someone is your soul mate doesn't mean you can raise a child and have a life together. When you have children, you have to get real," she insisted.

Her mother had recently given her this piece of advice: "No matter what you do, next time around, don't marry your soul mate." Stacy shrugged her shoulders as I listened intently. She looked both sad and composed at the same time. She explained: "Spiritually I love him, but when you have a kid you have to do it differently. Love alone is not enough. I had love alone and it destroyed a family. You have to have the practical things, too.

"We all want to marry Prince Charming," she concluded as her eyes welled up with tears. "I did and it didn't work." For Stacy, it wasn't, after all, about finding "the one": "You shouldn't fall into love. I think love should be a conscious choice. It is about making it work. It is not a gamble, it is a choice—to stop looking and stop choosing other people."

After I spoke with Stacy, I was stupefied. She had found her "soul mate," the ultimate find, to many of this generation; and it hadn't worked out. How could encountering your "soul mate" lead you astray?

Author and columnist Maggie Gallagher wrote about this generation's longing for a soul mate in an article aptly called "The Soulmate Generation" that appeared on the Townhall.com Web site. Gallagher told me, "The idea that if you just find the right person who completes you, you will be blissfully happy, and its corollary, that if you run into serious emotional problems—if you feel distant or lonely or bored or frustrated or sexually tempted, all of which are quite common in lifetime marriages—then that means you didn't find your soul mate and you are supposed to trade this person in for another—is catastrophic in its effect. If what you want is someone you can count on in life and you want a happy life and a family and a life partner, then the soul mate theory will not get you there."

I was disturbed at how unromantic this theory of soul mates sounded, so I decided to ask my parents, whom I had thought considered each other their soul mate. We sat down in their home in Los Angeles. My father is a commanding six-foot presence with black curly hair, graying sideburns, hazel eyes, and wild caterpillar-shaped eyebrows that seem to laugh along with him. He is a quintessential New Yorker from the Bronx. I asked him, "Dad, do you believe in soul mates?" I thought I was sure to know his answer, since he met my mother in a storybook way.

They were at a club on the Lower East Side of New York, called East Street Basin, on a Sunday night—"Latin Jazz night." The place was jumping and the bossa nova music was pouring out of the club. My mother paid the ten-dollar cover charge and entered with her friend. My mother, a petite and outspoken redhead with warm chestnut eyes and a graceful nose, still remembers exactly how she looked that night: "I wore my hair in a French roll, that was a popular style then. I was wearing a chocolate brown suit with a skirt, shiny-gold buttons, and heels." My father interjected, "I didn't really like that suit. It was too conservative." My mother recalled that she was talking to some young man she had just met and my father was standing behind him. "At that moment I said to myself, I am going to marry that woman," he said, with glee in his eyes and a smile. "He took my wrist and pulled me away from him and said come have a drink." My mother grinned. My father said with a hearty laugh, "Right off the bat, she asked my last name." He replied to her, "Why? Do you want to know if I am Jewish?" My mother, who is Jewish, admitted she was indeed investigating to see if there was long-term potential. She was relieved to learn he was indeed also Jewish. "She was a beauty," my father recalled with his raspy New York accent. What did my mother think? Her quick response: "I liked how aggressive he was and I liked his green eyes but he wasn't really my type." When she got home that night, her mother asked her, "Did you meet anyone?" She told her mother, "I met this one engineer. He is kind of cute, but I'm not sure he is for me."

More than four decades later, here we were sitting in their living room. My father answered my question about whether or not he believed in soul mates. His answer surprised me: "Sometimes," he said. So are they made or born? He said, "Oh, definitely not born. It takes time, a relationship is about growing together, creating something, building a family."

So I probed a little further: How did they know forty-two years ago that they should tie the knot? Because my father said he knew he was going to marry her the first time he saw her, I assumed they felt fated to be together forever. Because of this story and because of their seemingly happy marriage, I had assumed that it had been somewhat effortless—that they had just been lucky to find one another. This scenario in my mind had added to my own romantic confusion.

It wasn't until I actually interviewed my parents that I discovered how wrong I was. I learned that my understanding of what made them happy was based on my own generation's script of "soul mates" and had absolutely nothing in common with their script about what made the marriage work. I asked my mom what that inexplicable element that she had seen in my dad (her soul mate, I thought), that had made her marry him, had been. To my surprise, she said, "I really cared about him and we had a great time together."

I asked again, still wedded to my soul mate theory, "Didn't you feel he was your soul mate when you got married?"

Her reply stunned me: "No, I didn't, but he is now."

I was shocked by both my mother's and my father's responses. Why hadn't they sat me down ten years ago to correct the impressions I was getting from my culture—and apparently superimposing on them? I had always thought they had met and found their perfect other half—and the relationship had just blissfully moved on from there. What I didn't know until I actually asked them to tell me about their courtship themselves was that it *wasn't* the initial connection that had made the relationship so successful. Despite their rare recognition-at-first-sight meeting, according to my father, soul mates are made, not born.

My father's message was—belatedly, for me—clear at last: it was the work, the struggles, and the resultant joys over forty-two years that had made them—over time—each into a mate to each other's souls.

The title of Jack Kornfeld's book *After the Ecstasy, the Laundry* sums up what my parents were saying—that true love is about much more than the initial ecstasy or bliss. Based on my interviews with people who have said they found true love, I have heard that they accept two things: that there are difficult days and that bliss takes effort. Our generation has internalized the message that it should be all bliss all the time and that no one has to make an effort to rekindle the spark. And that when there are days of "laundry," or boredom, it is time to bail. I would argue that in the seemingly good marriages I've seen, there have been both a spark and the willingness to renew it when it inevitably dies down. And I've learned from happy couples that the difficult times can actually make the blissful moments even sweeter. While many older married people might think this is obvious, they are not teaching this to the young unmarried people of my generation. Evil Influence #5 (The "Why Suffer?" Mentality) combined with Evil Influence #2 (Multiple Choice Culture) have led many of my generation to believe that if their relationship requires work, they have made the wrong choice. I have heard several of my friends over the years, struggling in relationships, utter the phrase, "It shouldn't be this hard." But long-term relationships are one of life's most difficult challenges and greatest joys. How could they not take work?

I learned on my journey that both Gen-X approaches to looking for love are shortsighted. Our checklists have become roadblocks to potentially fantastic partners. And our fantasy of romance without work (and shared experience) is a distortion of the romantic love model.

Next we will see in greater detail how the expectations of Gen-Xers are not only often outrageous, but also contradictory.

4

Contradictory Needs, Conflicting Agendas

*"You want to be able to be the protector and provider, but know that you
don't have to be. You want the woman to feel you take care
of it all—but you don't want her to need it,
demand it, or expect it."*

—JOSH, 30

We, the first generation born after the women's movement, often try
to wrap our arms around opposing expectations. On the one hand,
we have absorbed the traditional gender roles of many of our parents.
On the other, we also carry with us the more egalitarian roles of our
own time. Rather than reconciling these two scripts, my unhooked
singles are burdened with both scripts running in their heads and
hearts—looking for an ideal that could really only be met by two separate people!

Derek, the man with the checklist of twenty-five requirements,
stressed that he wanted a modern relationship, someone independent
and his equal: "I want someone who can handle her own business."
Even though he loved his last girlfriend, Derek said, he resented that
he had to pay for everything: "I want someone that can contribute.
[Nora] wanted to quit her job, move in with me, and have me pay for
all our vacations," he complained. It was important to him to find
someone that he could share financial burdens with—and also learn

something from. This side of Derek came across as a nontraditional man who wanted a modern woman.

But another inner Derek wanted Mrs. Cleaver. He told me about his previous girlfriend, a woman named Tracy. She had seemed to be much more of what Derek said he was looking for. She was in sales and was flourishing in her career: "She could really hold her own. She was the kind of woman who gets whatever she wants, whenever she wants it," he explained. But Derek wasn't satisfied in this relationship, either. "The problem with her was that I want an independent woman and a strong woman—but I want her to be dependent on me for something. Tracy had it going on more than me and it was intimidating," he said.

Neither Nora nor Tracy had fulfilled all of Derek's expectations. But I had to wonder, how could a single human being? Derek was looking for two completely different types of women.

"Nora was highly needy," he went on, explaining further his contradictory longings. "But Tracy didn't need me at all. Some women are so independent they don't need a man. I like a woman who is independent . . . but that knows she needs a man for something," he said.

Derek tried to clarify for me, and for himself, what it was he wanted in a mate. As he spoke, it was clear that his needs were based on real masculine concerns. In his case, it sounded as if the relief of not being the sole breadwinner in a couple was not mitigated by the fear of losing the traditional male power and authority that that breadwinning brings. I don't fault Derek for his honesty; I think this male conflict is widespread, if maddening, in relationships. "The thing is," he concluded finally, with a glimmer of insight, "I want to be responsible for taking care of the other person financially . . . but I want to know that she can take care of herself if I fall short. I still want to be the man."

Men are not alone in wanting to share the responsibility without sharing the power; many commentators have noted that women often say they want men to share domestic work fifty-fifty, but are reluctant to share parental and domestic authority fifty-fifty as well. It is human nature to want the benefits of partnership without losing the privileges of the "separate sphere." But it leads to chaotic searches for love. This seemingly hypocritical expectation is one result of Evil Influence #4 (The Inadvertent Effects of Feminism).

Josh, thirty, a New York trader divorced from an even more successful investment banker, expanded on Derek's insight: "You want to be able to be the protector and provider, but know that you don't have to be. You want the woman to feel you take care of it all—but you don't want her to need it, demand it, or expect it. It's like when you are on a ship and there is a storm, you want her to rely on you, but you don't want to be the only one paddling."

I thought: This is the dilemma my girlfriends and I are all facing. How can we ever meet such contradictory longings in men?

Men our age may well feel just as frustrated by us. Many of the women I spoke to also had contradictory expectations for their potential partners. Claudia, mentioned earlier, is the thirty-two-year-old go-getter who started her own jewelry line in Chicago. She is a dark-eyed woman with freckles and a strong Midwestern accent. Her boyfriend of five years had been kind and sensitive—qualities that she said she loved. This man had also been extremely supportive of her career—unlike other men in her past who had been intimidated by her strong personality and apparent ambition. By all accounts, the relationship was going well until her ex-boyfriend said that one day he wouldn't mind being "Mr. Mom." "The moment he talked about being 'Mr. Mom,' my vagina closed up," she quipped. She found it a total turn-off that this loving, supportive man would want to take on the role of caretaker to his children. She broke off her relationship with "the love of her life" because, in her words, he "lacked ambition." "I may seem like a modern woman—but I am old-fashioned. I am used to my father being in charge and taking care of everything. I have worked seven days a week for the last five years of my life and

I want to be taken care of," she declared. She continued, "My ex-boyfriend said he didn't want to work hard—he wanted to spend time with his family. That would make him happy. I say fuck 'happy,' work hard. I am attracted to a man who is smart, aggressive, and successful," she declared. Even though she loved him, she said, "To me, he is not a man. I don't need Gordon Gekko (the ruthless stockbroker Michael Douglas played in the move 1987 movie *Wall Street*) but I'm not going to be with Mr. Mom. This is not what I waited so long to get married for. I want to work because I want to, not because I have to," she said. It is now years since she said good-bye to the love of her life, and Claudia is still single.

Claudia is not alone. Other women I interviewed, even career women, said they wanted a sensitive, kind man who shared the domestic work . . . but they also wanted him to be the primary breadwinner. Many women had a different set of traditional needs that clashed with their modern ones. Alexandra, a thirty-year-old with a heart-shaped face and an elegant nose, had an MBA from one of the country's top business schools and a job at a Fortune 500 company. She surprised me when she told me what she was looking for in a long-term relationship. She spoke fondly of time spent with an old boyfriend, Elliot. For the first time in our conversation, I saw Alexandra's toothy smile: "Martini night," she reminisced. She explained this ritual that she had had with her ex: "I used to put my slippers on, playing the 1950s housewife, and make him a martini while he was watching TV. I don't mind cooking and cleaning while he is out in the workforce. . . . I had the feeling of being taking care of. It was a feeling of being the woman you were supposed to be—dainty and cute."

Many women of my mother's generation would look at Alexandra's current life as a successful career woman with envy. Yet some part of Alexandra longed for something simpler. She explained, "I wouldn't trade my life. I know I couldn't have my brain and have my mother's life. But sometimes I envy women with fewer options."

Alexandra craved the exact parallel to what Derek wanted: that is, someone who would adapt completely to her changing needs. I imagined Alexandra and Derek in a boat in a storm and neither of them knowing how to paddle together. Alexandra said: "I want a guy whose number-one priority is my happiness. I want someone who will support me whether I want to be a traditional housewife or if I get really into my career and I want to work." I imagined the nice guys of my generation throwing up their hands at Alexandra's dictum, just as I had mentally thrown up mine at Derek's. This vestigial longing for some symbol of the traditional female role—the martini, romantic gifts, or the big diamond engagement ring—is so common among my friends, even the high-powered feminist ones, that I call it **"the Wilma Flintstone effect."** My friend Tara, a progressive post-Marxist feminist, confessed that when her first child was born, she was obsessed with her husband giving her diamond earrings. She is convinced that this longing is hardwired—an anthropological residue of the feather-the-nest reflex. Men, on the other hand, have their own symbols. Egalitarian men I know who are fully capable of cooking their own dinner—or ordering takeout—still have a vestigial longing for a meal cooked by female hands.

It may well help the women and men of my generation if they can learn not to confuse these deep symbolic longings with an entire life choice. Alexandra would become suicidal if she were expected to wear slippers and serve martinis every day after work. Derek would turn to drink if his mate never shouldered some responsibility for the tough choices. But the longing of liberated women for a gesture of male protection is a legitimate symbolic need—just as the longing for a symbolic role to be the provider may be legitimate for men. For people who really want someone to help them row the boat, that desire for real partnership can underlie those more superficial, symbolic exchanges. Maybe we need to learn to serve the martini or bring home the flowers—*and* help each other row the boat.

This kind of contradiction can undermine a relationship before it even begins. Chloe, a hard-charging thirty-four-year-old international management consultant from Dallas, with Gucci sandals and a French manicure, explained that it is very difficult for her to be herself on a date. "When I meet someone and I tell them what I do, my success gives this impression that I want to climb the corporate ladder. Most guys I meet don't like that. The truth is, at this point in my life I would rather build a family, but my job is necessary right now to support myself. I want to be able to say to a guy, 'I really do want to get married,' but you can't say that to a guy. He'll run in the other direction." Men, too, say they can't express their honest thoughts about their contradictory expectations of women.

The problem is that we have not yet distinguished the symbolic exchange of traditional roles from the partnership we long for. A handful of women who spoke to me said they would have no problem making more money than their male counterparts; some even said they would sign on to be the breadwinner. But these women were also aware that usurping the role of main breadwinner came with symbolic dangers. The thirty-four-year-old doctor living in San Francisco told me that the day her relationship with a lower-earning man she loved ended was the day she brought home a Porsche. Throughout their relationship, he expressed frustration that she made more money than he did and he broke up with her shortly after she brought the car home. The luxury car made their income difference even more apparent to him—and it made him feel too inadequate to stay with her. She still has the Porsche—which she loves—and is hoping to find someone who can handle what's in her garage.

Could men my age handle a woman earning more? It seemed symbolically castrating to many. Bruce, thirty-three, a laid-back marketing consultant from Chicago, used a notable term in his description of how this symbolic role reversal would make him feel: "If my girlfriend or wife makes more money than me, I would feel like a *pussy.* I would feel like less of a man if she made all the money." What a conundrum: here my girlfriends and I are working so hard to do

well in our careers—and the very qualities that are attracting potential mates are making them ambivalent as well. This duality of course
is also a result of Evil Influence #4 (The Inadvertent Effects of Feminism).

So here we are: we are trained to be successful women—but have
the impression that the greater our success, the more complex our
search for love. In romance novels of the 1960s, the secretary married
the CEO and the nurse married the doctor. Today, women may
be CEOs and doctors. Yet successful women often still add to their
checklist the expectation of marrying someone even higher on the
ladder. According to "the newlywed study" of 107 couples conducted by psychology professor David Buss, financially successful
women express an even greater preference for high-earning men than
do women who are less financially successful. In addition, these
women also want, more than their less-accomplished sisters, husbands
who are tall, independent, and self-confident. This can go a long way
toward explaining the common scene of a group of gorgeous, high-
earning young women together at a bar table bemoaning their love
lives. They are refusing to look anywhere but up.

Leanne, a thirty-two-year-old brand manger at a major packaged
goods company, with hair like gold silk and an angelic smile, had been
asking herself why she was still single. Leanne looks flawless even
without makeup. She glides across a room with her flaxen hair moving slightly with every step. She is confident, poised, and polite. She is
the kind of woman who comforts single women everywhere. If she
can't find herself a quality man, who can? We spoke over a velvety
cappuccino in Chicago's Lincoln Park. She explained that she started
exercising recently; she worries that if she loses her figure she will become "less marketable." "When I was growing up, marriage was not
a priority for me; but I didn't see myself being single at this age." She
sounded forlorn. She wants, she said, to find a "Fred Astaire and Gin-
ger Rogers" type of relationship.

I could see it in her face; being single had clearly become a source of angst. She told me how a recent round of wedding showers drove her to tears. And constant pressure from family didn't make things any easier. "My aunt always asks me, 'How are your boyfriends?' I am like, 'I don't have any.'" She attributed being single to the contradictory scripts that men of her generation often have: the men at her business school, she said, didn't want someone at her success level as a mate. "In business school, guys still want the schoolteacher, even though they say they want an equal partner. They say 'I want to be CEO of my household and I want my wife to be COO,'" she explained as she sipped her coffee. The truth for Leanne? As much as she longed for a family, she wanted the choice of whether to work or be at home; she did not want the choice thrust upon her. She did not wish to pretend to be someone she was not in order to attract a mate. Leanne's one-up checklist ("I want a CEO") was ruling out many good men; and the one-down checklist of the men at her business school ("I want a schoolteacher") was ruling out Leanne.

The Biological Battle

Just as contradictory needs can play a powerful role in keeping men and women apart, so can conflicting agendas. Evil Influence #7 (The Fallout from the Marriage Delay) affects men's and women's quests for love differently. At a certain age, of course, many women get serious about their search for a mate because of their biological clocks. Their long-standing concerns about losing their reproductive capabilities and aging out of the marriage market, two enormous pressures, have caused, for some, an anxiety that can border on hysteria.

Among the single women I interviewed in their mid-to-late thirties were some who were completely—if stereotypically—freaked out about their biological clocks. A thirty-three-year-old friend of mine—still single after many failed relationships—cried on her birthday when I visited her at home with a present. "I should just get inseminated already," she wept.

Some of these women spoke about their "backup plans." If Mr. Right did not come along in time, they would have children on their own with donated sperm. A few of these women had already checked out fertility clinics and had asked male friends if they would consider being sperm donors when the time came. Some were also considering single-parent adoption, and had consulted adoption services. Some of them referred to single-mom role models on TV: Rachel on *Friends* and Miranda—before she got married—on *Sex and the City*.

Other frantic women to whom I spoke were still reluctant to give up on the hope of finding someone special with whom to start a family. Andrea, an attractive thirty-four-year-old African-American lawyer from Minneapolis, said she doesn't want to be a single mother. Still, she is reluctantly considering it. "I am contemplating having a child on my own in the next year. I said I was going to do it when I was thirty, then again I said it at thirty-three. I know the longer I put it off, the harder it will be, but I haven't done it on my own because I really want to do it with someone. However, I don't know how long I can wait." Sarah, thirty-five, a travel agent from a suburb of Chicago, vowed sadly to go it alone: "Motherhood seems very natural for me—but year after year I don't meet anyone to be with. I could freeze an egg or have a donor. I am thinking about that now. I worry I will have the feeling of loss, that my life will not be fulfilled the way I dreamt, but I'm not holding out for the storybook romance and family anymore."

Although many of my unhooked subjects considered having a baby on their own, only one had actually done it. Sabrina, a thirty-nine-year-old executive assistant from a suburb in the Bay Area, got pregnant "accidentally" by her longtime boyfriend; she confessed that her carelessness about contraception had followed an overwhelming physical longing to become a mother. While the child's father was not completely out of the picture, the couple was no longer romantically involved when their baby was born. Both parents had agreed that she would raise the child on her own.

There was, to my surprise, another camp of women I spoke to—also hovering around the dreaded thirty-five-year-old mark—who seemed completely detached from the issue of their biological clocks. When they expressed angst about not having a partner at that age, these women hardly mentioned having children. They talked more about not finding their soul mate or the agony of a recent breakup than about the fear that they might miss their reproductive window. It was almost as if they were in complete denial of this harsh but inevitable reality. A friend of mine who is thirty-eight had one explanation for the seemingly unconcerned women: "You get to a certain age and you are bummed about being single. You either also worry about your biological clock or you take it off your plate. It's just too much pressure."

As women age, not only do they fear losing their ability to procreate, but many also worry that if they lose their youthful appearance they will be unable to attract a man to be a potential husband and father. Allison, a beautiful thirty-six-year-old magazine writer from New York, worried that, year by year, she was becoming less marketable and hence less marriageable. "More than my biological clock, I fear losing my looks," she exclaimed.

Allison is a curvy blonde with alabaster skin and no visible signs of aging. But after she turned thirty-three she started working out religiously, eating a low-carb diet, and applying under-eye cream every night. Her bathroom was like a beauty product museum: dozens of bottles, from body-building hair gel to cellulite reducer, covered her vanity and the top of her toilet. She worked long hours, but like many of her single, professional girlfriends, she fit in appointments after work or on the weekend for facials, waxing, weight training, and hair coloring.

She told me a story about her friend Fiona, also a well-maintained thirty-six-year-old museum docent. Fiona had met a man at a bar last week when she was out having drinks with her coworkers. An attractive man had walked up to her and bought her a drink. After talking for about twenty minutes he asked if she wanted to sit down and talk more at a table. They spoke for a while longer when he made a reference to his age. "My older brother lives in D.C.; he's thirty-three, two years older than me. I'm thirty-one." Fiona suddenly got uncomfortable. "How old are you?" he asked. Under her breath she responded, "I'm thirty-six." Moments later his eyes started to roam around the bar. He looked at Fiona and said, "I have to meet up with my friends now. It was nice meeting you." After hearing that story, Allison started to seriously consider lying about her age.

Of course youth and beauty have always been essential qualities for attracting a husband, but women today have in some ways a much tougher battle than had earlier generations of women who married in their twenties. A single woman of this generation looking to meet someone must maintain her youthful appearance for many years longer than in the past, in some cases even as she approaches middle age. Not to mention, a woman today has double duty maintaining her appearance on top of her perhaps time-intensive career. Worse yet, she must also compete with women in their twenties for the same pool of marriageable men. Some, however, might argue it is not only women who have to keep themselves up these days. For the first time in history, men—that is, "metrosexuals," a new breed of well-dressed, sleekly pampered males—may also feel pressure to maintain themselves. The difference is their biological clocks are not ticking as fast.

For these reasons, women's timetables speed up even as men's timetables slow down. In the past, men had a sense of time urgency to marry—because they were not seen as being fully mature or successful if they were long single. Now social pressure on men to marry is diluted, and in some cases completely gone. The strain on women has been amplified precisely because the pressure on men to marry has dissipated—leaving the genders further apart. Although the marriage delay is socially acceptable for both genders, women ultimately pay a higher price for it.

As women in their thirties date with more urgency, they risk pushing potential partners further away. Close male friends of mine have confided in me that nothing turns them off more than a woman who is aggressively looking for a man so she can get married and start a family.

Take, for instance, my friend Judd, a thirty-eight-year-old electrical engineer from New York. Judd is intelligent, with an acerbic sense of humor. He has spiky hair and wears glasses that hide his kind eyes. He came over to my apartment on his way home from work one night.

Our mutual friend Rachel was over. We had just ordered in sushi and watched *Ocean's Eleven*. Judd showed up with a sandwich he had picked up on the way. He took a seat in my oversize chair and put his feet up on my coffee table.

He told us he had just broken it off with a woman named Lily, whom he had been seeing for three weeks. Lily was the same age as Judd. He described her as being fun-loving, and having a great sense of style. They had a couple of nice evenings out—but finally Judd thought she was "too accommodating." He explained: "It wasn't that she was so into me. She was into the fact that I was in my late thirties and had a good job. She's ready to have kids and I could just tell I fit her picture." Rachel and I pressed Judd about how it was he knew she was itching to settle down. Judd insists he could simply hear her clock ticking loud enough for it to be audible across the table over dinner. He felt he could sense her agenda clearly. Although Judd really wanted marriage and admitted he was actually ready to settle down— and although he really liked this woman—the mere possibility that she was on "a schedule" scared him away.

At first Judd's story made me angry. He was holding it against Lily that she might be responding to real reproductive pressure. But then it occurred to me that what Judd was saying was no different from what women thirty years ago were saying. Just as women before the feminist movement didn't want to be valued only for their roles as the keepers of the house or the bearers of the children, Judd didn't want to be desired primarily because he could play the part of father and provider. Judd wanted someone to fall in love with *him*. He didn't want to get plugged into someone's life picture. Judd didn't believe that love and commitment should have anything to do with an "agenda."

Other men I knew also objected to being part of what I call **The "MAB" Agenda,** which stands for the "Marriage And Baby" agenda. Interestingly enough, it seemed that men my age had absorbed the postfeminist idea that they, too, should be viewed as an individual and not for the prescribed role they could fill in a relationship. Although they have many more options than women did in the seventies, perhaps men of my generation were having their own awakening—hard though that makes it on the dating scene.

Given the contradictory needs of the Alexandras and Dereks of our generation—and the conflicting agendas of the Judds and Lilys—how on earth can personal longing easily proceed to true love?

5

Wedded Dis
The Media

"If 'The Bachelor' can do it, why can't I?"
—GLENN, 28

Some very powerful scripts, of course, that influence many Gen-Xers, consciously or not, are the ones written by movie and television producers in Hollywood. To a remarkable degree, especially given the cliché that Hollywood's happy ending has always been matrimonial, many of the films and TV programs that are hits for this generation carry the not-so-subtle message that marriage is boring and single life is sexy. Although television was powerful in previous generations, television is the defining medium for our generation, and therefore we are most likely influenced by the images on television more than any other forms of media.

When I set out to look at how the mainstream media influence my generation's relationships, I was not expecting to find a clear connection. But when I spoke to singles all over the country, I learned it was very common for them to compare dates and relationships to characters and situations on their favorite sitcoms and reality TV shows, with no evident irony. For example, a hundred singles had gathered for an afternoon party in a dive bar in Dallas with pictures of Cowboys on the wall and picnic tables all around. Men and women wearing Mardi Gras beads were elbow-deep in crawfish. Behind the bar, a thirtysomething man lifted a huge vat of crawfish, steam pouring out, as a bearded man sang and strummed his guitar. A twenty-eight-year-old accountant named Glenn, wearing shorts and a T-shirt, explained that he was juggling women, dating three at the same time. "If 'The Bachelor' can do it, why can't I?" He smiled. Men and women in other cities, too, often referred to television hits as reference points for their experiences, or to justify their decisions.

Gen-Xers grew up watching singles-dominated programs in which friends were the new family. Older favorites such as *Family Ties* and *The Cosby Show* gave way to hits such as *Friends* and *Sex and the City*. In fact, an apparent shift from family-centered shows to ones dominated by singles was well underway by 1995, by which time five of the top ten television shows centered around the lives of singles. From *Friends* to *Sex and the City, Seinfeld, Will and Grace, Suddenly Susan, The Single Guy, Melrose Place, Ally McBeal,* and *Living Single,* hit shows that highlighted the single life replaced family shows. While programs that center on singles are certainly not new—*That Girl* debuted in 1966 and the early 1970s saw the introduction of *The Mary Tyler Moore Show, Rhoda,* and *Three's Company*—happy-family comedies were still the staple, two decades ago, of what was considered to be the family viewing hour, and the single people in those shows saw their status as a way station: their ultimate goal was a happy marriage and family life. Many of today's TV singles are ambivalent, at best, about leaving their exciting, self-oriented lives—perhaps as ambivalent as are many of their audience members. While I, too, find many of these hit shows entertaining, the messages they send can have marked effects on our own romantic lives.

The Sexy Single Life vs. The Marriage
Is Boring Message

HBO's 1998–2004 hit series, *Sex and the City*, is the most obvious example of the glorification of single life. The show, which continues on in reruns, centers around four single women in New York City, told through the eyes of relationship columnist Carrie Bradshaw. The show went on to a second life in syndication on TBS, but has become a ubiquitous icon to singles. Even after the show's finale, its legacy lives on as a flagship brand for the single life; it's safe to say that many more people of my generation are aware of the *Sex and the City* message about the single status than actually watch the show.

These women are so independent that, in their world, "compromise" became a dirty word. Carrie wrote that even in good relationships, romantic unions are inevitably a series of compromises. She asks how much we should be willing to sacrifice for the other person. Ultimately she questions the value of giving up some of one's own desires for a relationship.

From their parties to their Prada couture, the show's four main characters' responsibility-free lives present a picture of singleness as being exciting, liberating, and self-indulgent. Life for them looks pretty good. If being single is about consuming a steady diet of martinis, Manolo Blahniks, and multiple orgasms with multiple partners—why would anyone want to trade it all in for one man, a station wagon, and a screaming child?

This show—and others like it—don't just glorify the single life; they also make clear negative judgments—some subtle, and others overt—about marriage and family life. The frequent caricature of domestic life is that it is a deadly dull trap; the end of sexual passion, adult individuality, and consumer pleasure. While many critics condemned *Sex and the City*'s main characters' rabid pursuit of men, they overlooked the fact that marriage is practically portrayed as a death sentence. When Carrie and her friends went to the suburbs for the baby shower of their friend Laney, a former party girl who was depicted as having been transformed by marriage and family into a more tedious version of Carol Brady, the portrait of domesticity could not have been more off-putting. After seeing Laney, Carrie notes that Miranda is convinced that "marriage plus baby equals death." Very pregnant Laney, desperate for her former life, shows up at a party back in the city and tries—unsuccessfully—to reclaim her carefree single days. Laney's desperation makes Carrie, Samantha, Miranda, and Charlotte feel better about their own life choices. Laney says that she doesn't want to go home to the suburbs and is despondent about the loss of her dreams. This alone is a dramatic change from the media message of earlier generations. The picture of marriage and family life on television, once depicted as a dream come true, had in this case become a dream crusher.

Indeed, the picture of modern marriage on *Sex and the City* was so consistently that of a stale, predictable, and oppressive way of life that one episode had Carrie actually throwing up with aversion when she found an engagement ring in her boyfriend Aidan's bag. Although Carrie desperately loves Aidan, when he proposes marriage, Carrie has a breakdown. Reluctant to wear the ring on her finger, set a date, or plan the wedding, she finally agrees to try on a dress. What *Sex and the City* viewer can forget the episode in which Miranda and Carrie went to try on tacky wedding gowns? When Carrie put on a white-lace balloon-sleeved dress, she instantly broke into hives. Over brunch, she tells her friends that she can't get married and that her body is rejecting the idea of marriage. She asks the gang for one good reason why she should marry. While fear of commitment is not a new theme in television, this time a hit television show portrayed the woman as being the one with the fear of marriage. Carrie tries to get over her crippling fear and asks Aidan for more time—but, ultimately, he can't wait.

If Doris Day had looked frantically for the exit whenever Rock Hudson cleared his throat before a proposal—well, the fifties might have unfolded entirely differently. I am not advocating a return to the impossibly idealized images of marriage of the *Father Knows Best* past; what is striking, though, is how hard it is to think of reasonably appealing TV images of marriage and family aimed at this generation.

Although all of *Sex and the City*'s main characters are in or entering committed relationships or marriages by the series finale, that fact hardly erases the dominant message fans tuned into, season after season, when married life was either portrayed as a fate of drudgery or a Pollyanna fantasy. In fact, the program's message over the years was so antimarriage that the show's finale was criticized by many fans for having given in to the happy ending of marriage and monogamy.

Friends, whose series finale among the top Nielsen-rated television finales, also glamorizes single life and often makes light of the inability of the show's characters to make and sustain commitments. The program, a favorite among this generation, continues in reruns several times a day in many markets. On the first episode of *Friends,* Rachel flees the altar to avoid marrying her fiancé. She begins a new life racking up dates, casual sex, and leisure time with her buddies. Ross also revels in single life: he was divorced at twenty-six from an attractive woman who, after giving birth to his son, he learned was a lesbian. But we rarely see Ross's son; in fact, he does almost nothing to cramp Ross's single lifestyle. The other perpetually single characters joke about their inability to sustain relationships. Chandler once declared to his friends: "Between us, we haven't had a relationship that has lasted longer than a Mento." And on another episode, Phoebe said to Joey: "You're not in a relationship, you are over thirty and you have never had a long-term relationship—you go from one meaningless relationship to the next." Joey responded: "You're right. I love my life."

Marriage is also made to look somewhat meaningless on *Friends*—as in the marriage of Rachel and Ross as a drunken stunt in

Las Vegas. Both characters floated in and out of wedlock several times; by the end of the series, Ross had been married and divorced three times.

When the characters on *Friends* finally decide to get married and have children, they focus not on what they are gaining from these experiences but on what they are leaving behind. While women on the show are excited about the idea of marriage and, of course, the wedding, when it comes to real commitment, the excitement is often tempered with fear of what they are giving up. For example, on one episode, Monica panics about the prospect of never having a first kiss again and never experiencing sex for the first time with someone new: "I just keep thinking about all the things I am never going to have and it is freaking me out," she says. These characters are so reluctant to give up the prolonged adolescence of single life that when Monica and Chandler marry, their life still revolves around hanging out with their friends. Marriage for them is simply one more roommate rotation. When Rachel is pregnant, she bemoans the loss of her single life. On one episode, she said, "I miss dating: getting all dressed up and going to a fancy restaurant. I'm not gonna be able to do that for so long and it's so much fun. I mean, not that sitting at home worrying about giving birth to a sixteen-pound baby is not fun."

This glamorized portrait of single life on many shows also ignores the common reality of single life that many of my unhooked subjects often spoke about: loneliness. The characters on *Friends,* it seems, never experience that unfortunate aspect of single life.

A similar "single is cool, marriage is lame" message dates back to the time many Gen-Xers started to have real romantic relationships. *Melrose Place,* a popular glossy nighttime drama about twentysomethings who live in the same Hollywood apartment complex, which ran from 1992 to 1999, portrayed single life as a revolving door for sex. The only married couple had serious marital problems: the husband was having an affair.

Seinfeld, one of the most successful sitcoms in television history, is yet another example. A common running joke on this program is the ridiculous, though admittedly hilarious, reasons why the show's main characters break up with people. From Jerry's date, who eats her peas one at a time, to George's love interest who beats him at chess, not only are the show's main characters hesitant to commit, they are hesitant to even give potential partners a chance to audition. On one episode, in fact, George and Jerry discuss their childish dumping excuses and begin to question whether there is indeed more to life than being single. As quickly as they reach the conclusion that there is, Kramer tries to set them straight, calling marriage and family "man-made prisons." But George and Jerry are not convinced and agree to change their immature ways. Surprisingly, the reformed George immediately proposes to Susan. But, in typical George fashion, he is disappointed when he learns that Jerry didn't hold up his end of the bargain and has decided to remain single.

Just when it seems the inseparable single friends will have to split up, George becomes anxiety-ridden about his pending nuptials. Desperate, George weeps to his fiancée begging for a postponement. She concedes, but eventually George knows he will have to face marriage—a fate so horrible his only escape route is apparently his fiancée's death. As the show's writers had it, the Susan character develops an allergic reaction to licking the adhesive on the wedding envelopes—and conveniently dies.

More recently, *Will and Grace,* the NBC hit about a single gay man and his single straight female best friend, celebrates the single life, both gay and straight. On this show, friendship lasts but romantic relationships don't. Will and Grace enjoy their time together and both long for romantic unions, but can never seem to get it right. Grace does eventually marry in the fifth season, but a couple seasons later, she is already divorced from her cheating husband. Meanwhile, Karen, another main character, also discovers her husband had an affair. Other occasional characters, Will's parents, are also having affairs. His mother declares on one episode, "Cheating is fun."

She actually wants her husband to keep having an affair for the good of her sex life. On this show, marriage is hardly synonymous with monogamy and bliss.

While these programs have done single people a service by taking the stigma out of being single, in the process they have created a new stigma—one in which married people are the losers. It's great that the idealization of marriage in the media is over—but the disparagement of marriage in the media has definitely reached a new low. In fact, pro-marriage experts such as sociologist David Popenoe, PhD, at the National Marriage Project, claim: "Nothing could be more anti-marriage than much of popular culture." Critics point to television shows such as *Sex and the City, Friends,* and *Seinfeld* for this pro-single culture that is discouraging people from choosing marriage, and even stigmatizing those who do.

Let us think back to the comedies of earlier generations, such as *I Love Lucy, Leave it to Beaver, The Honeymooners,* and *All in the Family.* In those days, we had two images of marriage—one happily ever after, the other the ball and chain: the resentful Ralph and Archie were balanced by lovable Ricky and respectful Mr. Cleaver. Nonetheless, marriage was seen as an intrinsic good.

The Fantasy of Prolonged Adolescence

So why is this pro-single message so appealing to Gen-Xers? One attractive subtext of many of these programs is the message about extending the carefree days of youth. On *Sex and the City,* the women prolong their adolescence well into their thirties—with Fendi bags as their shiny new toys and New York City as their man-hunting playground. On shows such as *Friends, Seinfeld,* and *Will and Grace* the characters have very few adult responsibilities, giving them the luxury of focusing on bad dates and good sex. In addition, many of these programs feature a close-knit group of friends who either live together or very close to one another. Their characters share their most intimate thoughts and experiences and, in some cases, even sex. These close friendships replace the need for a family and indeed become substitutes for family life. The programs offer viewers a fantasy world in which there are no husbands to rain on one's shoe-spending parade or wives to interfere with one's drinking with buddies. The fantasy of a perfect family has been supplanted by the fantasy of hanging out forever with one's friends.

The movie *Old School* is to the bachelor what *Sex and the City* is to the bachelorette. The male version of the fantasy is the never-ending bachelor party. The 2003 movie is about three men in their thirties who start their own fraternity in a house near a college campus in an effort to flee their humdrum lives in committed relationships or marriage. The film opens with the character Mitch leaving a business trip early to find his live-in girlfriend in their bedroom primed for a three-way with a half-naked blindfolded man and another woman. Mitch is horrified. When he tries to talk to his girlfriend, her response is: "You have to admit it, Mitch, we haven't exactly been living the most exciting lives in the world." Clearly she was bored and felt she was missing out by being in a monogamous relationship with Mitch.

In another scene in the film, the movie's main characters host a blowout bash full of college students and scantily clad freshman women. Frank, played by actor Will Ferrell, leaves behind his new bride and goes to the party, but tries to remain on his best behavior. When a twentysomething party guest offers him a drink from the "beer bong," he explains that he shouldn't because he has a big day the next day. When the guest inquires about his "big day," Frank says he and his wife are going to Home Depot and Bed Bath & Beyond. In doing so, he describes a stereotypical day of married life, one that couldn't possibly hold any allure for a single man. The party guests look at Frank as if he is crazy, mocking his newly domesticated life. Within an instant, Frank takes a huge swig from the beer bong, presumably to show that he wants to be one of them.

Dysfunctional Family Entertainment

So what happens to television characters who do get married and start a family? From the look of many family shows on television today, their attitudes don't change much. The popular shows of the late eighties, *Thirtysomething* and *Married . . . with Children,* ushered in a new type of TV family, centered on dysfunction and angst. *Thirtysomething* focused on the whining of yuppies as they wrestled with marriage and child-rearing. This program was the first show about married life in which estrangement and tension were an ongoing focus. *Married . . . with Children,* a broad satire, went several steps further in sharing a cynical look at the nuclear family: the relationship between a chauvinist husband, Al Bundy, and trashy wife, Peg, is characterized by gross disrespect for one another, and verbal warfare. On one episode, when someone mistakes the neighbor for Al's wife, Al corrects him: "I'm not married to this lady, I'm married to that thing." Later in that same episode, he says to his children: "Kids, I admit it, I did not marry well."

Everybody Loves Raymond, which aired from 1996 to 2005, was a consistently top-rated show, even in its final years. This program, which continues in re-runs, portrays a resigned marriage and a semidysfunctional family. On this show, marriage itself is a frequent punch line. For example, on one episode, Debra is talking about her brother-in-law's then wife, Joanne. She says about the way Joanne treats Ray's brother, Robert, "She's always putting him down." Ray responds: "That's marriage."

Ray and his fed-up wife, Debra, often argue, but their fights are always outdone by the barrage of insults that fly between Ray's parents. On practically every episode, Ray's father disparages his wife with countless "ball and chain" remarks and constantly complains about marriage. On one episode, Ray's mother says, "We've been married for forty-six years. We've seen the lows, we've seen the highs." Ray's father responds, "What day was the high?" On another episode, when Ray's parents get into an argument and his mother takes up residence at his house, Ray remarks on how happy his father seems without his mother. He says, "It is like Dad is on parole from marriage prison."

While some married couples find this program humorous and even relatable, to a single person looking in on married life from the outside, the show makes marriage look like a nightmare. While there are occasional loving moments between Ray and his wife, the show zeroes in on the more mundane and even negative aspects of married life, rarely focusing on the positive, loving moments that come with having a spouse and a family. In fact the characters make several references about Ray finding time with the children "boring."

In one episode, Ray visits his brother at his new bachelor pad. For Ray, the trip is all about what he thinks he is missing out on by being married. When he arrives at the apartment, he finds beautiful, single women everywhere:

RAY: This is a fantastic apartment.
          (Robert complains about the apartment)
RAY: I didn't notice because I was too busy looking at all the women. There are women everywhere. Are you the only man in the building?
ROBERT: There are some male nurses and flight attendants.
RAY: So this is like your kingdom. Oh my god, the castle has a hot tub.
ROBERT: Good luck getting in there, the girls are always hogging it.
RAY: You haven't actually gone out with any of these women, have you? And if you have, please talk slow.
ROBERT: Come on, Ray, you have seen pretty girls before.

RAY: Yeah, before, way before. What the hell is wrong
            with you, Robert? This is a really nice place to live.
ROBERT: You really like it?
RAY: Are you kidding? I've never been more jealous of
            you in my life.

In Ray's household, misunderstandings, arguments, and complaints dominate daily life and paint a picture of family life that
makes the happy and passionate days of the Huxtables seem like a distant memory.

Marital discontent is the actual premise behind ABC's overnight-
hit show *Desperate Housewives.* The program is a satire of suburban life
centered around four discontented women in an affluent suburb. The
women are depicted as universally frustrated by their husbands or
boyfriends, and by their families. Affairs are rampant, resentment is
common, and happiness within one's marriage is rare. From the
stressed-out mother whose kids drive her to tears, to the wife who
strikes up an affair with her gardener, these married women are truly
portrayed as being desperate. The show often finds its humor in making fun of the idea of domestic bliss. For example, when one of the
husbands, Rex, pays his neighbor for sex, she indulges his sexual fantasies while the camera pans to a plaque on the wall that reads BLESS
THIS HAPPY HOME. Marriage in the suburbs is further mocked by the
fact that this woman is servicing many of her married neighbors. In
the show's first season finale, we see that no one finds domestic happiness: Lynette is on the skids with her husband, Bree's husband is
dead, Gabby's husband goes to prison, and Susan doesn't trust her
live-in boyfriend.

A bleak portrait of marriage unfolded in the 1999 Oscar-
winner *American Beauty,* which stars Kevin Spacey as Lester and An-
nette Bening as Carolyn. The film takes a grim look at suburban
family life. The story is told through the eyes of a lifeless husband
and father who is having a midlife crisis, is completely disconnected

from his wife. Lester tidily sums up the situation, telling Carolyn that their marriage is essentially just a facade. While they may pretend to be "normal," they both know they really aren't. The film's director, Sam Mendes, portrays the worst-case marriage scenario in which love and sex are all but extinct. In a dramatic scene, Carolyn and Lester argue one night when she discovers he is masturbating. He says with burning resentment that he is the only one with blood pumping through his veins. She declares that they no longer have a marriage and threatens divorce.

The chasm between husband and wife in this over-the-top portrayal of misery in marriage sums up the common attitude depicted in this generation's media, that the dream of the white picket fence has become a nightmare.

An even more recent movie, *Sideways,* although more subtle than *American Beauty,* focuses on a character who sees marriage as an oppressive fate from which one must escape. A divorced, failed writer, Miles, and his best friend, Jack, take a weeklong drive to wine country in California for a last hurrah before Jack's wedding. Jack, who proclaims, "I'm going to get laid before I get married on Saturday," sleeps with the first woman he meets; he insists to his friend this was something he "had to do" in his "last week of freedom." Negative comments about marriage run through the film: when Miles introduces Jack to a bartender and says, "My friend is getting married in a week," the bartender responds, "My condolences."

Gen-X Fairy Tales

In contrast to these exaggeratedly cynical programs and movies, reality television uses the commercial trappings of marriage to evoke the fairy-tale image of marital bliss—but nonetheless does away entirely with the idea of long-term commitment being taken seriously. Programs such as *The Bachelor, Temptation Island, Married by America,* and *Joe Millionaire* all glorify romantic multiple choice. As cartoonish as they are, these are the fairy tales for this generation—and as all fairy tales do, they can deeply affect those who pay attention to the fantasy involved. By making the search for love into a game of mix-and-match choices, luxury dates, public breakups, and hollow commitments, these shows reinforce the notion that a more perfect choice is always elsewhere. If the Internet turns a potential partner into a consumer item, *The Bachelor* does, too: by pitting twenty-five women against one another in competition for one man (or twenty-five men in competition for one woman). These shows turn the bachelor or bachelorette into a consumer, shopping for his perfect bride or perfect groom. The constant pressure on the bachelor or bachelorette to narrow the pool of potential mates shows viewers that rejecting candidates on the basis of snap judgments can ultimately lead you to your "one and only." Ultimately, the show trivializes marriage and commitment with on-camera engagements taking place after only a few weeks of shallow dates.

While our mothers grew up on Cinderella and Snow White fairy tales in which the heroines wait for their princes to arrive on white horses, our "fairy tales" are damaging in a different way. From limousines to lavish dates, the fantasies of these programs depict celebrity-style romance. This kind of gilded courtship is obviously unattainable in the real world. Furthermore, these programs often end with a proposal, in much the same way that fairy tales of our mothers' generation ended with a wedding. We never see the reality of what happens next—although we read about it in magazines when these couples break up offscreen weeks later.

The Media's Three Categories of Sex

The media's message about sex supplements this pro-single, anti-marriage rift. On TV, there are essentially **three categories of sex**: **hot sex**, **romantic sex**, and **married sex**. There is almost no hot *married* sex. As TV writers would have us imagine it, hot sex is clearly the best kind; marital sex is the worst; and romantic sex lies somewhere in between. Hot sex, the kind featured on practically every popular prime-time television show, is seen as being the sex at the top of the sexual food chain—an uninhibited, guilt-free pleasure that takes place spontaneously between attractive strangers or casual acquaintances in bathrooms, at parties, or out of doors.

Romantic sex, in contrast, is portrayed as being more sweet than hot: We tend to see romantic sex on TV as being likely to take place in a candlelit room after an elegant meal, on a cruise ship, or in some other dreamy venue. While the foreplay is gentle and the act is sometimes preceded by loving conversation, the sex itself is generally unremarkable.

Married sex is seen as being at the bottom of the heap—often depicted as a chore that is about as much fun as paying your taxes. TV married sex is generally prosaic, almost always happens in the bedroom, and is rarely spontaneous. The overwhelming message about married people and sex is that they rarely have it at all—but when they do, it is likely to be a missionary-style obligation. Miranda on *Sex and the City,* who couldn't get enough breathless one-night stands as a single girl, later, on her honeymoon, complains to Carrie about her new husband's insatiable libido.

I remember watching this episode, and noting the conflicting portrayals of sex from season to season. Later, I realized how much these media images shaped my perception of my own sex life—in spite of my conscious resistance to them.

Years ago, I had a casual sexual fling with a man whom I will call James. It was purely physical—reckless, wild, and unreliable sex—and James himself was selfish, insensitive, and also unreliable. He was six feet tall and lean, a little too lean for my taste, with copper brownish hair and eyes that oddly seemed to match. While James was not particularly attractive by most objective standards, his charm and subtle sex appeal won me over almost instantly. At the end of an evening out, after one or two or five cosmopolitans, we'd stumble into one of our apartments, hurriedly close the door—never even turning on the lights—and tear each other's clothes off. James would always start by kissing the nape of my neck. His fingers followed with little patience, first stroking the small of my back and making their way to my chest before unbuttoning my blouse. I could feel his heart pounding with excitement and smell his aftershave. The sex was fast, fun, and felt forbidden since we were not dating. It was like a drug.

The next day's recounting, when I shared the details with my women friends over brunch, was almost as much fun. After a couple of months, though, I started to expect more from James. He never delivered. Around the same time I became frustrated with James, I met a man whom I will call Ben. Ben was actually more physically attractive. He had thick, wavy charcoal hair with hints of gray and deep, penetrating blue eyes. We had much more in common, and I quickly became fond of him. I broke off my titillating tryst with James.

Ben and I dated briefly before we settled into a relationship. Once the excitement of the initial few months of sex with Ben wore off, I started to compare my sex life with him to the fling I'd had with James. I was in love with Ben; the sex was tender, gentle, and emotionally intense. Ben was just as good a lover as James—indeed, in terms of generosity, he was better in some ways. But the context made all the difference. Because Ben and I were close and went to sleep next to each other almost every night, an erotic connection with him felt more like slightly routine "lovemaking" than did the sex I had with the near-stranger James.

I was emotionally fulfilled—but I couldn't keep myself from thinking back to those wild nights with James. An irrational part of me thought I should be having sex like that every single night. I felt guilty as I compared the two men: everything from the differences between their touch, to the way our bodies fit together, even to the number of orgasms I had. I started to feel that sex with the man I loved seemed less exciting than those nights in an inebriated haze with James. The belief that a casual sexual fling is more exciting than sex with a loving and committed partner had sunk deep into my being. I was subconsciously comparing my sex life to the cultural images of casual sex—a mindset that eventually undermined the intimacy I had with Ben.

Nine months into my relationship with Ben, it was seven thirty on a Thursday night and I was primed for the couch and the television in my slippers and flannel pajamas. I had ordered Chinese takeout and was waiting for my boyfriend to come over. Meanwhile, I got a call from my friend Jana, a blonde with legs for days who had more dates in a month than I've had in my entire dating career. She needed help figuring out what to wear on yet another blind date. I had a sudden pang of envy as she talked about her predate excitement. She had never met this man, but a very trusted source, her sister, said he was tall and handsome and incredibly bright. We were on the phone fantasizing about what he would look like, what he would sound like, what he would smell like. How would he greet her? we wondered. I was more than familiar with both the good and bad parts of a first date—but now that I was no longer single, all I could focus on was the excitement of the potential my friend faced with this new man. I was jealous at the thought of the first kiss they might share— the tension, the apprehension. I could imagine being in her shoes, waiting breathlessly for him to make the first move.

For about an hour afterward, I was uneasy about my own relationship. It's not that I hadn't experienced those things with my own boyfriend; I had, months earlier. But the thought that I might never experience that first date, first kiss, again, made me wonder if I was ready to commit to a relationship. I realized that although I loved the man I was with, at times I was more in love with the fantasy of single life produced by HBO. Even though I knew on a cognitive level that it was a sensational, often unrealistic, television program, on a subconscious level I wanted that lifestyle again, at least temporarily. As I slid into the comfort of my relationship, I feared that my life had started

to look more like Edith Bunker's and less like Carrie Bradshaw's—
and it bothered me. I was afraid of losing my identity as the free-
spirited single girl.

My friends had also absorbed these glorified images of casual sex:
when I learned from my research that married people have more and
better sex than do single people in every single relevant survey of the
matter, I shared what I had discovered with a thirty-two-year-old single friend named Dean. Dean had smoldering hazel eyes and the
"cut" body of a water-polo player. He had had lots of casual sex and
reacted to this information with disbelief, since his assumption was
that all the married people he knew were having no sex to speak of.
I insisted it was true—but Dean simply couldn't believe it. Indeed,
whenever I passed on to my single friends this intriguing nugget of
information about married sex being better, they reacted with aston-
ishment and stubborn incredulity.

But married people *do* have more sex and better sex than do singles. MTV, take note: The 1994 National Health and Social Life Survey, which is considered to be the most comprehensive sex survey
done since the initial Kinsey report of 1948, found that married couples have sex more often and enjoy it more, both physically and emotionally, than do their single counterparts. Forty-three percent of the
married men surveyed reported that they had sex at least twice a
week. Only 26 percent of non-cohabiting single men said they had
sex this often. Married women have more active sex lives than do all
types of single women, except for those who live with a partner: 39
percent of married women had sex two or three times a week or
more, compared to 20 percent of single women. Both husbands and
wives were more satisfied with sex than were sexually active singles.

While no one can prove that the glorification of single life and
the erasure of images of marital fulfillment have led to my generation's romantic angst, these images certainly don't help. When I hear
from single people around me redundant statements such as: "I fear
that I will become boring and not seek out the world. I fear that mar-

riage means stagnancy"—even from people like the young man who
made this comment, whose parents have a close, fulfilling marriage—
I have to wonder if fantasy is overriding experience.

When I heard the story of a bride-to-be who was faced with
anti-marriage sentiment, again I had to wonder if negative media
messages about married life were at play. My cousin Rita recently attended the bachelorette party of a friend at a bar called Iggy's on
New York's Upper East Side. "American Woman" by Lenny Kravitz
was playing, and twenty- and thirtysomethings were packed into the
dive bar, with neon lights and two-dollar house shots, clamoring for
the bartenders' attention. The bride, Katherine, a slender twenty-six-
year-old with corkscrew curls, was dressed in a black halter top and a
miniskirt that night. Like many a bride-to-be, she also wore a veil—
attracting the attention of people at the bar. My cousin reported that
no less than ten people, both men and women, came up to the bride
and said, "Don't do it," or some very similar variation on that comment. Only one young woman approached the bride and said: "I
wish it were me." The bride was astounded by the number of
strangers who approached her to offer their unsolicited cynical opin-
ions on her upcoming nuptials. The bride laughed at first as she re-
adjusted her veil. While there is no way to know for sure if there was
a connection between the media and this situation, the scene in the
bar underlies an attitude among this generation, at least in some circles, that getting married is no longer seen as enviable. While that old
purely positive notion of earlier generations may not have been entirely realistic, today the negative stereotype of marriage as something
to dread is at the opposite end of the spectrum. While perhaps men at
bachelor parties decades ago might have teased each other with "the
old ball and chain" jokes, it would be hard to imagine women of earlier generations advising other women not to tie the knot.

Recently I overheard a group of men, two married with children
and two single, talking about their fortysomething bachelor coworker.
"He still goes out and parties. He has the best life," they noted.

Whether or not those remarks reflect men's true feelings, clearly it is an increasing social norm to be jealous of the single guy—or say that you are jealous. But my happily married friends assure me that, while their lives may not look particularly glamorous to others from the outside, given the choice between going to some trendy party and being home with their family, they would almost always choose being at home. They report that marriage and family life is anything but boring. In fact, studies from nearly every country have shown that married people are happier and healthier than single people. The data also indicate that men in particular benefit from marriage more. Interviews with 127,545 adults published in a report titled "Marital Status and Health, United States 1999–2002"showed that married people are less likely to be in poor-to-fair health, smoke or drink heavily, or suffer from such health problems as headaches and serious psychological distress.

In any moment of anyone's life there is the event—in other words, that person's experience—and there is the cultural interpretation of that event. While the audience of *The Bob Newhart Show* might look at a couple sitting at home quietly in their den together as blissful, a *Sex and the City* audience might view that same event as boring. The *Bob Newhart* viewer may see an enviable scene, but the *Sex and the City* viewer may think life is passing that couple by while Samantha is out dancing all night in her Manolos.

I can speak for myself, here, as a single woman dating in the *Sex and the City* era: I identify to a lesser extent with the *Bob Newhart* viewer. The picture of a couple nestled safely at home together is not one that resonates as particularly blissful with me. In fact, I can recall years ago lying in bed next to a boyfriend I'd been with for a few months in what felt like a similar scene. I was wearing a black silk Victoria's Secret camisole and he was tucked in next to me beneath my floral comforter in his Calvin Klein boxer briefs reading John Grisham's *A Time to Kill*. At that moment, I remember feeling completely frustrated. I was wondering why he was reading; why doesn't he want to have sex with me? This certainly can't be a good sign for our relationship, I thought. The mere fact that he was reading made me feel that our relationship had become routine and stale. It wasn't until years later that I realized that, in the best of marriages, there is a lot of reading in bed. But when the culture only shows you that a bed is for fireworks, otherwise you may as well end it all, it is hard not to be influenced. When *The Brady Bunch* set the standard for TV marriage and family life, the marital non-erotic kiss was the payoff, the happy conclusion of the episode. Today, the non-erotic marital kiss on TV is often code for a scene from a life in hell.

Given the fact that before single men and women even meet, they, too, are influenced by this anti-marriage landscape—how on earth can longing proceed without trepidation to courtship, and courtship, without ambivalence, to true, committed love?

6

The Collapse of Courtship and the Death of Romance

This is the first e-mail exchange of a couple who met on Match.com in 2002:

---
outdoorbabe@talkmatch.com wrote:

hey there,

Well I got to be honest and say I was perusing this thing and came upon you. What can I say? I thought you had some qualities that were appealing. Really appreciated your comments and photos.

You probably want to find out a little about me before you consider hitting the reply button.

Well, I work and live in San Francisco. I love to ski, windsurf, work, volunteer, and travel (there are probably more but I can't go on).

Anyway, I would love to hear back from you. When I saw the skiing photo, I said wow, I need to meet this girl.

---

jtlady@talkmatch.com wrote:

hi there,

Thanks for writing and thank you for the compliments. It does seem that we have more than a few things in common. Skiing is a sport I can rally around. Been doing it since before I can remember, so it's like second nature to me and I love to travel.

Ok, so I could babble on and on about who I am, what I like, and what I do, but that's probably not a wise use of my time. I would love to start a dialogue with you. So . . . let's chat.

Joanne

---

outdoorbabe@talkmatch.com

u have a killer smile . . .

and you ski, I love it . . .

where are you from?

This exchange went on for thirteen e-mails before the two finally met face to face. Amazingly, this banal, nearly anonymous introduction led to a passionate relationship. This kind of e-mail exchange has become a fairly typical way for men and women of this generation to connect. In fact, 26.6 million people visited personals sites in May 2005, according to comScore Networks, a market research firm that tracks Internet use. In our parents' generation, a man and woman would of course speak to one another and he would ask the woman out on a date. He would pick her up, take her out, and pay for the evening. The couples who continued to date would get to know each other's families, go steady, and eventually get engaged. Physical intimacy generally happened gradually. The dance steps for the boy and the girl were fairly clear and so was the progression of the relationship.

Obviously, today dating remains a popular way for a man and woman to get to know each other, but the rules of the game have certainly changed: going out is no longer a requirement for erotic contact, nor is there a presumption that the man pays. Courtship behavior that has kept us going for generations has broken down; indeed, the very concept of courtship is foreign to most Gen-Xers. When I asked some of my unhooked men and women if they knew what courtship was, they asked: "You mean, who pays?" or "Is that when the guy 'woos' the girl?" Very few knew what traditional courtship actually looked like, in practical terms. So, what is the definition of courtship? Sociologist Andrew Cherlin defines it this way: "[Courtship] was a process where parents and others kept watch while young people found a spouse. [The process] had rules; steps carried out in view of everyone. It was an elaborate routine of going steady, getting pinned, getting engaged, and then going on to marriage. You might not have sex until then." While the idea of courtship may seem like an outdated formality to many of this generation, for earlier generations it served several purposes. Courtship forced the suitor to pass a series of tests to prove that intimacy was safe and appropriate without risk to the man or woman's reputations. In addition, the suitor established himself as an upstanding partner to the woman's family. Finally, it helped to create and build romance with gradual steps toward intimacy.

When courtship was abolished by the sexual revolution, romance died along with it. The freedoms of the revolution blurred gender roles and introduced casual sex. The problem for us? No new rules more appropriate for our generation were ever established to replace the old ones. As a result, dating today is often characterized by confusion and uncertainty about what each gesture—each phone call, each night together—might mean. In fact, there are so many trip wires for dating today that is difficult for singles to know how to act. With all this confusion, it is hard to even get to a second date, let alone a relationship.

While few want to go back to the days when dating meant that the man struggled to get to second base and the woman struggled to hold him at bay, there are several real casualties of our inheriting the legacy of courtship's collapse. Trying to make it up as they go along, Gen-Xers have adopted some undefined, inconsistent ways of dating. The effort is brave; but many of these new approaches are so imperfect that they serve to keep us unhooked.

No Clear Etiquette

In the absence of clear dating rules, we make it up as we go along. While this strategy may seem like a good solution, the lack of clear etiquette can often result in miscommunication and potentially undermine a romantic connection. Dates are often set up for failure before they even begin.

"Confused Courtship"

Lisa, a twenty-six-year-old newspaper reporter, experienced firsthand how the lack of clear gender roles on a date can undermine a potential union. Lisa is a runner with an athletic, broad build and perfect posture. She has the famous haircut that Jennifer Aniston introduced on *Friends* in 1995. She lives in a duplex apartment in Cleveland, Ohio, decorated with distressed antique furniture that she has collected from flea markets and estate sales over the years. The walls are lined with black and white photos of her after-graduation trip to Paris, and she painted the periwinkle borders herself. It had been about a year since Lisa's last relationship and she was eager to meet someone. One of Lisa's friends had given her phone number to a single twenty-nine-year-old social worker, Sam, rumored to be attractive. Lisa was at home one night after work lying on the couch, watching *The Daily Show,* when Sam called. She was screening her calls and didn't answer. When Lisa heard his voice she was excited; he sounded gregarious and confident. But she didn't want to call back right away—for fear of seeming too aggressive. She worried at the same time, though, that Sam might be dating multiple women—and if she waited too long to call back, he might meet someone else. She finally decided to return the call the next day.

After a three-day exchange of phone messages, Lisa and Sam finally spoke directly. Their phone conversation lasted for twenty minutes, but it was filled with awkward silences. Sam finally ended the excruciating phone call with a blunt invitation: "I will pick you up on Thursday at eight o'clock."

Lisa was not deterred; she knew by now that the first phone conversation is always awkward. On Thursday, Lisa rushed home from work, flung open her accordionlike closet, and tried on four outfits. Her navy bedspread was covered with clothes: her Levi's, her new blue sweater from Banana Republic, a pink V-neck top, a Coach bag, and a celadon cardigan. At seven forty, still in her bathrobe, with Kelly Clarkson's latest CD playing, she took a final look in her closet, and settled on the outfit she had worn on her last blind date: a sheer white blouse and a Cordova skirt with flowers.

Sam arrived on time. When Lisa opened the door she was relieved to find a handsome man with broad shoulders and an endearing smile. They greeted each other and walked together to the car. When they arrived at his two-tone black-and-white Mini Cooper, Sam entered on the driver's side. Lisa was annoyed that Sam hadn't opened the door for her.

After they both got into the car, Sam turned to Lisa and said, "So . . . what do you want to do?" Lisa was disappointed once again. Her idea of a date is that a man plans the evening and takes the woman out. Lisa and Sam finally agreed on a Thai restaurant in the neighborhood. They had a nice time; conversation flowed and so did the wine. At the end of the date, the waiter placed the check, in the most politically correct way, in the middle of the table. Suddenly the fluid conversation was halted by a pregnant pause. Lisa worried that if she waited too long to offer, it would look as though she expected him to pay the bill; but if she grabbed too quickly for her wallet, she might insult him. She was hesitant to attempt her friend Rebecca's strategy: "the fake grab." Rebecca was infamous for reaching for her purse on dates before being stopped—without any intention of paying; sometimes Rebecca didn't have any money in her wallet when she made the move.

Confused, Lisa nervously lunged for the check. Sam said, "Let's split it." Although she had offered to pay because she feared offending him, she didn't really expect Sam to take her up on it. She thought maybe this was a sign that he was not interested in her or that perhaps he was cheap.

Sam took Lisa home. They sat in the car for a half hour talking, each trying to end the date but uncertain of the magic words to use that would allow closure without offense. Even though the evening didn't get off to a great start, Lisa had hoped that perhaps an incredible good-night kiss would have compelled her to see Sam again. She wanted to lean toward him for the kiss and see if they had any chemistry, but she thought she needed to let him initiate. Sam didn't—and the conversation lingered. Finally, Lisa couldn't stand it anymore. She decided to punctuate the evening with the obligatory good-night kiss on the cheek and bolted out of the car.

While Lisa found Sam to be interesting and attractive, the fact that he didn't open her door, make a reservation, or even kiss her good night turned her off. But she was willing to give it a second try: their conversation had been interesting and she found him attractive. To her surprise, though, he never called.

A few weeks later, her friend who set her up told her that Sam didn't call her for a second date because he thought she wasn't interested. She seemed uncomfortable letting him pay and he interpreted her cursory good-night kiss as her signal that she wasn't attracted to him.

Confusion over prescribed gender roles on the first date, part of Evil Influence #4 (The Inadvertent Effects of Feminism), can thwart the chances of a union getting off the ground. You may or may not share Lisa's expectations, but I have found that every woman my age has some very personal "script" of this kind. My friend Ava, a publicist who takes her independence very seriously, was put off because an otherwise lovely man did not place himself nearer to the street when he walked with her—a stipulation that I found ridiculous. But what is not ridiculous is that these private scripts are common, and often baffle communication.

I have had countless conversations with male and female friends and unhooked respondents about how unfulfilled expectations on a first date can impede a second meeting. My friend Jean, a thirty-three-year-old real estate agent from Washington, D.C., turned down a second date with a man because he didn't pick her up for their night out. And one of my female respondents, Pam, a twenty-six-year-old flight attendant from Minneapolis, recalled the time she went on a date with a guy who didn't open the car door for her. She decided to send him a clear message: she sat in the car and leaned on the horn until he came around and opened the door. As you might expect, there was no second date. My girlfriends will often complain, after a date, about at least one personal "rule" violation: he didn't walk her home or put on her coat or call a cab for her. Conversely, friends of mine—even feminist ones—have confessed that they fell in love with their mates when the men pushed in their chairs, or got their coats, or dropped them off at their destination and then parked the car.

Although it might seem that women are the ones caught up in obsessing about dating etiquette, men complain about it, too. While women's complaints seemed to indicate frustration with the lack of traditional courting, men are often at the other end of the spectrum, exasperated with women who don't seem to want to share the duties of a date—the planning or the expense. My friend Roy, a thirty-five-year-old wine salesman from Indiana, said he took a woman out to a nice restaurant and then out for drinks. She didn't offer to pay for a single cocktail. He decided not to take her out again. Other men complained of the exact opposite scenario; they said they wanted the women to let them pay for the date and take charge of the evening. Perhaps these dates would have made it to the second round, but the lack of clear rules resulted in a romantic misfire before a connection could even be made.

The closest thing this generation has ever had to a dating script was the 1995 bestselling—albeit controversial—book *The Rules* by authors Ellen Fein and Sherrie Schneider. *The Rules* sought to provide guidelines for singles of this generation—but the book proved to be no more than a passing fad. The thirty-five "secrets" armed women with dating commandments ranging from "always end the date first" to "never accept a date without a week's notice."

While I am by no means a *"Rules* girl"—in fact, the very thought of subscribing to such a contrived set of standards to win a man's affection is preposterous to me—the book's success is evidence that many young people longed for some clear set of guidelines. The book's secrets became popular folklore among single women, and the guide was passed from girlfriend to girlfriend, the way our mothers shared recipes. Men overheard the book's tips from their female friends—and a word-of-mouth dating script got around in some singles' circles. A handful of people I know credit *The Rules* with helping them find a husband or a boyfriend. Others, however, found the etiquette too hard to sustain or simply ridiculous. Interestingly, the rules weren't as foolproof as some people might have hoped. Five years after the book came out, one of its authors got divorced. *The Rules* may have provided for some a shortcut to getting the guy, but not necessarily to keeping him.

Almost a decade later came a book comically called *He's Just Not That Into You,* about how to read a man's actions in a world with no clear rules. *Sex and the City* writer Liz Tuccillo and consultant Greg Behrendt coined the bestseller's title and wrote the book after using the line "He's just not that into you" in a *Sex and the City* episode. The book seeks to decode male behavior for women by outlining all the ways in which men send covert signals that they are not interested. The authors urge women not to make excuses for these men, but instead to read these signals for what they are—messages of disinterest. At the end of the book, the authors urge women to adhere to some "standard suggestions" such as: "I will not go out with a man who hasn't asked me out first," to ward off a relationship that is doomed from the start. This book is yet another attempt to demystify the otherwise baffling process of dating in a postcourtship culture.

"Express Dating"

Busy Gen-Xers sometimes approach dating in unconventional and unromantic ways that are unlikely to result in any kind of real relationship. In the past it was clear what a proper date looked like. Today, men and women of other generations would be surprised by what some Gen-Xers consider to be a date. Take, for example, the date of one of my friends named Courtney.

I met Courtney and my friend Ellen at a Mexican restaurant on the Upper West Side of New York City. Courtney, a thirty-one-year-old speech therapist with platinum hair, a bubbly smile, and an outgoing personality, was eager to tell us about her "disaster date." We took a seat at the dimly lit place with oversized murals and waitresses scurrying around with colossal trays. We ordered a round of margaritas and Courtney started to tell us her story: Two months after Courtney's painful breakup with a man she had dated for a year and a half, she decided to go online. This was Courtney's first experience with Internet dating. She connected with a thirty-two-year-old chiropractor whose profile she thought sounded interesting: "He seemed intelligent and he looked cute in his picture." After trading e-mails and then voice mail, they finally spoke on a Thursday night. Neil sounded somewhat intriguing on the phone and seemed nice enough, so they planned to get together on Sunday night. They would coordinate the details that afternoon. Sunday morning, Courtney laid out what she was going to wear on the date: a green Juicy long-sleeved shirt that matched her eyes, her favorite pair of jeans, and black boots that gave her an extra inch. She ran a few errands and then went to the gym. As soon as she walked in the door, Neil called to discuss when and where to meet. Courtney told him she needed to shower and asked if he could call back in an hour. Courtney got ready for the date. When Neil called back he said, "I know this might sound crazy, but why don't we meet on a street corner; if we like each other we can go somewhere else." Courtney, who had showered, applied makeup, and was dressed in the outfit she had chosen that morning, was baffled by Neil's suggestion: "I thought it was crazy. I said, 'You don't want to meet for a drink?'" "I just think meeting on a corner would be easier," he replied. He wanted to meet her on the corner of Ninety-second Street and Broadway. "I was hesitant. I told him I would call him back," she said as she took another sip of her margarita. My friend Ellen inquired, "You were actually thinking about going?" Courtney explained, shrugging her shoulders, "I thought it was crazy, but I was already dressed. So I decided to get another opinion." Courtney called three trusted sources for counsel. One friend told her not to go. Her sister agreed, and the third friend said: "That's near my place, so go and then meet me afterward for dinner." Courtney called Neil back with no intention of meeting him: "It sounds like you are not into meeting. So, maybe we shouldn't." He quickly responded with an anxious tone: "You're misunderstanding me. I just think it takes the pressure off." She replied, "I will meet you at five fifteen, but I have to meet someone at five forty-five." We understood her need for a backup plan; at one point or another we had all booked dates that we expected to be disappointing that way. As she flipped her hair, she added: "I wanted him to know I didn't give a shit. I wasn't making my plans around him and I figured the date would suck, so I wanted something fun to do after."

Ellen, who disapproved of Courtney going on this date, laughed. "So, did you pass the curb test? Clearly he want to check you out, see what you looked like before he bothered taking you out for dinner or a drink. What a jerk."

"So what was he like?" I inquired curiously.

"I was so turned off at that point I doubt I could have liked him." She rolled her eyes.

"So what happened?" Ellen nudged.

"The minute he saw me he said, 'You are so beautiful. You look so much more beautiful than your picture. You can never tell from someone's picture if they are going to be ugly or not. Pictures can be deceiving.'" Courtney, not knowing what to say, just said, "Thank you." Then to her surprise, Neil asked: "Can we go somewhere else?" "I told you I was meeting someone at five forty-five," she snapped. He suggested that she change her plans. But she insisted, "I don't blow people off." Neil replied, "Well, can I take you and your friend to dinner?" Courtney looked at Neil and said sternly, "No, I have plans for the evening." "Can I call you, then?" he asked sheepishly.

Ellen and I were convulsed with laughter at this point. "He's got to be kidding," she said as she ordered another margarita. Courtney had no intention of ever seeing Neil again, but she looked up at him and said, "You can try me."

The next night, Neil called. She didn't pick up, and the following night he left a message asking if he could take her out for dinner. Courtney never returned his calls. Three months later, to her surprise, he e-mailed again. She didn't recognize his screen name so she replied. He wrote: "Remember me? We met on the street corner." She immediately replied: "I didn't realize it was you." "Can I take you out to dinner?" he wrote. She typed the words: "I just don't think we are meant to be" and shut down her computer.

Neil learned the hard way that he had lost his opportunity with Courtney. While the date on the street corner obviously reflects an extreme example, nonetheless it is on a spectrum with a type of dating strategy practiced by many Gen-Xers. Because Gen-Xers often have busy, overscheduled lives and many go on multiple dates, they often make dates short and casual. Some even **"double book."** "Double booking" is this generation's term for making two different plans for the evening. This kind of time-saving approach to dating, of course now facilitated by speed-dating services such as HurryDate or 8 Minute Dating, allows the user to meet dozens of people and spend only three or eight minutes with each, depending on the service. This type of dating obviously requires that you eliminate potential mates on the basis of quick, superficial judgments. A January 2005 article in the *Harvard Business Review* entitled "Why Smart People Underperform" makes the case that living in a sped-up world can actually undermine our lives at work by forcing us to become effective at snap judgments, but ineffective at making bigger, more important types of decisions. If that is the case, you can imagine what it does to our personal lives when you sit across from twenty-five potential mates and have to decide in three minutes whether or not you should consider him or her as someone with whom to spend the rest of your life.

Dating strategies designed to save time create an attitude of impatience and make it easier to discount someone without really getting to know him or her. Encounters like this are highly unlikely ever to result in a potential long-term match, regardless of who is on the other side of the date. The common mentality among this generation, that you should be able to have everything you want precisely when you want it, is clearly amplified in our approach to dating. Take, for example, a new book put out by Match.com entitled, *How to Find the Right Person in 90 Days.* The notion that finding true love should happen in an instant or in your time frame is ridiculous. The journey to lasting love is more like training for a marathon than running a sprint. Love takes time. This instant-gratification approach to love, whether Gen-Xers realize it or not, is a noninvestment strategy that practically guarantees that the date will result in failure. Risk-taking and time investment are two ingredients that are absolutely necessary for the success of a long-term relationship. By making such "express" dates, we are already looking for a way out of a potential relationship, rather than a way in.

"Cyber Courting"

In addition to the lack of roles and rules when it comes to dating etiquette, new technologies add yet another element to the already confused world of dating and courtship. Cultural rules have not caught up with our technology and this seriously affects romantic interaction. Take, for instance, the courtship between my friend Marissa, a thirty-two-year-old travel agent, and a thirtysomething lawyer named Phillip. Marissa has layered hair that softens her angular face and a light-hearted, ebullient disposition. She dated Phillip for a month and a half. She was set up with him through mutual friends. On their first date, they went out for a quiet romantic dinner. Marissa found Phillip, a 5'8" soccer player with a half-moon smile and a dry sense of humor, to be charming and attractive. At the end of the date, they said good night and Phillip asked for her Instant Message screen name. The next day, Phillip started to IM Marissa.

At first Marissa thought IM'ing with Phillip was a fun diversion from an otherwise boring workday. They continued to IM a couple times that week and then one day he IM'd, "I was thinking about going to a movie tonight, any interest?" Marissa replied, "Sounds good. Why don't you give me a call?" He IM'd back, "Meet me at the 7:30 showing of *Million Dollar Baby* at the Loews Cineplex near your house." They went to the movie and had a nice time, but after that he continued to communicate with her only on IM. He IM'd to chat, to ask her out for dates, and even to flirt with her. After a couple of weeks Marissa started to complain to her friends. "It really annoys me. He never calls. Maybe he is really self-absorbed. He won't give his time. It is rude and a real turn-off that he only communicates with me over the computer."

Marissa's friends understood why she was so frustrated. Her best friend, Leah, recently found herself e-mailing more than talking with someone she recently started dating. Leah suggested she stop signing on. "If you're not on IM, then he will have to call you." Marissa agreed and for a week she didn't sign on. But to her dismay, her strategy didn't work. A week later she told Leah, "I stopped signing on for a week and he never called. He even went on vacation and I didn't know about it. He got back from vacation and he e-mailed me. 'I didn't see you on IM, where were you?'" A frustrated Marissa recalled, "If he really wanted to know where I was, he would have called. He only IM's. What is wrong with him?" Marissa started to analyze what his using only cyber communication meant: "I wasn't sure if he was a pussy or if he was just not that into me." Despite her frustration, she kept dating him because, when they were together, she enjoyed herself. And, after going on so many dates with men she had no interest in, she thought she would stick it out with Phillip. She explained that she never asked that he call her, because she wanted him to call her only if he truly wanted to, not because she asked him to. One night, after coordinating plans via e-mail, they went out and had a great date: dinner and dancing, followed by several cocktails. She was very attracted to him and, of course, the vodka didn't hurt. She started to forget about her IM frustration. His voice and titillating touch made her forget that the only real communication she had with him between dates was over a computer screen. At the end of the evening, they went back to his place. They talked for over an hour and then they had great sex. Before they parted they told each other what a good time they had.

The next day, although she didn't expect flowers, she thought communication between them would certainly be different. After spending the night, she felt confident he would call. But once again he IM'd, "Last night was fun. What are you up to for the rest of the weekend?" For Marissa, that was it. She was frustrated, not to mention embarrassed that she spent the night with him. She IM'd back: "I was really drunk last night" and signed off. Marissa explained with a sharp tone, "I just thought he had to hide behind a screen. It was like he was afraid of getting to know someone and afraid of intimacy. It had no chance to grow." After that, Marissa stopped IM'ing Phillip. "I never logged on. I ended up changing my screen name, so the communication fizzled." She explained, "We never got to explore the potential. If you only communicate through IM, you can't establish communication or really get to know the other person." Marissa never saw or communicated with Phillip again. A month later, Marissa's best friend went out with a group of coworkers and ran into a friend of Phillip's at a bar. He immediately asked, "What happened with Marissa and Phillip? He really liked her." Leah replied, "Then why didn't he call her? He only IM'd her." The guy responded, "Really. That is why they never went out again?" Leah nodded and the minute she left the bar she called Marissa and told her what Phillip's friend said. Marissa explained, "I was shocked to hear he really liked me, since he never called!"

Marissa and Phillip's courtship is an example of how a potential relationship was thwarted because of technology, part of Evil Influence #2 (Multiple Choice Culture). Phillip hid his feelings behind a computer screen, leaving Marissa baffled about his interest. Technology ultimately created emotional distance and miscommunication, and got in the way of a potential relationship.

Some of my single subjects also complained about their problems with prospective dates and technology. They said these men (or, theoretically, women, too), rather than asking them out and committing in advance to a real night out, would instead rely on cell phones, text messaging, or BlackBerries to get together on the spot. The instantaneous connection this technology provides not only makes **"booty calls"** convenient but it also makes the formality of having a real date, that was planned ahead of time, a thing of the past. Technology makes it difficult to know the intention and commitment level of those who use it as part of dating. Finally, people feel more comfortable blowing off a date they meet and communicate with over a computer screen than at church or through a friend.

No Clear Signposts

Another casualty of courtship's collapse is the lack of signposts that indicate where a relationship is headed. In the pre–sexual revolution past, the point of romantic courtship was clear: finding a marriage partner. Sociologist Barbara Dafoe Whitehead, author of *Why There Are No Good Men Left,* explained the essential role of courtship best: "Romantic courtship is a process of mate selection closely connected to marriage. As it has been elaborated and codified in social practice over the ages, it is organized as a linear progression, or ladder, toward marital commitment." Contemporary dating is not necessarily about mate selection for marriage—just as teen dating was not necessarily for marriage in the 1950s. In this way, though—many adults cycling intimately through one another's lives without the necessary intention of marriage—we are a historical generation. Today, adults date for many other reasons: short-term companionship, raw sex, emotional stability, or to find a live-in love. Evil Influence #1 (The Cult of I), Evil Influence #3 (The Divorce Effect), Evil Influence #4 (The Inadvertent Effects of Feminism), and Evil Influence #7 (The Fallout from the Marriage Delay) are all factors that have helped contribute to changing dating motives. The intention of dating these days often depends more on what life stage you're in than whether you have found "the one."

Graduated steps marked progress in the courtship process of previous generations: "going steady" or "pinning" or engagement. Today, the absence of such signposts can lead one or both people in the relationship to make incorrect assumptions. Singles often invest physically, emotionally, and financially in their relationships—living together, getting to know each other's families, taking vacations together—without any markers of intensifying commitment. So, if the relationship ends, it can come as a dramatic, unexpected blow to one member of the couple. He or she may feel betrayed after investing heavily in the relationship.

In a low-commitment culture, getting into a relationship can start to feel like gambling at a Las Vegas casino—you invest and you lose, you play again and lose—and the pattern continues. Each time, it seems you are left with nothing, and you have to start again from scratch. And, though I mentioned it earlier, it bears repeating that the more failed relationships one experiences, the more scar tissue that grows around your heart, therefore adding to this generation's cynicism.

For example, my friend Marni, a thirty-four-year-old financial analyst from Los Angeles, reports that she looks for signs that a man is noncommittal on the first date. She was in a five-year relationship with a guy who spent all of his time out drinking with his friends. Ultimately, he never committed to her. Now, if a man she dates talks about partying with his buddies or hasn't been in a relationship for a few years, she is reluctant to give him a second date. She fears investing in something that has little potential to get serious. Her past experience has made her fearful of commitment and therefore limited her ability to even get past the courtship stage.

Without signposts on the road to romance, Gen-Xers are, understandably, trying hard to invent ways to assess the strength of the commitments of their boyfriends or girlfriends.

"The DTR" Talk

"The DTR" is an expression some people of this generation use that stands for "the defining the relationship" conversation. Because of a lack of guideposts, there comes a point in many relationships when someone asks the question: "Where is this relationship going?" The couples that have these stressful conversations are actually the lucky ones, because at least then they know where the relationship stands. Those that don't have "the talk" are often in the dark for months or even years. My friend Allen, a charming thirty-five-year-old engineer with a cherubic face and expressive eyes, told me that he was caught off guard by "the DTR" six months into a relationship with a woman named Cindy. He complained to me as we talked over a Corona on his couch in Boston: "We had 'the DTR' last night. She said she needed to know where things were going and what my plans were. I was just having fun. I wasn't ready to define things. I wasn't thinking about it," he said. He seemed to really like her but, ultimately, Allen told Cindy he wasn't sure where their relationship was going. They broke up a couple of weeks later.

Although the DTR is perhaps one of the only ways to gauge whether or not two people are on the same page today, I have to wonder what would have happened had this couple continued in their relationship and let it evolve naturally. If, for instance, there were some more graduated cues in place of the DTR, some more current incarnations of a corsage, a fraternity pin, other less intense—and indeed less dire—markers of growing interest, perhaps the couple would have had some clarity without disrupting the natural flow of the relationship. Courtship of the past had a romantic progression to it, while the DTR approach is reactive and abrupt. Also, the DTR can put premature pressure on a young relationship and may be off-putting to the person who doesn't initiate the conversation.

Even more important, according to Allen, nothing turns a man off quicker than being forced to have the DTR. The marriage delay, as I mentioned earlier, has given men an advantage in the dating market. While they face little pressure to date on a time frame, women still face considerable biological pressure and therefore are often the ones to initiate the DTR. It is also understandable that a generation that dates without direction would feel a need to define the terms of the relationship. But this approach may be too constraining for many Gen-Xers, who value the freedom to change their minds, and it may actually undermine a relationship that has potential.

"The Bling Ultimatum"

For those who have invested deeply in relationships but bypassed the DTR, there is a more drastic approach. Shelly, a thirty-five-year-old makeup artist from Los Angeles, a second-generation Korean-American woman with purplish-auburn hair and porcelain skin, experienced firsthand the dangers of living with someone without a commitment. Shelly had dated John, a thirty-six-year-old actor who has a boyish Matt Damon appeal, for two years before they moved in together. They bought a small three-bedroom house in North Hollywood with black granite countertops in their kitchen and plenty of room for their Ansel Adams photos and a black leather couch from his old bachelor pad. The couple had grown quite close: they enjoyed many of the same leisure activities, liked each other's families, and entertained regularly. But, like many Gen-Xers, they never discussed what moving in meant for their relationship.

After three more years together (now a total of five years), Shelly began to wonder if they were ever going to tie the knot. Since she was now in her mid-thirties, she became nervous that her childbearing years might be passing her by. Shelly finally expressed forcefully what she wanted—marriage—although she had mentioned it subtly many times before. This time she said to John in a stern tone: "John, when are we going to get engaged?" John looked up from his *Sports Illustrated* magazine and replied: "I just started a new television pilot; you want to get engaged now?" Over the next few weeks, he walked around the house in a daze. He seemed to be having an internal dialogue about what he should do. Finally, he told her that he was happy with the way things were. She was extremely disappointed.

After two months, her sadness turned to anger and she gave him **"the bling ultimatum"**: "If we don't get engaged within the next couple of weeks, I am moving out." John felt blindsided. Meanwhile, Shelly felt that she had been waiting for John for years. A month passed and to Shelly's surprise there was no ring in sight. Shelly packed all of her belongings and moved out. John looked dumbstruck. He didn't really believe that Shelly would do something so drastic. But Shelly believed the engagement ring should have surfaced even before they moved in together. She had given up on John. She got herself a new apartment and began to rebuild her life after their five-year relationship—a life that she had hoped would result in marriage. They had built a future together: they made their house a home; they went to church together on holidays and cooked dinner once a week for their parents. Now she was starting over.

John and Shelly stayed in contact over the next few months. Meanwhile, Shelly actually became quite content in her new apartment and her new life. She even started dating. Seven months after the breakup, John called her on a Saturday afternoon. He wanted to have dinner with her the following night. She agreed. He picked her up and took her to the romantic, upscale L'Orangerie restaurant for dinner. Over their gourmet, five-course feast, surrounded by elegant French windows, white lilies, and candlelight, they caught up on their lives. When the chocolate soufflé arrived, John had arranged for a violinist to play their song, Andrea Bocelli's "Con Te Partiro," and he pulled out a one-carat princess-cut ring. Shelly was silent. Just the night before she had had a date, her third, with another man, and now John was proposing with a ring in hand. Shelly's heart was pounding. She looked squarely at John and said: "I have to think about it." John, with a puzzled countenance, replied: "This is what you said you wanted." But Shelly explained that in their time apart, she had done a lot of thinking. She was resentful that she had invested so much time with this man. What bothered her even more was that it took an ultimatum for John to propose.

The next two nights Shelly didn't sleep. Her mind was racing. As she lay awake that night she thought about John, his proposal, and also about this new man in her life. The next morning, she woke up and

immediately called John: "I can't marry you. You lost your chance."
"What?" he replied. "Are you kidding me?" She tried to hold back
her tears: "I waited for you for five years. It is too late." She could hear
John's voice trembling over the phone. She figured he was crying. But
Shelly felt John was too late. She questioned whether John was eager
to share a life with her or if he was just lonely. She had moved on from
the relationship. John had missed his window of opportunity.

The story of the post-cohabitation "ultimatum" is not an uncommon one for this generation. In relationships where couples live
together, as so many Gen-Xers do, cohabitation can be a deceptive
sign of progress. For some, living together is a step toward marriage,
while for others, it is merely a matter of convenience. Sometimes
both of these attitudes live together in the same apartment or condo-
minium. For many the act of "moving in" doesn't necessarily mark
any progress at all. Sociologist Barbara Dafoe Whitehead, author of
Why There Are No Good Men Left, explores the problem of cohabitation as a modern form of courtship: "People can slide into living together without any serious discussion or mutual understanding as to
its meaning or purpose." She argues that since there is a lack of formality in cohabitation-as-courtship, there is the risk of miscommunication and faulty assumption, not to mention the risk of a broken
heart. While I do believe cohabitation can be a good idea for many
couples today, cohabitation without commitment can often result in
conflicting assumptions and disappointment.

The "bling ultimatum," which of course can be a line in the
sand in noncohabiting relationships as well, can often be the only
communication between a couple about where the relationship is going. Sometimes it occurs, as in this case, when it is too late. Ultimatums have become another inevitable reality for men and women
living at a time when the marriage delay is so prevalent. Some of my
friends and subjects attest to the fact that often the pressure of the ultimatum is necessary because one person may want to put off marriage for as long as possible. "If I never pushed, we would have been

dating forever," said Anna, a thirty-two-year-old trend researcher, who says she has been happily married to her husband since she gave him an ultimatum three years ago. On the other hand, many men and women talked about how these ultimatums played out to the detriment of their relationships. Tammy, a thirty-year-old guidance counselor from Dallas, gave her boyfriend an ultimatum after two years of dating. He did eventually propose. They were engaged for six months when they began to fight all the time. He said he just wasn't ready to get married. Finally, they agreed to call off the wedding. In this case, her ultimatum pushed him to do something he clearly was not ready for. Of course men, too, can give their own type of ultimatum, but not surprisingly, more often than not it is the women initiating these conversations, in many cases because of biological pressure. While ultimatums are common, of course no one ever wants to be the person who has to give one. In the case of John and Shelly, a forceful and painful ultimatum could have been avoided with some clear signals about where the relationship was going. Perhaps it could have even saved their relationship.

The First Date Interview

Those singles who can't stand ambiguity from the very beginning develop a more direct dating approach. Meet, for instance, Steven Kaplan—as several of my girlfriends did. I was on yet another blind date—my third in the last two weeks. Here we go again, I thought, as I walked out my front door, and waved to the night doorman, Stan. Stan was my friend, and he had watched me return home forlorn from every date in the last month, except for one night when he happened to catch the end of a good-night kiss—albeit from a man who never called me again.

Like most of my friends, I had a careful semiotic clothing code that I had worked out for different kinds of dates. Tonight I was in full date battle mode: wearing my new fitted red V-neck sweater—the effort was to be attractive but not too slutty—paired with Diesel jeans, to give a "casual" impression. I had avoided my usual uniform of black cigarette pants, black top, and Gucci bag (on sale, but no one needed to know), because I did not want to convey that I was too high-maintenance. Hey, I am being honest here.

I was on my way to meet a friend-of-a-friend named Steven Kaplan. I didn't know much about him, except that he was supposedly a good-looking, thirty-six-year-old Jewish oncologist—with a full head of hair. In my mother's mind, of course, he was already fully qualified, sight unseen, to be my husband; in mine, he sounded like he could go any number of ways, but it was at least worth meeting him for dinner on a Tuesday night in the West Village.

I arrived at a cozy, unpretentious restaurant, Gradisca, and looked for someone fitting his description: "I'll be wearing a green sweater and I have salt-and-pepper hair," he'd told me during our short phone conversation. The first person I saw was a man wearing a green shirt—with the largest nose I had ever seen. As I walked toward this man with trepidation, trying to stay focused on the beauty of the soul, someone tapped me on the shoulder. "Hi, I'm Steven," this man said.

I breathed a sigh of relief. He fit the description, and was actually better looking than I had anticipated: 6'2", with thick, wavy salt-and-pepper hair and, thankfully, an entirely ordinary nose. We sat down right away. The restaurant was buzzing with beautiful people. We were seated at a quiet table in the corner, away from all the activity.

I was impressed by Steven's sophistication: he perused the wine list and selected a full-bodied red wine; it was delicious, and we lingered over the bottle for about twenty minutes before ordering dinner. By then, I had a nice buzz, and I was beginning to feel chemistry between us. Steven looked particularly handsome with the shadow of the candle flame flickering on his face, turning his eyes into deep reflective pools. Hmmm, I thought. . . . He asked the usual first-date icebreaker questions: "Where are you from?" "What do you do in your free time?"

Who in New York has free time, anyway? I thought vaguely, as I admired his deep voice and silky lips. I was wondering what it would be like to kiss him.

Before we'd had a chance to order, however, the scene shifted from *Last Tango in Paris* to *Nine to Five*. My date had started to put me through a job interview:

"Do you want to stay in the city for the next couple of years?"

"Why did your last relationship end?"

"How many kids do you want?"

I was floored. I was thinking what it would be like to make out with him, and he wanted to figure out where we were sending our kids to school! When the waitress came and rescued me from his relentless battery of suitability questions, I was thrilled. The romantic mood had been extinguished the moment he seemed to scan my résumé for the position of Mrs. Kaplan.

He sensed my unease, politely walked me home, and gave me an obligatory kiss on the cheek.

I wasn't the only one of my circle, as it turned out, who'd had a date that ended up as a job interview. A few days later, I was having drinks with some girlfriends, and we were comparing our recent dates. I told them about Steven Kaplan. "He was really attractive and sophisticated, but he grilled me about my long-term life plan ten minutes into the date," I complained. Rory, thirty-four, a blunt casting agent with baby-blue saucer eyes, explained my baffling evening to me in her own terms. Her clinical analysis of the different stages in which people approach courtship helped me to understand why so few of these dates we were all going on seemed romantic in the slightest: "He's just trying to figure out what phase you are in. There is **'Phase One'** and there is **'Phase Two'** for people in the dating process," she said. "Phase One involves buying some nice clothes and looking after yourself—for instance, taking care of your apartment, your job—and having lots of sex. I did that until I was about thirty, and I loved it."

Rory continued, "Then there is Phase Two: This is when you want to put your money into building something for your future, you want to make your place a home in preparation for a partner and eventually a family, and most of all you want to share the life you've built with someone. For a woman in Phase Two, it can be challenging: you can try to put a Phase-One guy in a Phase-Two situation, but it rarely works," she explained. Of course, the same applied to women, she said. That was clearly part of the disconnect between Dr. Kaplan and myself. But Rory felt she was now too often on the Phase-Two side of the equation, waiting for a Phase-One man to commit, and she was tired of it. I knew all too well what she was talking about, since I had spent much of my dating years chasing noncommittal men.

But the interrogation on the first date is not particularly romantic. Besides, this tendency of young people to be either partying wildly or on a manic Google-like search for "the one and only" complicates the hope of simply falling in love; if we did not assign ourselves these rigid life categories, we would perhaps be more open to being persuaded to move, by the connection with another person, from Phase One to Phase Two—or even better, to simply want to be close to someone and intimate for its own sake, rather than for the fulfillment of an external timetable. But as long as we continue to approach our search for love this way, perhaps we'd be better off if we wore visible distinguishing signs: "NC" for noncommittal or "R" for ready.

I never saw or spoke to Steven Kaplan after that. I heard he got engaged to someone six months later. I was not surprised. The first date interview was an obvious, but unsubtle, way to weed out those who were not in the same place in their lives. Many of the people I heard from talked about the tormenting challenge of trying to find someone with whom you "connect"—that central word again—who is "ready" for the same things you are. On the whole, more women than men whom I interviewed had this complaint, but there were plenty of men who were pining after women who were "not ready." The **"readiness factor"** was usually a sense of one's own place in one's life, rather than a reaction to the pull of the relationship itself. Steven Kaplan was ready, and he wasn't going to waste any time trying to figure out whether I really was—or, for that matter, whom I really was.

On more than a dozen occasions, I had lent an ear to tortured friends who had waited and waited for a commitment, constantly hoping for clues, signs that their potential mate was coming around. I told the Steven Kaplan story to one of my ex-boyfriends, a semi-reformed noncommitter who had broken my heart over ten years earlier. Years after the breakup, he had said, "Jillian, it wouldn't have mattered if you were Cindy Crawford—I just wasn't ready." Here we were now, friends, and he explained my date with the doctor this way: Most guys don't necessarily end up with the woman they love the most. "It's like a game of musical chairs; you sit down in one chair, then you sit in another, and when the music stops, whatever chair you are sitting in is the chair you end up in." It was the most unromantic thing I had ever heard and I thought I would never be able to buy that line of thinking. While this approach provided a shortcut to finding a mate in an ambiguous dating culture, I doubted that in the long run it resulted in many happy, permanent matches.

Gen-Xers are accustomed to figure-it-out-as-you-go-along dating and seem to resist any early pressure in a relationship, no matter what phase of dating they might be in. The Gen-X approach gives men and women the ability to get in and out of their relationships as easily as they change their jobs or apartments. The lack of formal romantic cues give this generation freedom, but with that freedom often comes a price: the inability to decisively commit.

The Hookup Culture

In our parents' time, romance was obviously an important part of courtship. On the first date of one of my friends' parents, he brought her yellow roses and took her to the then-impressive, candlelit restaurant the Spindletop at the Plaza Hotel in New York. Over the course of the next few months, they took long walks on the beach, drank wine by his fireplace, and watched the sun set together. Their romance led to sexual tension that built over time. It wasn't until their fifth date that they became physical, which at that time meant they "made out" in the back of his car. After six months they spent the night together, but sex, of course, was out of the question. Finally, on their wedding day, they consummated their relationship. That was a typical progression of intimacy in our parents' generation. Today, dating often works backward: the physical part often comes first and then if the sexual encounter is good, a relationship potentially comes next. Many social critics have declared the "death of the date" and the rise of a "hookup culture" on college campuses. A **"hookup,"** of course, is this generation's term for spontaneous sexual encounters with strangers or acquaintances that range from kissing to intercourse. An eighteen-month study, published in 2001, called "Hooking Up, Hanging Out, and Hoping for Mr. Right," commissioned by the Independent Women's Forum, surveyed one thousand college women. These students reported that dates were rare; they said that, instead, young men and women "hang out in packs." In addition, four in ten women in the national survey said they had experienced a "hookup," and one in ten reported having done so more than six times. Although these findings made news, they were not surprising to me. Another study of one school in the Northeast conducted in 2000 by Dr. Elizabeth Paul, chair of the psychology department at the College of New Jersey, and published by the *Journal of Sex Research,* reported an even higher percentage of women who "hook up"—78 percent. The study found that the same percentage of men "hook up." Although this behavior is only formally documented on college campuses, any Gen-Xer can tell you it happens among singles everywhere. Author Tom Wolfe, in his insightful book entitled *Hooking Up*, describes "hooking up" as "a term known to almost every American child over the age of nine, but to only a relatively small percentage of their parents."

Some of my singles spoke of hooking up as a way to "break the ice" when getting to know someone. Ellis, twenty-five, waiting tables in Los Angeles while trying to sell his screenplay, explained: "It is best to have sex first and get it out of the way. You don't want to waste a month of your life getting to know someone only to find out you are not sexually compatible." A common mentality in this "hookup culture" is that the tension of a first date or first meeting, which was to earlier generations an alluring part of attraction-building, is now seen as a nuisance; it can be bypassed with a make-out session—or even with the removal of each other's clothes. If there is in fact chemistry during the hookup, then one might be inspired to invest time into getting to know the other person. This idea of hooking up as a precursor to a relationship is like taking a car for a test drive before you decide to buy.

One of my own hookups happened the night I went to a party in downtown Manhattan at a hip nightclub with crimson walls, a translucent spiral staircase, and a mammoth chandelier made of huge crystals. I was wearing my new silk tank top and dancing with friends to Beyoncé's "Crazy in Love" when a handsome man approached me and started to dance with me. After a few more songs, he asked me if he could buy me a drink. We spent the next two hours chatting at the bar. He was a thirty-three-year-old financial consultant named Todd, with a chiseled jaw and sleek hair, dressed in a navy suit. Todd was friendly, intelligent, and interesting; the kind of guy you hope to meet at a club as swanky as this one. We had another drink, and then another. We talked about our families, where we grew up, and about our work. Finally, he asked me if I wanted to walk for a few blocks. Before I knew it, we were walking straight toward his high-rise apartment complex. We arrived at the mahogany entryway of his bright lobby and he asked me to come up. I stood there, confused about what to do, while the doorman checked me out. I felt pressure to make a quick decision as the lights were beating down on me. I was interested in Todd and I felt if I left at that moment I might never see him again. But the prospect of a "hookup" with this complete stranger seemed a bit dangerous to (cautious) me. However, since we had spent the whole night together, dancing and talking, I decided I needed to stay long enough to give him the opportunity to ask for my number. So we took the steel elevator up to his apartment. We were chatting and laughing, the kind of giddy, embarrassed laughter you have with someone with whom you know you are going to hook up. We walked into his apartment, with its oversized windows and majestic views. I wondered if the impressive decor of his place, festooned with contemporary furniture and David Hockney prints on the wall, was his work or perhaps that of an ex-girlfriend. As I checked out the view, Todd started to fumble with the CD player. He put on some slow music that I didn't recognize. He sat down on his pristine, white leather couch. I decided to take the armchair; while I was very attracted to him, I wasn't completely at ease. "You're so far away," he said. I stood up from the chair and walked toward him. He lunged forward and immediately started kissing me with long passionate kisses while the music played in the background. Then he pulled me on top of him so that I straddled his body. I could feel his chest pressed up against mine. He took out the rubber band that was holding my hair back and shook out my hair, as if he were letting a bird out of its cage. I started to trace his shoulders and then his sinewy arms with my nails. He made his way up the front of my shirt. At that moment I asked myself how far this was going to go. As many of the women in my generation may relate to, I was thinking, if ever there was a night to hook up this was it: after all, I had just had could cause you to rule someone out for a relationship. "In the past I waited and then I realized there was no point or benefit to waiting," she declared. From my own experience, too, I knew how laughable this concept of waiting is to many of my peers. I once went out with a guy who said on our first date: "I'd love to get a bottle of wine and go back to your apartment." I laughed. "That is pretty presumptuous of you." He replied with a half-crooked, devilish smile: "A little mystery is good, too." Is waiting until the second date to fool around with someone what we now consider "mystery"? Although I think my date was content to wait, and it probably was for the good of the relationship, at that particular moment I am sure he would have preferred the alternative.

On the other hand, there are some glimmering signs of courtship's rehabilitation. Although conventional wisdom says that men want cheap, easy "sex on tap," some of my male informants revealed a different picture. A few of the men I spoke to said that they wanted to wait to have sex with a woman whom they cared about. Surprisingly, almost all of these men explained that they were the ones who had asked their girlfriends if they could put off sex until they knew each other better. I know it may sound strange—it did to me as I sat across the table from these handsome, virile, otherwise sexually active men who seemed to have no trouble getting dates, or sex, for that matter— but it is true. Some of these men confessed to early careers in casual sex that got in the way of their ability to develop lasting relationships. And now that these men were older, they said, they knew the potential dangers of having sex too quickly. Gil, a thirty-year-old architect in Minneapolis, explained: "If you like the girl, you risk the loss of the buildup, the excitement, and that is the best part. If you don't like her, it doesn't matter; it is just good sex. But you also risk waking up weeks later and saying to yourself, what is this person really about? It is easy to confuse good sex with a good relationship."

I was also surprised to hear from a handful of women that they sometimes held off from sex with the men they liked and instead slept

with the men with whom they had no real interest. They feared un-
dermining a potential relationship, but they also didn't want to give
up sex. So, ironically, they shared the most intimate sexual experiences with the men they didn't care about, while they withheld from
the ones they did. Dina, a twenty-seven-year-old Bay Area woman
who worked for a nonprofit, explained it this way: "If you are going
to go to the trouble of calling it a date, then you don't have sex with
them on the first night." *New York* magazine reported anecdotally on
women who kept their online dates and sex partners separate: the
women hopped on one Web site for sex and another for dates. They
didn't want to jeopardize a potential relationship by having sex too
soon.

"Friends with Benefits"

In this "hookup culture," another pattern has emerged that would
shock our parents. **"Friends with benefits"** or **"fuck buddies"**
are terms unique to this generation: men and women who hook up
with friends with the understanding that there are no strings attached. Since friendships among men and women are much more
common among this generation, access is easy. And "friends with
benefits" provides safety, not to mention convenience, on the dangerous highway of casual sex. This topic was important enough that the
New York Times explored its prevalence among high school and college students in an in-depth magazine story in 2004. And a 2001 survey, conducted by Bowling Green State University in Ohio, found
that of the 55 percent of local eleventh graders who engaged in intercourse, 60 percent said they had sex with a partner who was no
more than a friend.

I know from my own circle of friends and my unhooked subjects
that "friends with benefits" is also popular among the postcollege,
twenty- and thirtysomething crowd. Sean, the thirty-two-year-old
software salesman living in Los Angeles who gave up his girlfriend

when he went to business school, talked to me one afternoon in his upstairs loft apartment as the sun streamed in his bay windows. He welcomed me into his bright living room with a blue-and-white Pottery Barn rug and began talking faster than I could type. His pronounced nose and thick, blond curly hair gave him an unusual look. His laid-back personality made him more cool than handsome. His apartment was lined with dozens of photographs of suntanned California-looking friends. He was athletic and casual, dressed comfortably in his khaki shorts, T-shirt, and a pair of Tevas. Sean loved spontaneous travel, often hopping on a plane to Vegas or San Francisco with little notice to "party" with his buddies. Though Sean had had his share of love interests, he has even more women friends. He continued to speak at high speed, but caught my attention when he mentioned the ongoing arrangement he had with a handful of these women friends. He explained that he and his friends would rely on each other if they hadn't been dating anyone for a long time. He was not big on one-night stands with strangers; he preferred to dabble in the familiar. While "friends with benefits" was a fairly common practice among the people I interviewed, Sean told me he had a staple of half a dozen friends, many of whom lived out of town, who would even get on a plane and travel halfway across the country for a hookup. I had never heard of such an arrangement. Over the years, this setup worked out well for Sean, until one of his friends got emotionally attached to him. In order to maintain the friendship, the benefits had to stop. With some communication, they were able to resuscitate the friendship, but their arrangement had definitely taken its toll on their relationship.

While I know of no official, scientific studies on twenty- and thirtysomethings having sex with friends, *Playboy* magazine's online casual sex survey conducted in 2003 reports that of their 10,000 respondents, 40 percent of men and 53 percent of women have someone they see just for sex—in other words, a "fuck buddy."

I never had an ongoing "fuck buddy," but some of my friends are

7

Gen-X Sex

"Regular sex is not enough—people are like,
so, you haven't had a threesome?"

—PURNIMA, 33

"I just want to have casual sex—to me, that's love," says actor Colin Farrell. Though Farrell is a celebrity known for his bad-boy behavior, this attitude is not so rare in our generation. We have taken casual sex to a whole new level of casualness: our access to partners is multiplying, and pressure on us to perform is intensifying. The separation of intimacy from emotion has never been so commonplace. We have transformed "casual sex" into **"consumer sex."**

Last summer, I was at a pool party in the Hamptons, New York's summer getaway at the beach, where affluent thirtysomethings party like college kids. One afternoon, I found myself part of a group of single people drinking wine, sprawled out on lounge chairs that overlooked a well-manicured lawn and a black-bottomed pool. A virtual stranger—with gelled hair and a husky build, wearing blue Polo swim trunks—turned to me and asked, "So are you getting any?"

My initial reaction was shock. But as I stumbled to find a suitable response, more disturbing than the answer I did not give—that I wasn't—was my realization that, in some circles, sex truly had become a kind of mundane currency. It seemed to me this man wanted to get a sense of where I was on his barometer, measuring status and power by the number of orgasms I was having that summer, rather than by the kind of car I drove or where I lived in the city.

When I told him I thought his inquiry rude, he pressed on: "So you're not." I didn't want to sound prudish, but I refused to reveal anything about my lackluster sex life that summer. Meanwhile, to my amazement, other people I barely knew started to share candid details of their adventurous sex lives that quickly got my attention, but seemed unremarkable to the group: One guy told us about the time he popped pills secured from his father's Viagra prescription in order to bring a female friend to orgasm. Another woman, an ordinary-looking brunette who worked as a hair stylist, described having had sex with five of her friends—three men and two women—simultaneously. A girlfriend had dared her to do it after a few drinks one night.

This kind of conversation would have been unheard-of to most previous generations, except in subcultures at the margins of society. But here, at an unremarkable party among mainstream young professionals, no one batted an eye. At a time when finding "the one" seems virtually impossible, marriage is delayed; personal freedom reigns supreme; and consumer culture constantly nags at us, hot casual sex has become the ultimate commodity.

The New Revolution

When the sexual revolution broke new ground in the 1960s and early 1970s, casual sex was an expression of liberation, freedom from the chains of chastity and unwanted pregnancy. In the seventies, if you had casual sex, you were often not just "doing it"—you were doing it, in some ways, for the revolution. Today, casual sex has almost no political resonance; it is not a transgression of the social order—it *is* the social order.

In our parents' day, the idea of casual sex was still titillating—and so, according to many reports from the front lines of 1970s eros, was the practice of it. For our generation, plain old casual sex has been done; it's so last week. To titillate, casual sexual behavior today must be amped up in some way: be more public, or more outrageous, or involve more partners, or more orifices, or new kinds of technology. Casual sex has a whole new tone.

It is still an open question as to whether people have more sexual partners now than in the original sexual revolution, according to sex experts. But it is not necessarily the number of partners that has changed; rather, it is the approach to sex that has changed: you can choose your sex partner from potentially millions, rather than only from the people you happen to meet and feel attracted to. "What is going on now is making the sexual revolution of the '60s and '70s pale in comparison," said Eli Coleman, a professor of human sexuality at the University of Minnesota. Your ability to select sex partners today, as opposed to your parents' wild-oats days in the 1970s, is like a six-lane highway versus a rural road—same idea, but a different speed, and a different rate of collision.

Many commentators have noted, of course, that in the 1960s and '70s, casual sex became a mass-market consumer item. But if the sexual revolution forty years ago opened up the notion of turning sex into a consumer item, the Internet today has created efficiencies of scale for consumer sex by putting it on a production line. In the '60s, a young man or woman would have been lucky to find himself or herself in the right hot tubs; today, all he or she has to do is log on to the Net in order to dial up hundreds, if not thousands, of outlets for sexual fantasies.

In our frenetic working world today, sex can be seen not as an escape from workaday life, as it was in many ways in the original sexual revolution, but rather as a maximizer of our working life. It is about obtaining, performing, maintaining. Some of the singles I interviewed described having casual sex as being just like going to the gym: a stress reliever, a bodily function, an item on a to-do list. The phrase "I need to get laid" is shared openly, even in mixed-sex company. Meanwhile, in those same circles, the desire for true intimacy in a relationship has become embarrassing to express. Sex for its own sake is seen as a mundane need, like the need to eat or sleep. But the desire for emotional intimacy, also a basic human need, is often viewed as weak or pathetic. My friend Cole, a thirty-two-year-old video editor who has been pining over an ex-girlfriend for a year, has asked me to set him up countless times. Yet when I ask him, "Do you want a girlfriend?" he always responds, "I just need to get laid." I assure you this is not for lack of casual sex partners. He has no trouble finding those. He clearly is looking for something more, although he won't admit it.

Today, casual sex has a recreational appeal. This generation has taken the separation of sex and love to a new level. It is practically an unspoken code that there should be no strings attached to sex. I was recently at a bar and overheard this conversation between two women:

One woman to her friend, "We left the party and we had sex. The next day he asked for my phone number and put it in his phone. I just deleted it when he went to the bathroom. Let's be honest, he is never going to call and really I don't expect him to."

Her friend quickly replied, "Of course you shouldn't. It was just sex."

The no-strings-attached mentality is further heightened by technology, part of Evil Influence #2 (Multiple Choice Culture). The Internet provides the means to further compartmentalize sex and emotion by giving users the technology to locate different partners for these different needs. Singles seeking sex can hop onto any number of Web sites such as Adultfinder.com, "the world's largest sex and swinger personal Web site," which boasts over seven million members. Users can choose from a pull-down menu with a host of options: discreet relationships, group sex, bondage and discipline, cross-dressing, kinky fetishes, sadism, and masochism. Sex partners and love connections are often even possible on the very same Web site: the mainstream dating site, Lavalife, allows users to select a partner under the categories "dating," "relationship," or "intimate encounters," while Craigslist also has one section for dating and another, "casual encounters," just for sex.

Simon, a thirty-year-old man who worked for a record label in Chicago, certainly reaped the Internet's sexual benefits. I met him in Chicago's Wicker Park neighborhood at a dimly lit bar with emerald lights and a large bamboo tree in the corner. An under-aged DJ played No Doubt's "Hollaback Girl" while young girls in Seven jeans hovered around the bar and smoked skinny cigarettes as they sipped cosmos. Simon met me at 10:00 p.m. on a Sunday night. His job allowed him late nights and kept him in the know about cool places around town. He entered the bar with a laid-back walk; his long strides accentuated his lanky frame. I could barely make out his face under his shaggy mop of dirty-blond hair that covered his iPod earbuds. His outfit, a faded shirt and vintage jeans, looked as though it came straight off an Urban Outfitters rack.

Simon quickly revealed himself to be a reformed online dating addict and a self-proclaimed commitment-phobe. Although he said he went online looking for a date, he soon discovered the Net's other perks. He explained that he had gone out with fifty women he had met online over a two-year period and he had slept with half of them: "You're in an environment of multiple dating, it is so easy," he explained. Simon looked at me with his honey-brown eyes and explained that for a commitment-phobic man, the Internet is the perfect tool to keep you free, sexually satisfied, and on the market. "I'm shocked at how easy it is to get women into bed. What blows my mind is that I want what I can't have and women are giving it away. Women on the first date want to have sex and I don't." He smiled. A shy and awkward Simon claimed to be turning down offers for sex: "I

tell women we can't have sex because I don't have any condoms and
they say they don't care. I have to tell them I do. It isn't that I really
won't have sex without a condom. I use it as an excuse instead of
having to turn them down outright." One might assume that a generation that grew up in the midst of the AIDS epidemic would breed
a more careful sexual environment, but most of my unhooked singles
seemed unfazed. Simon didn't view these women as being promiscuous; he understood the demands of the sexual marketplace. "I don't
see them as sluts. I think they are competitive. They think you have to
bring something to the table or someone else will," he declared
matter-of-factly.

Simon was caught up in a sea of sexual opportunity. At the beginning he enjoyed the countless offers for sex but, like any junkie, he
came down from the high feeling worn and tired. It no longer mattered how many proposals for sex he could garner; his promiscuity
only increased his desire for real intimacy with someone he could
take out and talk to. Simon wasn't looking for the quick fix anymore.
He said sincerely, "More than anything, I want to fall in love."

I was surprised at Simon's proclamation, and intrigued that someone like him wanted a reprieve from his high-octane, sexually ram-
bunctious lifestyle and was now in search of a different kind of
connection. Many of the women I spoke to inquired about the men:
"What do they say? What do they want?" They were so convinced
that men didn't want relationships. But, in many cases, they were
wrong. Simon, like the majority of men I spoke to, ultimately—and
intensely—wanted a deeper relationship with real intimacy. But these
men are in a real bind: they are getting far more social affirmation for
seeking out the latest conquest than for confessing to a search for real
love.

I realized that my own stereotypical characterization of men as
being in one of two camps—either that of "the player" who is always
on the hunt for as much casual sex as he can get, or "the sensitive
guy" who wants a relationship—was one-dimensional and largely in-

accurate. In fact, I found that these two "types" of men I had imagined were actually often cohabitating in one body. Both personalities coexisted in many of the men I spoke with: they wanted relationships but they also wanted casual sex. The reason many of these men, and women, too, seemed more ready to opt for casual sex was because relationships had become so difficult in this dating landscape—and commitment so undervalued. Meanwhile, sex was easy to come by and carried the status and cachet that a mere relationship didn't.

A New Reality

Technology hasn't just created new access to real sex partners in this atmosphere of "consumer sex"; it has also created a new way of looking at fantasy sex partners. Internet pornography brings porn straight into people's offices and homes, turning Web sites into private and convenient fulfillment zones. In the 1970s, there was a whiff of loser around a man who turned to pornography on a regular basis; what was he missing in his sex life? Today, though, dependency on porn has become standard issue; younger men and women who do have real, responsive sex partners still often find they need to look at porn as a way to amp things up. One of my unhooked singles, Lena, a stunning twenty-seven-year-old Chinese-American woman from San Francisco studying to be a sommelier, told me, "In my last relationship, when I found my boyfriend's porn, it made me feel like I wasn't doing my job. He couldn't have an orgasm just with me. I couldn't measure up." An issue of *New York* magazine whose cover reads "Gen XXX" features a story that argues that porn, for some younger viewers, has become a replacement for sex. This new lens through which we view real sex partners is, of course, not limited to the computer screen: strip clubs and erotic shots of models in magazines also affect our generation's perceptions of "the real thing"—leading many of us to feel that sex isn't sexy enough if it is not pornographic.

My friend Susan, a film publicist with blond highlights, Angelina

Jolie lips, and a voluptuous figure, experienced this firsthand. One night, she found herself at a party that was dying down. She had been hoping to get lucky with one of two men she had met that evening—and she believed she had a shot, since both of the men had shown interest in her. The brooding photographer, Harris, had brought her a drink at the party early in the evening, and the chiseled lawyer, Scott, had stroked her hair during a quiet conversation. She had flirted with both men at different times during the evening, indicating clearly to both at different points that she was indeed ready for a hookup with either one of them. Susan was by any measure very attractive; and she was feeling particularly sexy that night, wearing an apricot slip dress displaying her bronzed décolletage.

As the last party guests were leaving, Susan and these two men, who did not know each other before that night, hopped in a cab together, looking for a place to go dancing. To her surprise, the two men took her to a strip club. She sheepishly entered the club and the men paid for her twenty-dollar cover charge. She followed the two men downstairs into a large room. The walls looked like a Jackson Pollock painting: wild colors were strewn about, and the blaring techno music was deafening. She was surprised to find quite a number of women at the club, among the preppie fraternity boys and the older men drenched in bad cologne.

In the center of the room stood a huge stage with a black marble finish, with two phallic poles at either end. Women in short skirts served martinis and beer while strippers pranced around in Velcro dresses and leather microminiskirts that could slide off in a second. Susan had no idea what she was doing in a strip club at that moment; it was her first time. Although she had felt desirable all evening, once she walked into the club, packed with the most beautiful, toned female bodies with gravity-defying (mostly fake) breasts that she had ever seen, she suddenly felt outmatched. One of the men looked at the other and said, "The talent is good tonight."

It was as if Susan were suddenly invisible. How could she compete, she wondered, with these pole-dancing dynamos? It had never before occurred to her that she might actually need to compete with a stripper for a man's attention. At the table to the left, three men flagged down a redhead named Brandi, wearing a turquoise halter-dress and three-inch pumps. One of the men bought a lap dance and turned to Susan's table and said: "This one is for my buddy. He's getting married next month."

Well, Susan said she knew she could never compete when she saw what Brandi did next: Brandi pulled her dress off over her head; underneath she was wearing nothing but a hot-pink thong. She nestled herself between the man's legs, which were spread apart. First she turned toward him, thrusting her naked breasts with their pastie-covered nipples in his face. He had an awkward, embarrassed grin that soon turned to a delighted smile. Brandi shook her head, tickling his face with her long, fiery mane. She then turned around and shimmied her buttocks in his face. At this point he began to relax and sink into his chair. He followed the rules, keeping his hands by his sides—no touching. His friends looked on, drinking and laughing.

Finally, Brandi turned around one more time and repeated the dance. When the song ended, she put her dress back on and walked away, leaving the man turned on and alone, with nothing but the smell of her vanilla perfume.

Meanwhile, a woman with frosted short hair and glossy, ruby lips sat down at Susan's table. Her makeup was tasteful, not overdone, and she was wearing a crisp white blouse and skin-tight blue jeans. She struck up a conversation with the lawyer. Though the woman didn't look like a stripper to Susan, it became clear that she worked there and that the lawyer was a regular. The two men talked to her for a few minutes until she said good-bye with a round of kisses. Harris and Scott turned their attention to the stage for the main attraction: twins with the names Cinnamon and Sugar. The two men gazed like drunken zombies.

Susan pulled out all of her flirtatious stunts that night, from twirling her hair to touching the men's shoulders, but nothing seemed to draw the men's attention away from the professionals. Fair enough: the stripper was naked and Susan still had her clothes on. Nevertheless, Susan felt so rejected that she had to excuse herself from the table.

Susan went home alone in a cab that night; she never saw Harris or Scott again. It didn't matter how enchanting or ravishing she looked that night. The two men wanted the anonymous fantasy, the commodified version of sex, instead of the very real thing Susan was certainly considering offering.

In this new "consumer sex" climate, a purchased image of a woman enhanced with balloon-shaped breasts, pouty lips, and a sex-kitten pose has an allure that couldn't possibly be matched by an actual, attainable woman. The fantasy woman, a picture of perfection, willingness, and carnal sexuality is in a completely different league from that of a wife or a date. Anonymous sexual arousal offers an easy and appealing shortcut to this impatient and disconnected generation. But not without consequence: Our ordinary fantasies are ratcheted up to impossible standards. That night, Susan felt like an old Cadillac next to a souped-up BMW with a CD player and a GPS system. She felt outmoded, outdated, and out-inflated.

New Sexual Expectations

This "consumer sex" revolution has also created an expectation that, as sex partners, we must reach new heights of performance. My girlfriend and I were at a dark bar with flickering candles when I overheard three men in their late twenties at the next table talking about sex. These men were undeterred from their candid conversation about the kind of women they wanted to "hook up" with that night. A dark-skinned, exotic-looking man took a swig of his Amstel Light and said to his friends: "You don't want to sleep with the beautiful girl because she will be bad in bed." The stocky one sitting across from him replied: "Yeah, you don't want to be with a ten." The third man, with a shaved head, interjected: "You want the girl that was shy in high school and blossomed afterward. She's humble, she likes sex, and she wants to please you. It is like buying a stock that is undervalued. You want to buy it before people realize it is the place to be." The exotic-looking man chimed in, "I think of it like you are looking for the perennial that came out of the ground and no one knows it's there. She's the one you want to close the deal with." (**"Close the deal"** is a popular expression among many of my generation for intercourse.) Suddenly, the men were sidetracked from their conversation by an attractive blonde who entered the bar wearing blue jeans and a pink ruffled top. "Now, she's cute," said the man with the dark skin. "Would you hit that?" "How's the backyard look?" replied the man with the shaved head. My girlfriend explained to clueless me that "the backyard" was a term for a woman's rear end. I knew from many of my white male friends that a big behind could be a deal breaker. No wonder every white woman in America was asking her friend if her butt looked big.

The obsession with pleasing our partners sexually, and being pleased by them, has reached new levels; women's magazines and books promise to teach us how to unlock the secrets to our partner's orgasms—from a recent article in *Glamour* magazine called "The Sexual Aptitude Test," about the way men and women score each other after the first time they have sex, to *Cosmopolitan*'s "Advanced Sex Tricks," both sexes are said to be pushed to extremes to perform.

In 2003, the *New York Times* reported that single men who do not suffer from impotence are taking Viagra "as psychological palliatives against the mighty expectations of modern romance." Several months later, a study of Viagra users in the *International Journal of Impotence Research* confirmed that prescriptions of Viagra skyrocketed 312 percent among men aged eighteen to forty-five between 1998 and 2002. The *Times* article—titled, "In an Oversexed Age, More Guys Take a Pill"—attributes this rise in the use of sexual enhancement medication among sexually healthy young men to the need to keep up with the intense marketplace of online dating. These young men are taking impotence drugs because they feel the pressure to keep up with the sexual demands of their evaluating partners.

The Evil Influences of consumer choice and the fast-paced nature of our society and technology, not to mention pornography, create the expectation that sex must always be exciting, outrageous, and nonstop. Studies show that 75 percent of impotence cases in men under thirty-five are "psychogenic"—that is, caused not by physical problems but by stress, according to the *Times*. In other words, the constant pressure to produce a big, hard cock on demand results in performance anxiety. A thirty-four-year-old quoted in the *New York Times* article, an otherwise healthy Viagra user said: "We live in a crazy, high-velocity world, and if you're dating in New York right now there are no road rules. It's a very tumultuous sexual arena, and it's exhausting."

New Pressures

In addition to the expectation to perform, there is cultural pressure to get a considerable amount of casual sex under your belt. In previous generations, it was men who often coerced women into sex. Today there is pressure on both sexes to be sexually seasoned. Some of my unhooked singles talked about how powerfully societal messages weighed on their own choices to have recreational sex. Robin, the thirty-four-year-old doctor from San Francisco mentioned earlier, told me that programs like *Friends* and *Sex and the City* made her and her peers feel as if they were the only ones not "doing it." Furthermore, they felt that if they didn't have casual sex with the men they were dating, there were plenty of other women who would. Eventually, most of them did indeed succumb to the pressure.

Laura, the thirty-four-year-old physical therapist from Minneapolis mentioned earlier, expressed sheepishly that she had slept with "only" five men in her life. She is charming and attractive; not asexual in the least. Laura grew up in the Midwest and was raised Catholic. At the time of our conversation, she said she hadn't had sex in years. She explained, "People make all kinds of judgments about the number of people you have sex with." By the age of thirty-four, friends thought it was odd that she had slept with only five people. As a Catholic, she didn't believe in casual sex, and as a woman she didn't feel comfortable with it, either. The judgments her friends made about her "modest" behavior also made her uncomfortable. And among her sexually active friends, she began to feel that she was missing out: "You get to the point that you feel asexual. You don't feel sexy or pretty; you don't feel like you exude any femininity. It is because you are not using your sexuality," she explained.

In the absence of a real relationship, she thought that it would be easier if she could just get comfortable with the idea of having casual sex. So she, to use her words, thought she should "get back up on the horse." She continued, "It made me sad that my sexuality was passing me by." So she did eventually succumb to her own internal pressure to have casual sex. The guy never called her again, and she regretted it: "It wasn't fulfilling. I wish I hadn't done it." But more than her regret over what she had done was her frustration that she didn't enjoy it the way her friends had. "It would be easier if I could," she explained. Sadly, Laura now felt even worse about her sexuality than she had before. She punished herself when her sex life didn't follow that of her peers or a Hollywood script.

A man I know named Jerry got divorced after ten years of marriage. He was surprised at the advice of his friends. They told him just weeks after his separation: "This is your chance to go out and have fun and get laid. It is what you need to do." He ignored their advice and immediately became involved in another relationship. Even the woman he was seeing asked him: "Are you sure you don't need to play the field after the breakup of your ten-year marriage?" His response was that casual sex wasn't for him and that it seemed unfulfilling. But two years later, when his relationship got more serious and his girlfriend wanted to get engaged, he found he wasn't ready. They broke up. Months later, she found out through mutual friends that he did in fact have a plenitude of casual sex with multiple partners after the split. Ultimately, it seemed, he felt he needed to recuperate after the loss of his marriage with the obligatory post-breakup fiesta of recreational sex, even though it went against his natural inclination. The panacea was short-lived: casual sex palled, and he ended up in another serious relationship.

Women, too, talked about using casual encounters after a breakup as a "Band-Aid." Rhonda, a thirty-year-old marketing assistant from Chicago, explained: "After my breakup, I was angry and I went on a sexual rampage. It was a power trip. I thought, I am in control." She said she enjoyed it in the moment, but almost as soon as the sex was over, the pain of her breakup returned. Like shopping, sex is sometimes used by people our age to numb painful feelings, to distract us from grief or loneliness. But in many cases, according to my unhooked singles, casual sex often made them feel worse.

Fringe Acts Go Mainstream

In the sixties, fringe sexual experience was for a subculture: swingers and fetishists and S&M types, not to mention those who were into group sex, were seen as either deviants or pioneers, depending on one's viewpoint. Casual sex, for most people then, had a more vanilla flavor. Today, though, once-fringe sexual experience has gone mainstream. Just as gray is the new black, anal is the new vaginal, and three-way is the new missionary position among this group of otherwise quite ordinary men and women. People with good parenting and solid values, from every class and ethnic background, are seeking out "extreme sex," the sensations of which dim unless they are continually ratcheted up. There are mainstream social groups throughout cities in America in which singles carry around tales of their one-night stands, their thrill-seeking threesomes, and even their adventures in anal sex, as trophies. Nice girls at brunch—that is, young people with perfectly normal values—compare extreme sexual stunts, each outdoing the other; nice guys at poker games share stories of their three-ways of the night before.

Tim, a twenty-six-year-old graphic artist, lives in downtown Minneapolis. He is average in every way: an average-looking guy who came from an unexceptional family, with a bland apartment in an unremarkable neighborhood. He has had his share of real relationships and even heartbreaks. Nevertheless, Tim is the new face of edgy, consumerist sex.

I met him at a Starbucks in downtown Minneapolis. He had responded to my ad on Craigslist. I sized him up as he walked through the door confidently, with a bit of a sway in his step. Tim was 5'8" and stocky, with a boyish buzz haircut and a round baby face. He wore an oatmeal Abercrombie & Fitch sweater, a distressed leather jacket, and jeans. He placed his order and the upbeat barista shouted out, "Decaf venti latte."

From the moment he sat down, his stories made my eyes widen. He boasted about his sexual encounters with well over one hundred women. "It's amazing that I don't have AIDS," he said. He sank into the chair and took off his jacket. He was eager to tell me about his favorite encounter, with a porn star he had recently met in Las Vegas, a woman named Summer Rose. She was a platinum blonde with collagen-enhanced lips, a heart-shaped butt, and the bountiful breasts God gave her, Tim recalled. He had worked his way into an adult-entertainment expo at a nearby hotel and he struck up a conversation with her. This was Tim's opportunity to fulfill his wildest fantasy: for a professional porn star to perform oral sex on him. He confessed his wishes to her, and Summer said she was willing to oblige. They went back to his room at the MGM Grand and as Tim looked out his hotel window at the city's bright lights, Summer made his fantasy a reality. Then the two of them went to Rain, a popular nightclub, to scout out more women to join their party. Tim drew two young, waiflike women into the back of the limo he had rented, and they became part of what was now a traveling drunken orgy: while Tim and a male friend watched, the women caressed each other's breasts, exchanged deep kisses, and struck raunchy positions, indulging all the young men's fantasies. Tim clearly didn't subscribe to the "What happens in Vegas stays in Vegas" mentality. He was thrilled to share the details. While I was certainly wondering if this man was spinning an erotic fable because he was enjoying shocking me, his stories were confirmed by a credible independent source.

Tim bragged about his ability to spot women who would go to bed with him. "I can walk into a bar and tell what a woman will do and what they like with only a small margin of error. That is my God-given gift, reading people," he laughed. He told me I had caught him at a good time. "Last week, I had one of the most amazing sexual weeks of my life. I hooked up with five different girls—I got sex from two, blow jobs from two, and the most incredible hand job of my life."

He shared a story about the time he met a married woman who had two children. She complained to him, "I'm not happy and I want to cheat on my husband." Tim's voice went up an octave: "I thought it was fucked up. She was persistent. She wanted me to go out of town with her. She seduced me, and finally I felt if I didn't do it, someone else would," he exclaimed. Tim shrugged and gave me a guilty look, but it was clear that he didn't need my reassurance.

It was important to Tim to differentiate between what he does—"being a player," a term from the hip-hop world—and "womanizing." He insisted that he was not a womanizer: "'Womanizing' is when guys use women to make themselves feel better. 'Being a player' is a good thing. It's just going out and having a good time."

At the end of our conversation, which involved more descriptions of threesomes and hookups, I saw another side of Tim: he confessed that what he really wanted was to find "Mrs. Right." I asked Tim how he intended to find her this way. His response: "All these sexcapades are part of a never-ending search for fairy-tale love. I'm passing the time in a fun way. Wasting sexual lust is like throwing money away." In Tim's view, it would be senseless for two people to share a sexual attraction and not act on it.

I followed up with Tim several months later and was surprised to learn he had traded in his casual sexual adventures for a relationship. He has been seeing a woman for the past few months and reports that he is quite happy. But he explained that the escapades he once bragged about were coming back to haunt him: "I can't go many places without running into a girl I've slept with. My girlfriend is picking up on old behavior and she really likes me, but she is grossed out by my past." Tim didn't blame her.

While his story may seem extreme, it is a snapshot of one part of the current cultural climate that sees sex as an attractive but inexpensive and disposable consumer item. Tim's story also underlies that in this world of plentiful, readily available sex, practically anyone can be a player.

"The Sexually Aggressive Woman"

Meet Tim's female counterpart: Heather, a tall, slender thirty-year-old advertising executive who loves sex. The sexually aggressive woman has become a vivid character in popular culture (e.g., Samantha from *Sex and the City*) and she is indeed a reality of this generation's single scene. Heather is a real-life Samantha. She is blond and has pretty blue eyes that sparkle, with tiny brown flecks. She exudes confidence. In contrast to the plunging necklines Samantha wore on the hit television show, Heather is dressed in jeans and a white T-shirt. Her flirtatious smile is her accessory. She doesn't need flashy jewelry, fake Fendi bags, or Prada pumps to boost her sex appeal. Yet, when she opened her mouth and started talking about her sexual escapades, it was nearly impossible to avoid the comparison to the infamous *Sex and the City* character. Within moments of meeting me she told me that she had slept with sixty men, but hoped to get to seventy-five by the time she married. She had had two affairs with married men, the first one when she was twenty-four. She lost her virginity when she was thirteen because "there wasn't that much to do in my hometown. I had sex with a lot of people. It was not a big deal," she said.

I wasn't the first person to make the connection to the *Sex and the City* character, but she strongly objected to it. "Everyone tells me I am the slutty one on *Sex and the City*. I don't feel like a slut. I feel like I am in control. 'Slut' means anyone who wants her can have her. I don't have a disregard for sex. We [women] have come too far to be reduced to the Samantha character. She is trashy," Heather declared.

Both Tim and Heather still felt they needed to justify their sexual behavior. But clearly, Heather had the more damning cultural stereotype to fight. I wondered if Heather was the one in a relationship now whether her boyfriend could accept her past the way Tim's girlfriend did. The double standard that labeled a sexually aggressive woman "a slut" has begun to fade only slightly, and its persistence, despite the proliferation of sexually aggressive women, is surprising. I asked the men I interviewed whether a woman having sex on the first date would cause them to rule her out as a potential girlfriend. Half of them said it would. I wasn't sure if the other half were telling the truth. A nonscientific poll conducted by *Cosmopolitan* magazine in 2001 confirmed that the double standard still existed: 76 percent of male respondents said there would be no second date with a girl they slept with on the first date.

Sean, the thirty-two-year-old software salesman from Los Angeles with several "fuck buddies" mentioned earlier, was not one of these men. He said he welcomed signs of promiscuity in a girlfriend: "I want someone a little promiscuous. I don't want to end up with forty years of missionary sex. A girl who waits until the nineteenth date to have sex is not suddenly going to become this erotic sex machine."

Heather would have been Sean's dream girl—at least for one night. She didn't worry about possibly scaring away potential relationships with early, up-front sex. She wasn't in search of a relationship. She was in **"play mode,"** a term some Gen-Xers use to describe the state of "having fun and not ready for a commitment." She dodges phone calls from men who want romantic dates, but takes the calls from those who want only hookups. "I don't like guys who say, 'I miss you,'" she explained. She told me she laughs at her sister and her friends who envy her carefree lifestyle—but can't manage to have sex without feeling vulnerable emotionally. "Most women get emotionally attached when they have sex. I don't," she asserted. "Sex is not an emotional thing at all, but it is very intense."

To Heather, it is all about sex, all the time. She met her "current ongoing hookup" at a party: "He is only twenty-four." She smiled devilishly. "I don't date. I can't remember the last time I went on a date. I have one-night stands. I meet people at house parties and clubs. I don't go out and think 'I am going to get laid.' I don't put on the skimpy underwear. It is not like a game. I just say, 'That is the hottest guy in the room and I'll go home with him.' Guys do it, so why can't I?" she asked.

Nothing drives her crazier than when a guy calls her after a one-night stand. "People who are hung up on sex and 'the rules,' I feel bad for them. I am so lucky to go out and carry on like this. It is guilt-free and fun," she exclaimed. In fact, she pitied those who became mired in feelings of attachment after sex.

Heather seems to be quite self-assured. Her promiscuity was not the result of a bad childhood or of low self-esteem. Her parents are happily married, her family is close, and she loves her high-powered job. She answered every one of my questions about her sex life as quickly as I could ask them. And, as I listened intently, I couldn't help but admire her candor.

Like any pickup artist, she bragged about approaching men—and even suggested I try some of her techniques. Her courage impressed

me because I had never approached and picked up a stranger. She became animated as she told me about using her friends to fetch attractive men she spotted across the bar. Her voice went up a notch: "That
is my version of sending a man a drink." One of her favorite techniques was to wear a cowboy hat and sit at the end of the bar: she said
it provided men with a conversation starter that made her easy to approach.

In addition to her flings with men, married and single, she talked
about experimenting with women. "I made out with a girl who gave
me a lap dance at a strip club. . . . People were staring at me. It was
cool," she said, giggling. Heather, like many of her female peers, enjoyed flirting with the stereotypical male fantasy of a lesbian encounter, particularly when she had an audience. It was obvious that
she lapped up men's reaction to her the way an actress basks in ap-
plause. She loved to see the shock on their faces and reel them in.

Heather said she eventually does, in fact, want a relationship and
marriage. She surprised me when she mentioned wanting a wedding
with traditional trimmings. She suddenly seemed more Charlotte
than Samantha. It was quite a contradiction to the picture she had
painted of herself as a purveyor of no-strings-attached sex. However,
she explained, she is in no hurry to marry: "If someone told me I was
going to meet the man of my dreams tomorrow, I would want two
more years to be single." She doesn't feel pressure to find a boyfriend,
even though coworkers and friends constantly comment on her single status: "Such a pretty girl like you, why aren't you with someone?" they often inquire. Her stock reply is: "I haven't met anyone I
like yet." But she looked at me with a knowing nod. "What I really
want to say to them is, do you know how many people I slept with?"
she explained, as if that were a source of pride.

Heather, it seemed, wanted to be a modern version of the character in Erica Jong's 1973 *Fear of Flying,* the novel that helped open the
floodgate of women's sexuality. The then controversial imagery of a

woman enjoying her sexuality without shame had resonated with me since I first read the novel as a curious virgin in high school. Today, fifteen years later, I still remember Jong's words. "The zipless fuck was more than a fuck. It was a platonic ideal. Zipless because when you came together zippers fell away like rose petals, underwear blew off in one breath like dandelion fluff," Jong wrote. For Heather, the zipless fuck was easy to achieve. Understandably, women like Heather embarked on exploring their sexuality with enthusiasm when they could—without penalties. With the sexual revolution, Nancy Friday's *My Secret Garden,* a book heralded for bringing women's sexual fantasies out of the closet, confirmed that women were likely to find the fantasy of sex with a stranger erotic. Friday's book, however, described fantasy. Today, women of my generation actively ventured into casual sex, some confidently, some hesitantly. The reports back from the field are mixed.

My friend Diane, who prided herself on having had thirty sex partners before her thirtieth birthday, called me, crying, a week after her first date with Wes. She had had mind-blowing sex with him— and then he never called. Even Diane—who seemed to love sex for the sake of it—was miserably disappointed when Wes didn't call and she realized he had no interest in getting to know her.

Many studies show that most women are not lastingly into casual sex. For example, the 1994 National Health and Social Life Survey of men and women ages eighteen to fifty-nine carried out at the University of Chicago found that women are twice as likely as men to say they find the idea of anonymous sex "not at all appealing." However, you can get little real insight from the studies of our generation's sexual attitudes: Women are unlikely to confide to a stranger that they like fucking strangers.

So, in the absence of data, listen to women's own anecdotes. In my interviews with dozens of women, it became clear that women like casual sex—for a while. Many of the women said they enjoyed it at first, or when they were younger, but the thrill wore off with time. But I heard the same reports from the men. No researcher I found had done a longitudinal study of responses to casual sex over time. I believe that if they were to look at both men and women, their findings would echo the themes I heard in my face-to-face interviews: Men and women both were delighted at the beginning to explore casual sex, but got sick of it years into the fray.

My friend Chris, a twenty-seven-year-old medical researcher from Chicago, surprised me when I asked him if he had ever regretted casual sex. Chris is Irish and fair-skinned with a husky build. He is extraordinarily shy at first meeting, but when his sarcastic sense of humor comes out he is a different person. Chris had dated Mary, a petite and perky receptionist at a hair salon, for two years. She broke up with him because she said he wasn't spending enough time with her. Chris understood her complaint, but explained that he was in graduate school when they were dating. Despite what Mary said, Chris claims he was crazy about her. When they broke up, he was devastated for months. They stayed in touch over the next year, dropping each other e-mails or making an occasional phone call. Chris had thought of her often. He knew she was dating, but was relieved that she didn't have a steady boyfriend. One night, Chris, after not seeing Mary for six months, invited her over for dinner. They ordered in Chinese food, caught up on their jobs—and had wild and uninhibited sex. Chris admits he had every intention of sleeping with her that night. He explained, "It felt completely new with her. Before, when we were dating, the sex was comfortable, but I always thought there was something better out there." Now he said he realized that, because he had missed her, there was nothing better for him. That night, Mary confessed that she had wanted to sleep with him, too—but particularly because, she admitted, she hadn't had sex in months. The next morning, Mary left. They never discussed what, if anything, that evening meant. Chris referred to it as **"a booty call with a twist."**

Chris and Mary did what many people of this generation do—they **"recycled,"** a term many people of my generation use to describe having sex with an "ex." It is not surprising, given the "consumer sex" culture, that my generation would come up with such a term. Shortly after Chris and Mary slept together, Mary invited Chris to go to a wedding out of town. Chris booked a room at a nearby hotel. At the wedding, they drank, they danced, and they laughed. By the end of the night, they stumbled back to their hotel room and darted into bed. They started making out until Mary expeditiously stopped Chris and made the terms clear: "I don't think we should sleep together tonight because I don't want you to think we are getting back together."

Chris replied, "No, it doesn't have to mean that. I am fine with it." With that understanding, they had sex. He explained his take on it. "I knew it wasn't going anywhere and it was just going to be fun. So it was more just about getting the job done." According to Chris, the sex wasn't particularly good. The next morning, Chris dropped Mary off. "I still wanted to be with her. It might sound lame, like I am the girl in the situation, but maybe she was just using me," he said with an embarrassed grin.

"Afterward, I gave her a hug good-bye. It was a lifeless type of hug. It felt cold, like a handshake. I had just had sex with her ten hours earlier. It was so weird. She left and I went on with my day." He averted his eyes. Chris says he regretted it: "I was bummed. I knew it was just sex and I wanted more. I was still thinking about it a few days later. It definitely set me back. Sleeping with her brought everything back to the surface." Contrary to conventional wisdom, according to Chris and other men I spoke with, men did at times regret casual sex.

Many women used the phrase: "I failed at it"—meaning that they felt they had failed at casual sex because they felt attachment afterward. To become attached after sex is to be human—but both men and women of this generation considered this a human failing. I thought to myself, if fucking a stranger and enjoying it is now a sign of success, things have certainly changed: beating yourself up because you can't use your body without involving your soul is quite the twenty-first-century dilemma.

Was cold, robotlike sex really a sign of empowerment this many decades after the feminist movement? The conflicts among my women friends and my unhooked subjects suggested not; the disappointment and ennui of many of the men suggested not, as well. I am not suggesting we return to a time when women denied their sexuality. But after speaking to these singles, it was clear to me that the explosion of casual consumer sex lacked any lasting liberation for either gender.

It became obvious that beneath all the erotic aerobic activity, for many people, casual sex served as a substitution for real emotional intimacy. Having sex is easy for this generation, but connection and commitment are hard. Sex is a temporary solution to solving the problems of this generation. While physically close, we're more distant than ever from each other. Often, Gen-Xers have sex quickly and then wait for the emotions to catch up with the physical sensations. I think of how our mothers, some of them virgins, must have felt on their wedding nights—trembling with excitement and fear at their first sexual experience. That situation certainly had its downsides—but sex becoming unimportant was not one of them.

Casual sex has become an inalienable right, a freedom of the young and single that requires no commitments beyond the sex itself. Today, sexual flings, seemingly fun but fleeting, are now a dime a dozen. I couldn't help but wonder whether casual sex wasn't losing its appeal due to its sheer availability. After all, it is the luxury goods that we can't afford that most of us want—not the knock-offs that we can afford.

Today, we have sex if we want to on the first date—and then we decide whether there is potential for more. Simon, the reformed online dating addict from Chicago, said he was sick of the in-your-face sex:

"I've been asked to have a threesome four times in my life. I turned all those offers down. My ultimate fantasy is to find one person to share everything with—not two."

For many men and women, the more casual sex they had, the more numb they felt. Purnima, a light-skinned thirty-three-year-old Indian woman with doe eyes and perfect makeup, who worked as an assistant marketing manager, exclaimed: "People don't know if they want a guy or a girl or both. Everyone is so sexually bored. Regular sex is not enough—people are like, so, you haven't had a threesome?" Her comment rang true to me. There was nothing left undiscovered. For our generation, now that we have done it all, what is next?

Wendy Shalit, in her book *A Return to Modesty*, makes the case that in an oversexualized society, what women really need is to revert back to more modest sexual behavior. She writes, "Maybe we're not having fun because everything is permitted. Maybe without modesty, we forget what is erotic." While I don't agree that this is a woman's task alone, Shalit certainly has a point, if we apply this insight equally to both genders. I began to see things differently after talking to these singles. For me and for many others, casual consumer sex often dampens eroticism and potentially undermines sex with those we actually care about.

I thought about the words of Robert McElvaine, historian and author of *Eve's Seed: Biology, the Sexes, and the Course of History:* "Free love is the supreme oxymoron. Someone who is genuinely in love cannot be free; to be in love is to be connected, tied, bound to another. . . . Totally free people can have sex, but never love, because to have love is to give up freedom."

8

Marriage Lite

"I don't know if I will get married. People don't stay married.
I never want to get divorced, so maybe I won't get married."

—EVE, 34

It is not surprising that the experiences Gen-Xers face—from childhood, to adolescence, through early adulthood—lead them to feel
conflicted about marriage. By the time they reach a marriage-
appropriate age, they have witnessed or experienced a number of
failed relationships. These circumstances lead them to a paradoxical
attitude about marriage: they tend to be at the same time very hopeful and extremely cautious. This attitude is what I call **"the pessimism paradox."**

The Pessimism Paradox

The people I interviewed often reiterated an unfortunate paradox.
They desperately wanted a lifelong bond, but at the same time, they
expressed serious doubts that marriage could ever supply this bond
for them.

As often as I heard a deep longing for connection, I heard—from the same men and women—expressions of a paralyzing fear that "forever" could ever really work. As Christine, thirty-six, a video artist, confided to me at a dive bar in an edgy San Francisco neighborhood, "I have a fear of saying yes to forever. I would like to find 'the one,' but things change so much." Her fear that love could ever last was absolutely characteristic of our generation, I found.

More than any previous generation, Gen Xers are products of divorced families. In our postdivorce culture, many of my unhooked singles found themselves lacking role models for a strong, lasting relationship, unsure of their skills within intimate relationships, and doubtful of ever beating the grim statistics about marital demise. In a 2001 study of young Americans' attitudes toward marriage by Rutgers University's National Marriage Project, one of the top fears expressed about getting married involved the real possibility of divorce.

That fear of divorce is a massive inhibitor of intimacy and trust in marriage within people of my generation, even among those without divorced parents. For Sean, the thirty-two-year-old software salesman from the Los Angeles area mentioned earlier, fear of divorce had kept him from deepening his love relationships. He told me that he had been in love several times, but was always too cautious about commitment to tie the knot. The reason? He was so afraid of divorce that he had become afraid of marriage itself. As he described his dilemma, while his family expected marriage to be for keeps, he was not sure he could deliver: "No one in my family is divorced. I take the sanctity of marriage very seriously; I think that is why I am still single. I am scared of disappointing my family because the chances are good that divorce could happen." In fact, it seemed many of my single informants, like Sean, were single precisely because they took marriage so seriously and they feared they would screw it up.

It's not that this divorce-scarred generation eschews marriage itself; in fact, the marriage rate in this country still remains surprisingly high despite our firsthand experience with the prevalence of divorce: most of our generation is going to marry before too much of their life passes by. Nearly nine out of ten people will marry sometime in their lives, according to a 2002 report by the Census Bureau. Nevertheless, in recent decades, Americans have become less likely to marry. The marriage rate in 2004 was 30 percent lower than in 1970, according to the National Center for Health Statistics. As I stated earlier, some of the decline—it is not clear how much—results from the postponement of marriage. The difference in our generation is not statistical so much as attitudinal. It is not that we don't marry—it is that we marry without confidence.

Divorce has forever changed this generation by making marriage seem ultimately disposable. In spite of the reasonably high rate of marriage, the National Marriage Project reports, "In survey after survey, young men and women express a growing pessimism about their chances for a successful marriage." At the very same time, though, a horrifying paradox of pessimism becomes apparent: a majority of the same young people identify a happy and lasting marriage as one of their highest personal goals in life—even as they doubt they can ever really trust they can get there. Journalist Maggie Gallagher, author of *The Abolition of Marriage*, sketched out the same paradox for me. She argues that "compared to the generation before, young people are more desiring of a stable and loving marriage and are more uncertain about whether they will get it."

The marriage-is-forever mentality that many of our parents began with seems unfathomable to many of us now. Some of us watched our parents grow apart. Many Gen-Xers have attended weddings of close friends, witnessing their sacred promises before God and family—only to watch them divorce a few years later. Sean recalled, "I've been a groomsman twelve times; in slightly less than half of those weddings I stood up knowing they should not be married. Three of them are already divorced."

As I explained earlier, my own pessimism about the possibility of a stable marriage intensified after I had dated three men—sequentially, please—whose parents had all gone through ugly divorces. Almost all of the significant love relationships in my life have been with children of divorce. I overheard telephone arguments over which parent would come to family graduations or weddings; I heard from my boyfriends about parents' affairs, malevolent court battles, and venomous arguments. Though none of them were really "confirmed bachelor" types, each of these men was leery of marriage and had problems with commitment. They all earnestly sought intimate monogamous relationships, but once they became involved with a woman, they could never seem to move on to the next level of closeness and trust.

Even though I was not myself a child of divorce, these lovers' parents' divorces affected my own worldview. In this sense, the divorce epidemic among my peers' parents is geometric in its effects: each of these divorces had a legacy effect, not just on their own children, but on all of their children's partners over the course of their years of courtship.

By the time many of my friends reached their late twenties and early thirties, we had moved into the years in which hooking-up relationships were getting old, and dating turned into commitment: my peers were starting to get married. The weddings were lavish: productions in Long Island country clubs, or overlooking the Pacific Ocean on a Santa Monica beach, or at the Fairmont Hotel ballroom in Chicago. But only six years after the bouquet-throwing festivities, three of the couples had split up; one couple called it quits after only a year. My faith in marriage wavered even more. It seemed to me that more rigor had gone into choosing the flowers than into preparing the newlyweds for the emotional challenges of the first few years of married life.

Was I alone in my growing pessimism that coexisted with my longing for marriage? I started to ask a lot of questions, but it wasn't until I interviewed these hundred men and women that I confirmed just how widespread this combination of hope and pessimism was. To my shock, I found that this "pessimism paradox" preyed equally on children of divorce and those young people with happily married parents.

Thirty-five-year-old Reed, an engineer living in a suburb of Chicago, mentioned earlier, echoed the reservations of many of the other men and women I interviewed who came from happily married homes. "I think it is good to have a commitment, but it is not so realistic. My grandparents were married, like, seventy years. I can't imagine keeping a relationship for that many years," he told me. Thirty-four-year-old Eve, an attorney in Minneapolis, spoke the sentiments of many of her peers whose parents are divorced: "I don't know if I will get married. People don't stay married. I never want to get divorced, so maybe I will not get married." It became quite clear that we need to reckon with the effects of divorce, not just for its impact on the kids, but also for its impact on the romantic air we all breathe. Despite completely different childhood experiences, children of intact as well as divorced couples are clearly disillusioned about the possibilities of marriage.

Marriage Heavy vs. Marriage Lite

Many of the qualities that are seen by marriage experts as constituting the bedrock of successful marriage are at odds with this generation's core eject-button values.

John Gottman, PhD, a leading marriage expert and author of *The Seven Principles for Making Marriage Work*—based on his research that was able to predict marital success with 91 percent accuracy—describes some of the key components of successful marriages: compromise, tolerance, and forgiveness. These make up just a few of the core characteristics of a successful committed marriage—what I call **"marriage**

heavy." Look at how the core qualities needed for a committed, successful marriage conflict with our generation's core values:

Characteristics for Marriage-heavy	Values of Gen-Xers
one partner	multiple choices
fulfillment of partner	fulfillment of self
the marriage above all	personal happiness above all
compromise	personal checklist
connection	independence
forgiveness	entitlement
tolerance	desire for change

To solve this problem, many Gen-Xers have turned to what I call **"marriage lite."** They have come up with elaborate coping strategies that allow them to engage in close romantic relationships, while avoiding what they perceive as being the dangers of marriage. Marriage lite is the Holy Grail for this generation: intimacy without risk, commitment without traps. Through the voices of those I heard from, it became clear that these young people's fears of real, old-fashioned, till-death-do-us-part marriage had led them to invent alternative ways to be close without the risk of profound disappointment.

Strategy 1: The Waiting Game

Liz, a thirty-two-year-old urban planner with a bronze tan and sun-kissed hair, met Adam at a Fourth of July party on the beach in Los Angeles. Adam is thirty-five. He is 6'4", with a muscular build, washboard abs, and pronounced facial features. Adam was working at a hedge fund after having spent years as a bartender, "partying" and drinking to excess. Despite their hectic corporate jobs, they both had active, even wild, social lives.

Adam frequented strip clubs and dabbled in recreational drugs.

Liz went to the trendiest clubs, followed the live-music scene, and smoked pot recreationally. The two started seeing each other; their dates were playful and passionate. They would usually have dinner at an ethnic restaurant and then head to a bar, where they quaffed cocktails and talked all night. Sometimes they would go late-night dancing and "get dirty"—their group's term for sexy dancing—on the dance floor; or they would end up at one of their apartments for a raw make-out session that ended just short of sex. Their dates always ended well after 2 a.m., and left both of them exhausted and hungover.

After five months of dating, Liz wanted to know why they weren't having sex, but was reluctant to ask directly. Adam finally brought up the subject. "You know, Liz, I don't believe in casual sex," he said. He didn't give Liz a reason. She was stunned, and when she told me the story, so was I. Adam was not the kind of man whom you would expect to say that. Judging by his good looks and rugged sex appeal, one might guess that he bedded a different woman every week. Liz didn't know what to make of his comment, except to understand it as a clear message that he was dating her only casually. She had strong feelings for him, however, and was ready for a relationship.

It was not just intercourse that Adam put restrictions on; their playful evenings together and unmistakable chemistry notwithstanding, Adam limited their dates to one a week. Much to Liz's frustration, this pacing went on for six months. At one point, Adam mentioned that he wanted to get married someday, and that he eventually wanted children. Liz took that as an encouraging sign that they wanted the same things in the future, but she also wanted more from him right now.

Eventually they did have sex—which was fine but unremarkable. Liz still wondered where the relationship was going. After almost every date, she would give me a frustrated recap: "He doesn't act like I am his girlfriend. We have a great time together, but he never stays for breakfast. He's always going to parties and hanging out drinking instead of seeing me. But I don't think he is seeing anyone else, so I don't understand it," she complained. Her voice sounded shaky; she began talking very fast, and at one point I thought I saw a tear in her eye. This time, I felt her angst profoundly, and I recalled many of my own frustrating moments, trying to read someone who seemed indifferent to me while I was consumed with pining away for him.

After Liz and I talked, she decided to confront Adam and have "the DTR" conversation. Liz tried, but was unable to really accomplish much; she didn't want to ask Adam directly for what she hoped for—an exclusive relationship—so she circled around the subject. She said: "I get asked out all the time and I don't know what to do."

Adam stared at her blankly. Finally Liz, teeming with anger, looked at Adam and said, "Maybe you have commitment issues."

"You're right, I probably do," was his only response. She was able to get no more out of him in the entire course of the conversation.

"The DTR" had failed—from Liz's point of view. Perhaps it had succeeded from Adam's—Liz and I may never really know. At this writing, Liz continues to date Adam on his own unilateral terms. They remain, as so many relationships in our generation do, completely undefined.

Adam, in his complete lack of any sense of urgency for commitment in a relationship, represents millions of young men, and young women, too: according to virtually all of the data available, they are delaying marriage longer than did young people of previous generations. This statistic bears repeating: according to the Census Bureau, the average age of first marriage for women is now twenty-five and for men twenty-seven. This is the first time in U.S. history both sexes are choosing to marry so late. The heartbreaking irony of this cultural tendency—I would say pressure—toward delay? Many of the people with whom I spoke said that they had met wonderful potential life partners when they had still been in their early or mid-twenties, but had resisted commitment not out of a lack of love or compatibility, but simply because they felt they needed more time at that age to "play the field." Ironically, Liz herself almost got engaged to a man she had dated years earlier, but when he was ready to propose, Liz wasn't ready for marriage. She wanted to get dating "out of her system" and continue "seeing what else was out there" before settling down. So they broke up. Now Liz was the one who was ready and was frustrated that her new man was not.

A thirty-year-old New Jersey real estate agent named Ivy expressed what many of the singles told me: "I do believe in marriage, which is why I am not married. I am not ready to be married." Meaning: even at thirty, Ivy did not feel herself to be ready to make the real commitment she felt marriage required.

Reason 1: The Desire to "Play"

Over a cigarette and a couple of drinks in a dark, cavernous bar in Chicago, thirty-three-year-old Rob, a loquacious civil engineer, told me that he had been engaged at twenty-five to a woman he truly loved, but broke it off because "I really wanted to be the single guy. I had only slept with four girls, and then entered a seven-year relationship." Had he met his ex-fiancée a year ago, he said, he would be the happiest married man alive; but at the time, even though he said she was right for him, "I wanted to pick up chicks, have one-night stands—be the man."

It struck me just how familiar and apparently reasonable Rob's need to "play the field" sounded to someone of my age, almost as if it were a developmental necessity, like the obligatory Grand Tour of Europe fifty years ago. Rob didn't strike me as being particularly immature; he'd had long relationships, and he spoke with deep feeling about all of the women who had been part of his life. In previous decades, his resistance to commit would have earned him a reputation as a marginal man, a Peter Pan or Casanova type; but, by today's standards, he simply was in "play mode."

Rob represented the perspective of many men who spoke to me who were not ready for commitment. A 2004 survey of men ages twenty-five to thirty-four commissioned by the National Marriage Project and conducted by Opinion Research Corporation found that 74 percent of men who are delaying marriage agree with the statement, "At this stage in my life I want fun and freedom." The men surveyed gave additional reasons for their delay, including: work obligations made it difficult to date; the need to achieve financial viability for a home or a wedding; and the search for a partner was in itself too difficult of a struggle. These findings may reassure those of us who have been rejected by noncommittal partners. Many women I know think their boyfriends aren't seeking to tie the knot simply because the love they feel is not sufficiently strong. In truth, many of the reasons why partners won't commit are not at all personal—they are societal. And it's not just the men who feel the societal pressure to commit only when everything in their lives is in place. Women who report their own aversions to commitment have parallel reasons for the marriage delay, reasons that would seem flimsy to many from our parents' generation.

Delayed marriage means prolonged adolescence for this generation. In our parents' generation, a man in his mid-twenties was likely to be starting on a career path that he would perhaps continue for the rest of his life while supporting a family. These days, a young man around that age is more likely to be thinking about what bars to go to, rather than worrying about taking care of a family. Norval Glenn, a sociologist at the University of Texas, explained to me in an interview that since there is less societal pressure to marry today, men and women can grow up more slowly than ever. "If you are a man, you can postpone a lot of adult responsibility," remarked Glenn. Even after marriage, men today don't have the full responsibility of supporting a family the way earlier generations did. This lack of responsibility allows today's young men, he concluded, to focus more steadily on their own gratification than did men of the past. Evil Influence #1 (The Cult of I) enables such prolonged adolescence.

The people I spoke to talked about experiencing a sense that they would somehow miss out on casual dates and sex if they chose to marry young: "I felt like I should be dating more and having more sex. That is what you are supposed to be doing at a certain age," said Jamie, a six-foot-tall, twenty-nine-year-old sociology student and sculptor from New York. She was having trouble getting over a breakup with her boyfriend of five years, and, to add to her misery, she felt that she had missed out on something by spending much of her twenties in a committed relationship.

While marrying young was seen as a sign of accomplishment in our parents' generation, we have turned away from that ideal in the extreme. In fact, there is considerable cultural pressure to get a lot of romantic and life experience under your belt before you walk down the aisle, for both men and women. Today it is the exact opposite of our parents' experience. Now, if you get married "too young," you are seen as immature or naive. Even Dr. Phil, an opinion maker and relationship expert for this generation, on a show called "Married Too Fast, Too Young" declared what he thought was the appropriate age to marry: "I think you ought to be thirty."

I'm not saying the answer is to marry early and start a family, or to give up career goals. But I do believe there is a real dilemma for us today. If you focus on yourself and your career at the expense of love and romance, you may find yourself unhappily single; if you marry early, you may feel you gave up the self-exploration that we as Gen-Xers feel is our right.

Because of Evil Influence #2 (Multiple Choice Culture) we are obsessively conditioned to keep our options open. As a result, no matter what choice we make we always feel we are missing out. We need to find a level of comfort with whatever choice we make; to be happy, we need to learn not to focus on what we are giving up, but rather on what we are gaining with each choice we make.

Reason 2: There Is Plenty of Companionship—Why Commit?

In addition to the societal pressure to delay marriage, big cities where singles often tend to populate make single life so comfortable that there is little pressure to commit. Author Ethan Watters coined the term "urban tribes" to describe communities of singles in urban areas: never-married, generally twenty- and thirtysomethings who congregate in close-knit groups. In the past, a long-single man or woman would have been socially marginalized; now, in many urban centers, singles have a vibrant community of peers who have made the same choices that they have—and are having a great time in this stage of life. Without the social stigma of being single, why trade in this gratifying lifestyle for commitment?

Reason 3: The Need to Be "Economically Set"

Another factor influencing the "Waiting Game" is the emphasis, by both men and women of this generation, on achieving career and financial stability before marriage. In a 2001 Gallup survey of men and women in their twenties for the National Marriage Project, 86 percent of men and women agreed with the statement, "It is extremely important to you to be economically set before you get married." No wonder singles are taking so long to settle down.

For many, part of being "economically set" may mean giving up individual economic freedom. While young couples in the past threw their lot in together and accepted a certain level of selflessness as they tried to build security for the family, professional singles in their thirties have the luxury of spending money only on themselves and may be reluctant to give up that perk for marriage. After so many years on their own, the thought of giving up vacations with their friends, pricey nights out, or expensive hobbies for the good of the team may not seem so appealing. When singles get married, they often have to shift their spending habits. Money once earmarked for leisure and entertainment must go toward saving for practical needs, such as a home and family. For some, this may feel like a painful sacrifice.

Gen-Xers who are living in an age of celebrity obsession are often affected by Evil Influence #6 (The Celebrity Standard). The images of the opulent lives of the rich and famous are so prevalent in our culture that it can inflate our tastes. A recent front page *New York Times* story that looked at status and class in America quoted Juliet B. Schor, a professor of sociology at Boston College, who has written widely on consumer culture. She said, "The old system was keeping up with the Joneses. The new system is keeping up with the Gateses." The American dream of simply owning a home and having a comfortable family life, for some, has shifted to an obsession with wealth, status, and luxury. Tying the knot can certainly get in the way of the pursuit of a self-focused lifestyle that revolves around spending money frivolously. A thirty-year-old woman named Corinne, a brand manager for a major food company in Los Angeles, who is married, struggles now with her lust for luxury in her relationship. She explained: "In my career, I have always been able to afford a certain level of luxury—but my spending habits drive my husband insane. He doesn't want extravagant vacations. He is practical and wants to save for the future. But I resent having to give those things up." She confesses that spending freely on herself is one of the things she misses about being single. Similar sentiments about not wanting to give up material possessions were expressed by Ivy, the thirty-year-old real estate agent, who is single. She said, "My friend who is married says, now that she is part of a couple, she can't justify buying certain luxuries. I don't want marriage to be about depriving myself of things. I work. If I want to spend one hundred dollars on jeans I should be able to."

Today's conventional wisdom is that marriage is strongest and most attractive if you are financially stable before you commit. But, ironically, for many of those whom I interviewed, the longer they waited, the more the luster of marriage began to fade. Nick, the thirty-year-old legal recruiter from Chicago, thought he would be the first of his friends to marry, but now he is one of the only single people left among his social network. Today, he's not so sure he wants to get married at all. He contrasted the lives of his married friends with his practically responsibility-free existence of work and play, a life that revolves around hanging out with friends, going to parties, and spending (not saving) his disposable income. I wouldn't be surprised if Nick decided to delay marriage indefinitely. Putting off marriage for some becomes a dangerous trap. The longer the delay, the harder it can become to leave this period of life behind. A friend of mine, Damen, a thirty-four-year-old mortgage broker from San Francisco, anxious on the eve of his engagement, explained it this way: "Today you think about all the things you are giving up when you get married, not all the things you gain."

Strategy 2: Virtual Marriage: Living Together

The ease of cohabitation in our culture supplies another strategy that Gen-Xers use as a way to get close without committing to marriage. Forty-nine percent of American women ages twenty-five to twenty-nine and a slightly higher percentage of women ages thirty to thirty-four have ever cohabitated, according to the Centers for Disease Control. Living together is "the perfect compromise," said one couple with whom I spoke. Natalia, twenty-nine, is a documentary filmmaker. Gary, thirty-three, is a photographer who has already gone through a messy divorce. Natalia is part tomboy, part femme fatale. She has a muscular build and arms that look as though they have been sculpted by an artist. She wears ruffled skirts and always smells of French perfume. Gary has mastered the downtown New York look: thick, funky black-frame glasses, and Comme des Garçons slacks. Natalia explains, "We've been together for four years. He wants to get married, but I'm afraid of it. So we moved in together." They seem content with this as a permanent arrangement, and their friends described them as "practically married." For this couple, a "virtual marriage" seems to bring the benefits of physical and emotional intimacy without the risk of divorce. They say they have a lifetime commitment to cohabitate instead of marry. In this respect, Gary and Natalia's arrangement is very European. Committed cohabitation is more popular in the United Kingdom, France, Germany, and throughout Scandinavia today than it is in the United States. (This is no doubt due to laws in these countries than grant many of the legal rights to cohabitators that couples in the United States can gain only through marriage.)

For other Americans of this generation, living together is not a permanent solution (or a replacement for marriage); rather, it is a kind of marriage on training wheels; a smart way to practice marriage before taking off for real. The majority of couples marrying today have lived together first. Isn't this a good thing? How can we be blamed for wanting to "try out" marriage? If you could, wouldn't you want to try out a house before taking out a mortgage? You test drive a car before signing a lease. According to a 2002 survey of men and women in their twenties conducted by the Gallup Organization for the National Marriage Project, the belief that living together before marriage is a useful way "to find out whether you really get along," and thus avoid a bad marriage and eventual divorce, is now widespread among young people. Marriage has always been a leap of faith, but many people of our generation try to reduce that risk as much as possible with such a "trial."

Some marriage advocates, such as sociologist Linda Waite, coauthor of *The Case for Marriage,* warn of the danger of cohabitation; critics of the trend, especially religious conservatives, claim that cohabitation undermines marriage and actually contributes to divorce.

My friends, who are far less conservative, would be astonished to learn that those critics may be onto something. Couples who live together before marriage have a dramatically increased risk of separation or divorce according to most research, including that of the Centers for Disease Control—51 percent within fifteen years of marriage—12 percent higher than those who did not live together first. Commentators against cohabitation, for their part, often respond by pointing out that people who live together before marriage are less traditional, so they are less reluctant to divorce later.

I don't believe that cohabitation causes divorce any more than I believe that marriage causes divorce. But it seems to me that some young people who decide to live together first may fail at marriage later because they made the choice to start with "marriage lite." On some level they have a fear of "forever." They eventually marry, but perhaps never fully commit. The ease of divorce helps them revert back to their preferred commitment-free state.

While some want to try it out and see how it goes, living together is not always marriage lite. For others it is a natural course of intimacy.

It is clear, however, that the distinction between living together and being married seems to be fading for lots of Gen-Xers. Marriage is no longer the only and ultimate sign of commitment. Of the people I spoke to, some saw living together as being a commitment equal to marriage—either because their lives were already completely enmeshed by living together or because these people saw the marriage contract as arbitrary. "I was no more committed to my husband after our wedding day than I had been before," said Ellie, who finally married after she had lived with her boyfriend for three years. You can read this as one of those classic Gen-X palimpsests of ambiguous love: is she saying she was already fully committed before she got married—or that marriage did nothing to mark an absolute increase in her commitment? Either way, it is clear that for her and many of her divorce-wary generation, cohabitation has become an attractive option.

Strategy 3: Hedging Our Bets

"Hedging our bets" is one more way Gen-Xers protect themselves in relationships. My friend Dana married her husband, Jordon, when she was twenty-two. I met her six years later. She is an überglam strawberry blonde full of moxie. Sporting a luminescent three-carat ring, she looked like a kid wearing a toy she'd pulled from a Cracker Jack box. Dana never left the house without putting herself together, from her perfectly coiffed hair and makeup to her meticulously coordinated couture. Her bags were generally Prada and her shoes were just one step down from that. She is the kind of person who would mortgage her home to wear the latest fashions. She and her husband are an attractive couple who seem to adore each other. She radiates sex appeal and she knows it. She loves attention from strangers, who gape at her at the gym or the supermarket. When we met, she was working in a high-end retail store; Jordon is an accountant. I remember that even though they seemed to complement each other, I could not fathom being mature enough to choose a lifelong partner at the age Dana was when she married Jordon.

Later, when I got to know her, I asked, "How did you know it was going to work? You were so young when you made the decision to be with someone for the rest of your life." She said quite cavalierly, almost with a smile, "I always figured if it didn't work out, I would get divorced."

I was stunned by what she said, and the casual way in which she said it. Her statement stuck in my mind for years. A few years and three kids later, she did in fact get divorced. I couldn't help but think perhaps there was a correlation between her comment and the divorce itself.

This "divorce as a safety net" mentality is yet another strategy some in our generation use to get close without making an ultimate commitment. Many of the men and women I talked to describe this kind of hedging-their-bets approach to relationships. An acquaintance of mine actually asked the priest to rework her wedding vows. Instead of the words "until death do us part" she opted to change her vows to end with the words "from this day forward." She explained the new vows to a friend this way: "We're going into it with no promises of forever. We hope it will work out. If it doesn't, it doesn't." While this example may seem extreme, the attitude behind it is actually quite common among Gen-Xers. When my friend Abby's boyfriend of ten months asked her to move in with him, she was willing. But she wouldn't make the move without limiting the risk; she kept her own apartment, just in case it didn't work out. "That way I can see how it goes while I still have my apartment. I want to keep [my place] as a fallback," she explained. Of course, Abby and her boyfriend have since broken up. When Richard Gere swept Debra Winger off her feet at the end of *An Officer and a Gentleman,* you can be sure she did not whisper in his ear that she was keeping the lease on her apartment. While I am not advocating headfirst, heedless decision-making, it certainly sends a message of ambivalence about a relationship if one's partner sees some prime real estate being held in abeyance just in case things fall apart.

The same sentiments were echoed by Marlo, a thirty-year-old book editor living in the Midwest, who was a child of divorce. Marlo told me that she wanted to keep a separate checking account after she got married, "just in case." Her husband, whose parents were still married after more than three decades, was crestfallen about the separate checking account: he interpreted it as a safety net clause to their marriage. Many couples separate their finances and it does not signal ambivalence; but obviously something in her affect, or his response to it, was turning the checking account into a symbol of impermanence. He interpreted her stance as having only one foot in the marriage.

A study by sociologists Paul Amato and Stacy Rogers entitled "Do Attitudes Toward Divorce Affect Marital Quality?" published in

1999 in the *Journal of Family Issues* confirms the hypothesis that the hedging-your-bets mentality can, in fact, undermine a relationship. The study looked at 2,033 married people to assess whether couples with more favorable attitudes toward divorce are more likely to dissolve their marriages. The initial results found that people who saw divorce as an option often had less satisfying marriages and were more likely to divorce. "Ironically, by adopting attitudes that provide greater freedom to leave unsatisfying marriages, people may be increasing the likelihood that their marriages will become unsatisfying in the long run," they concluded. My peers—who think they are being prudent by checking every escape hatch and fire exit, as if that were a way to defend the stability of the marriage—would be surprised that the very awareness of exits can destabilize the commitment they seek.

Strategy 4: Policy of Disengagement

Yet another strategy that people in my generation use to achieve intimacy while keeping their options open emotionally is the retracted engagement. This is a drastic measure, but it struck me profoundly that almost all of the young people who spoke to me either knew someone who had experienced a broken engagement, or it had taken place in their own lives. Is this meaningful? Only if you consider the traditional step of engagement—that is, I select you in a formal way as my future mate—to be meaningful. Again, we go back to the issue of choice: if a serious step toward a final choice can be so easily retracted, it seems that the act of choosing is less permanent and less deep. The act of engagement, it seems, has far less meaning that it used to a generation ago. Just as marriage has gone from a permanent commitment to a "let's see if it works" experiment for some, an engagement today can seem like a trial run. But, for a generation so fearful of divorce, the broken engagement seems far less drastic in comparison to a trip to divorce court. In fact, a friend of mine who experienced "pre-wedding jitters" a few weeks before her wedding was comforted by her mother, who told her: "If you have any doubt, even as you walk down the aisle, I will support you." Presumably, in earlier generations, the bride would feel compelled to sound the alarm bell earlier.

Though the flowers had been ordered, the hotel was booked, and the advance wedding presents had already arrived, Amanda and Evan were not getting married as they had planned to on the August date they had selected. Amanda, who worked in television animation, has jet black hair in a choppy, short cut and flawless skin. She is convivial with a bit of a hard edge. Her eyes welled up with tears throughout our interview. She sipped a glass of wine as she told the painful details of her called-off wedding.

Evan was an Ohio State graduate and in sales; they had met through mutual friends. From the moment they met they had been inseparable. It had been blissful at first, said Amanda: "There was never a doubt about it. I thought, you get one shot in your life for a relationship like that." Evan and Amanda had talked about getting engaged for a year. He surprised her one morning while she was sleeping. He made her breakfast in bed and got down on one knee and presented her with a pear-shaped diamond set in platinum. She was thrilled when they told their respective families. All the parents and siblings were delighted; Amanda was already practically a member of Evan's family. Over the course of the following year, the happy couple planned an elaborate wedding for three hundred at a historic hotel in downtown Chicago. Amanda chose navy, floor-length sleeveless bridesmaids' dresses, white roses, and a marzipan-decorated wedding cake. The honeymoon to Fiji had been booked and paid for.

But . . . "Eleven days before the wedding, I went on a business trip to Los Angeles. I got back to my apartment to find condoms scattered on the bed in our bedroom," she reported. The woman was gone, and Evan was in the shower; but it was clear that Amanda's fiancé had just had sex with someone in their bed. I shuddered in disbelief.

Evan wasn't apologetic. His response? "You know what? Maybe this relationship isn't right."

I didn't know what to say to Amanda. She had been blindsided by her soon-to-be husband and was beyond fury. She called his parents and said, "The wedding is off; your son fucked another girl in our bed." The parents were shocked and horrified at what their son had done.

Amanda decided to turn her devastation into action. She transformed her already-planned bachelorette party into a "Fuck Evan" party to celebrate that "he was an ass and I didn't marry him."

Days later, she ran into him at a bar; he was holding hands with another woman. Was this the woman who had been with him in their bedroom on the eve of the wedding? Through a cursory investigation, the kind only a scorned woman could pull off, Amanda found out that someone from Evan's office had actually set him up on a blind date five days before his planned wedding day.

Just when I was thinking that this guy—not to mention his office mates—could not get any worse, Amanda told me that in the next conversation she had with Evan, his main objective was asking her for the ring back.

Amanda shot back, "No way."

"The Miss Manners book says you should give the ring back," Evan insisted.

"What do you think Miss Manners would say about having sex with another girl in our bed right before our wedding?" Amanda snapped.

Amanda looked up at me, with tears streaming down her face. "That was the most expensive fuck he ever had," she blurted out. Amanda's raw bitterness penetrated me at that moment and I shook my head. I couldn't imagine what it would have felt like to come home to evidence that your fiancé had slept with another woman.

Although we had spoken more than three years after the broken engagement, Amanda's vitriol was still apparent. I couldn't blame her.

She fantasized enthusiastically about ways of getting back at Evan. She had seriously thought about taking an ad in the local paper: "Beware of dog. He cheats and roams. Paid for by the friends of the ex-fiancé"—and posting his picture. She decided against it, however, fearing a libel suit.

But beneath her acerbic exterior lay a tender, softer Amanda who had simply wanted to understand how things could have gone so terribly wrong. She told me that in the month before the wedding date, their relationship had indeed been strained. "He had said, 'This wedding is tearing us apart,'" she told me. Amanda admitted that her focus had become the wedding itself, rather than the relationship, and that Evan had been petrified of the wedding as it loomed. Perhaps she had been mistaken not to speak with him—or, say, a counselor—about the origin of his true fears. In Amanda's case, the wedding had been treated—if only temporarily—as a focus, at the expense of the relationship.

When Amanda moved through her bitterness and started to have some insight into what Evan's unexplored fears of marriage might have been, she became more compassionate. "The infidelity was so out of character; sometimes I think what he did was a desperate act. I just don't think he was ready to get married. I loved him dearly—this was one of the best relationships I ever had. I never got the chance to know what was wrong," she sobbed. There seemed to be nothing more for me to say. I placed my hand on hers and could feel a slight tremble. I was overcome with my own sadness for her.

Amanda and Evan's situation may seem extreme—and, of course, in some ways it was. But not as extreme as people may think. Startlingly, their story is just part of a big picture: in an online national poll of 565 single adults conducted in August of 2003 by Match.com/Zoomerang for *Time* magazine, 20 percent said they had themselves broken off an engagement in the past three years, and 39 percent said they knew someone else who had done so.

Is this scene of a broken engagement yet one more script for our generation, which wishes to become close, but also fears to? Pop culture is filled with images of people our age fleeing the ultimate commitment after the engagement has been announced. In 1967, when the heroine of *The Graduate* ran away from the altar with Dustin Hoffman and boarded a city bus in her wedding dress, the image was shocking. Today, the image of a woman running away in a bridal gown has become familiar TV and movie fare: Rachel on the hit TV series *Friends* left her dentist fiancé at the altar; and Julia Roberts, who backed out on her own engagement to Kiefer Sutherland, starred in *Runaway Bride* as a woman who just could not tie the knot. The latest *Spider-Man 2* has Gen-X glamour girl Mary Jane grinning as she runs away from a formal wedding in church and races across urban parks in her white wedding dress to her true love. Of course, many celebrities also break their real-life engagements offscreen.

Rachel Safier is the coauthor of a book that I find it hard to imagine would ever have been published in a previous generation, *There Goes the Bride: Making Up Your Mind, Calling It Off and Moving On.* She maintains that "this is a growing phenomenon." She claims that about 15 percent of all engagements are called off each year. Pamela Paul writes in a *Time* magazine article entitled "Calling It Off" that this kind of slippage can be accounted for by "the lengthening period of engagement; the vogue for mega-weddings, with their attendant stresses, expenses, and complications; and the fear of divorce. The longer the engagement, the more time for disillusionment and the greater the likelihood that the wedding will be called off."

I personally am aware of five people in my own social circle who have called off their weddings—male and female—and my circle of friends is not particularly dysfunctional.

One of my friends canceled her wedding three months before the wedding date. Judy is a thirty-three-year-old social worker. She is an unusually kind woman and a staunchly loyal friend. Judy grew up in Los Angeles and her parents have been happily married for thirty-six years. Judy and her fiancé, Brett, had dated on and off for two years and lived together.

A couple of years prior to this, I remember running into Judy at a Mexican restaurant as she ordered a margarita at a bar. We hadn't seen each other for years. She said she and Brett had broken up. We quickly struck up a conversation, and within a few minutes she asked me: "Are you ever upset that you are thirty and not married with no children?" I quickly replied, "No." I hadn't looked at my life in those terms, at least not until that moment. I realized that her comment wasn't about me; it actually reflected her own disappointment that she wasn't where she thought she should be at that age.

The next time I saw her, only a few months later, I was surprised to learn that she and Brett were back together and had gotten engaged. She was thrilled to finally be getting married and to begin the life that she had always envisioned for herself. We went out to celebrate with her friends, drank champagne, and ogled the ring. She booked a two-hundred-person wedding at the Bel Age hotel. She was busy meeting with florists, picking linens, and interviewing bands. But as the day inched closer, Judy told me that she and her fiancé were constantly fighting. Still, she continued to charge forward with the wedding plans. After several arguments and long discussions, Brett broke off the engagement. He explained that he just wasn't ready to settle down.

Months after the canceled wedding, with a little perspective, Judy sat down with me to talk over what had happened: "I wanted to get married so bad. You fall in love and think now you can finally get married. I think I really wanted to put a square peg in a round hole." She said Brett kept raising red flags and she tried to ignore them: "I was so happy to be engaged that I didn't listen. Right before I was going to the florist, he said, I don't know if we are compatible. I went to the florist in tears." But, she says, she still went. Her fiancé astutely sensed something was not right: "He thought I was too into the wedding. He wanted to downplay it because he wasn't sure if I wanted to get married or if I wanted to marry him." Judy says he was right about her eagerness for marriage. Judy told me about how her mother had always pushed marriage on her and cautioned her not to wait too long. She explained, "My mother married at twenty-seven, which was late for her generation. She told me not to wait too long because she said you don't want to be an old mom." I'm not sure whether her mother's goals for her actually became her own and I'm not sure if Judy knew. I remembered her once telling me that, after her sophomore year of college, she had seriously considered going to law school, but she changed her mind because she believed pursing a demanding career might keep her from having what she really wanted—a family. She said then, "I didn't apply to law school because I just didn't want to take years away from my social life." After graduation, she worked in less demanding professions; first for a nonprofit and then as a social worker.

For Judy, the wedding planning became synonymous with the idea of marital bliss. Judy says in her case she used the wedding festivities to mask the problems in her relationship: "If you're anxious about the relationship, you channel that into the wedding: the details and the worrying about the flowers. People who are confident in the relationship don't have to have the big wedding. I wanted my wedding to be perfect because my relationship wasn't perfect."

Some young couples break their engagements, many others make it down the aisle and then get divorced a year or two after the wedding, but often the mentality is the same: there is a strong focus on the idea of the wedding, but not necessarily on what comes next.

It struck me that the extended family and community really has a role to play in preparing young couples to work through their natural fears on the way to the altar; some communities encourage couples to have prewedding counseling by a priest or rabbi, which gives the couple a chance for fears to be talked through. Could some focus on the reality of marriage beforehand—not just the spectacle of the wedding—have saved Amanda from Evan's acting-out infidelity, and Evan from himself? What about Judy? There is no way to know, but it struck me that it sure couldn't have hurt.

Have other cultures prepared young people better for the realities of life after the wedding guests go home? Definitely. In other countries and during other periods in history, cultural messages about life after the wedding helped couples to understand the reality of a marriage commitment, but not here, not now, in "happily ever after" America. In high school curricula in the 1950s, "family life" was a standard part of a basic hygiene and social development course; the realities of marriage got a good sharp look. Currently, in the United Kingdom, the government mandates as part of the new National Curriculum that schools must teach children from the age of seven about the importance of marriage. There are still places in American culture where preparation for the realities of marriage is stressed—for instance, the Catholic Church requires premarital counseling. However, many of the urban, educated young middle- and upper-middle-class men and women with whom I spoke don't live in that world. And minus the religious content and socially conservative leaning of such counseling, the kind of ongoing intergenerational advice about marriage that has typically sustained unions in traditional societies is simply no longer passed down in our mobile society where the generations can live thousands of miles apart. In the past, one's grandmother might have told one's mother, "Never criticize your husband in front of somebody"—or a grandfather might tell one's father, "Always remember her birthday," or " 'Yes, dear' are two of the most useful words in the English language . . . eventually it will get you whatever you want.' " But our models are too often unavailable, distant, or unrealistic.

So this leaves the day-to-day workings of marriage as a big mystery, but the Big Day as a clear opportunity to shine.

Strategy 5: "Starter" and Multiple Marriages

Another approach to managing the fear of forever is to have more than one marriage. A strategy that many of the Gen-Xers I interviewed alluded to—a strategy so prevalent that a book has been written about it—is *"the starter marriage."* A "starter marriage" is a recent term, coined by Pamela Paul, author of *The Starter Marriage and the Future of Matrimony,* for a marriage that lasts five years or less and does not produce children. Today, almost half of American weddings include at least one spouse marrying for a second, third, or fourth time, according to *Time* magazine.

Paul asserts that these brief unions are a "growing trend" among Gen-Xers. According to her anecdotal findings, they often involve children of divorce. And according to Paul, although the parents of people in starter marriages are often divorced, and the bride and groom themselves see divorce as a viable option, the newlyweds truly believe that they will not be divorced.

This hope-against-hope attitude was described best by Greg, who recently ended his "starter marriage." The thirty-five-year-old, conservatively dressed New Yorker who works in public policy, reflected, "My parents are divorced. My wife and I talked about how we didn't want to [do that]. I toasted at our wedding, 'Here is to marriages like those in our grandparents' generation.' I prided myself on how strongly I believed in marriage. I thought my marriage was different, but it wasn't. If my parents hadn't gotten divorced, I would have pushed the eject button and [ended] my marriage even earlier." Greg claimed his marriage failed when he became obsessed with his career. He and his wife then grew apart and he had an affair. His determination to make it work before he walked down the aisle didn't save him from divorce.

Other Gen-Xers tie the knot more than twice, hoping to get it right with multiple marriages, Elizabeth Taylor–style. Multiple

marriages are an obvious and dramatic example of this generation's dogged determination to attain intimacy, but our failure over
and over again to sustain it. Multiple marriages, popular among
celebrities—from Jennifer Lopez, who is on her third marriage at
this writing, to Tom Cruise, recently engaged to be married for the
third time—are becoming more common. Taylor's eight marriages
may be some sort of record, as is Britney Spearss' fifty-five-hour
marriage to friend Jason Alexander: easy in, easy out. She moved
on to the next eight months later, with her marriage to backup
dancer Kevin Federline; at the time of this writing they are still together.

But ordinary people, too, think marriage is worth repeating—
and repeating. In one out of an estimated seven weddings, the bride
or the groom—or both—is tying the knot for at least the third
time; this is nearly twice as many as in 1970, according to *Utne
Reader* magazine.

The multiple-marriage phenomenon speaks to this generation's
generally low level of skills regarding how to sustain intimacy. Un-
derlying this phenomenon may well be the belief that marital success
is just a matter of finding the right person—and if you don't succeed
the first time, try, try again. This phenomenon is no doubt a result of
a blend of Evil influence #2 (Multiple Choice Culture) and Evil Influence #5 (The "Why Suffer?" Mentality). But perhaps a lack of real
commitment in many of these marriages is part of why they fail. It
seems to me that is precisely the reason why multiple marriages have
a lower success rate. Despite an assumption that some experience in
one marriage would help to sustain others, second marriages have an
even higher likelihood of ending in divorce: 60 percent, according to
Judith Wallerstein, divorce expert and clinical psychologist. Given
the unlikelihood of these multiple marriages lasting, it certainly says
something powerful about this generation's profound need to connect that we try over and over again, despite the likelihood of failure.

Strategy 6: "The Grass Is Greener" Affair

Even for those Gen-Xers who do make the leap to a supposed death-do-us-part marriage, some still seek to maintain an escape hatch through the age-old tactic of having an extramarital affair. While they may not technically be single, their attitude, when it comes to commitment, may be no different than that of a single person. They, too, are "unhooked."

Different studies draw different conclusions about how widespread infidelity is. In 1948, Alfred Kinsey, author of the landmark and controversial Kinsey Report, reported that 26 percent of wives and 50 percent of husbands said they had had at least one affair by the time they were forty years old. *The Janus Report on Sexual Behavior,* forty-five years later, found 26 percent of married women but 35 percent of married men reporting at least one extramarital sexual encounter. The 1994 National Health and Social Life Survey, considered the most recent comprehensive sex survey, put the numbers lower, estimating one out of five married people is unfaithful: 25 percent of men and 15 percent of women. I am reluctant to draw any hard conclusions about whether cheating is on the rise based on surveys, since surveys on affairs are notoriously unreliable. I believe that listening to people's stories about infidelity sheds the best light on current attitudes. The one trend that may be verified is that, among cheaters in marriage, women are now increasingly as likely to confess to infidelity as are men. In 1991, the National Opinion Research Center at the University of Chicago asked married women if they'd ever had sex outside their marriage, and 10 percent said yes. When the pollsters asked the same question in 2002, the yes responses rose to 15 percent, while the number of men stayed flat at about 22 percent. "The best interpretation of the data: the cheating rate for women is approaching that of men," said Tom Smith, author of the NORC's reports on sexual behavior. Recent headlines such as *Newsweek*'s cover story "The New Infidelity: From Office Affairs to Internet Hookups, More Wives Are Cheating Too," also report that the gap between men having affairs and women having them is closing.

Of course, affairs are not unique to this generation. What is different today is the increase in opportunity to cheat and a decrease in the stigma associated with it. Women in the workplace and the technology of cell phones and e-mail provide private communication and create an environment in which affairs can easily take place. Without question, though, it is the explosion of Internet sites for married people looking for people who want to cheat, such as MarriedandFlirting.net and Philanderers.com, that have opened up the playing field and made finding a partner to cheat with as easy as clicking a mouse. Whatever the data on affairs may indicate, what we can know for sure is that, these days, for my generation, adultery is not a scarlet letter. Some of our favorite television characters cheat on their spouses; famous men often leave their wives to marry girlfriends; and mistresses of public figures become overnight celebrities.

Earlier, I explored the high expectations of members of this generation, many of whom are on a quest for constant and complete emotional fulfillment. The expectation that our husbands or wives should connect with us on every level the way our friends, therapists, or colleagues do may make our marriages ripe for the projection that something is missing. This may be why we hear more and more about "the emotional affair." Those higher expectations may, in fact, be partially responsible for affairs. According to Shirley Glass, PhD, author of *Not "Just Friends,"* expectations are just as much to blame for affairs as bad marriages. She contends that individuals with high expectations can become easily dissatisfied because they expect more than any one relationship can provide. Today's men and women expect more out of marriage, she writes: "Both husbands and wives are looking to their spouses for love, companionship, intellectual stimulation, emotional support, and great sex in the high-stress environment of dual careers and Little League carpools. An attractive person who appears to offer any of the components missing from this picture of perfection can be very tempting." The exceedingly high expectations of Gen-Xers keep them not only from choosing a partner, but also from sticking with one.

Harlan, a thirty-seven-year-old Australian musician living in Chicago who looks like a character out of *Boogie Nights,* has been down that road. He has silver hair, distinctively long sideburns, and was wearing square blue sunglasses the day I met him, even though it was a cloudy day. He was dressed in striped pants and a rumpled dark shirt, and looked as though he had just woken up.

I met him in front of his walk-up apartment on a desolate street in Chicago's Ukrainian Village on a crisp fall morning. We got on the number 66 bus together to get to a café; within moments, he had told me about the affair that had ended his seven-year marriage. With no apparent embarrassment, he told me straight out why he had initiated the affair: "I thought marriage was going to be everlasting excitement, and it wasn't," he said. "So I went out looking elsewhere for happiness. I had an affair and realized that wasn't going to be [happiness]. I fucked up my marriage. I desperately loved my wife, but it was over and I had to move on."

Although he spoke frankly, it was clear from the anguish on his face that he was far from having moved on. The bus stopped abruptly and Harlan and I exited on Damen Avenue. Harlan led me into a hip, modern café with purplish walls, the color of the sky after sunset. It is the kind of place that serves beverages with names such as "Atomic Blast." Harlan kept his shades on inside and was chain smoking at 10 a.m.

He described himself as a "hopeless romantic." He spoke about his ex-wife, Trish, in glowing terms: "My ex-wife is kind, giving, compassionate. She is the person I wished I could be. She made me a better person," he said sadly. Trish is three years younger than Harlan.

He describes her as "conventionally beautiful." And she has a great sense of style, he says; she loved to refurbish old furniture she found at flea markets. Harlan recalled: "She is feminine and sexy with a curvy, voluptuous figure." He took another drag of his cigarette and started to explain what went wrong: "People say to me, you must not have been happy in your marriage. But I was. Life was fine, but a little bit gray. I wanted that sensation of being in color. I projected that onto the relationship. I thought that there was something she didn't have that I needed." Gen-Xers such as Harlan are encouraged—specifically by the influence of therapeutic language, which comes from Evil Influence #5 (The "Why Suffer?" Mentality)—to pursue euphoria as our birthright, and to resist settling into a situation which is uncomfortable or lacking stimulation for more than a moment.

Harlan's friends' assumption—that affairs only take place when the partners involved are trapped in unhappy or unloving marriages—is a common one, but it is out of date. While it is true that an affair may result from an unhappy marriage, it is not uncommon for people who describe their marriages as being happy to have affairs, as well.

Shirley Glass, called "the godmother of infidelity research" by the *New York Times,* concluded this from her 1980 "airport study." Dr. Glass gave a questionnaire to one thousand men and women at Baltimore/Washington International Airport and at an office park and received three hundred back anonymously. According to her study, 56 percent of men and 34 percent of women who had had extramarital intercourse said that their marriage was happy. The "unhappy marriage causes infidelity" mantra is a message that is often repeated in popular media, particularly on daytime talk shows and in books of pop psychology. But as I listened to men and women, some of whom had had affairs in spite of good marriages, this notion—that discontent in the marriage always precedes the affair—seemed to be useful for some of my unhooked subjects as a rationalization for a choice they had made that was not inevitable. The truth was that many Gen-Xers seem to have affairs not out of the anguish of being badly matched, but just because they wanted to see what was on another channel.

I spoke to a number of married Gen-X men and women who told me they had had affairs; some were indeed in unhappy marriages, while many others said that there was nothing really wrong in their unions. Like Harlan, many of my unfaithful informants looked to an affair to bring color to their otherwise "gray" lives. A thirty-year-old woman I interviewed, Renee, who lived in Los Angeles, cheated on her kind, adoring husband because, as she put it, "I missed the attention I used to get from men when I was single." Many of my unfaithful men and women expressed unwillingness to face the possibility that life within marriage—just as in any lifelong commitment—can sometimes become mundane. Men and women of my generation often seem unwilling to tolerate a love relationship in marriage that unfolds in anything less than Technicolor and surround sound.

As Harlan finished his third cigarette, he explained how his affair seemed to solve his problem, at least temporarily: "I had the feeling of being in love again. I wanted to get high on that again, and someone walked into my life and made it easy."

Harlan's affair began when he was on the road with his band. The night he played in Boston he met Monique at a party of a friend. Monique was a painter, and he was instantly drawn to her. "She was artsy. I liked that. My wife could appreciate that stuff, but she didn't do it for a living," he explained. "With my girlfriend, we connected on an intellectual level and a spiritual level. I thought maybe that was what I was missing with my wife. . . . After an hour with her I wanted to marry her." Monique and Harlan spent the next evening together at a bar talking. Then they hid in the back of the women's bathroom so they could make out. "I thought the person I married was perfect; but, because I wasn't completely satisfied with everything in my life, I thought this person was *more* perfect," he explained.

When Harlan went back home, the two did not contact one another. Harlan thought maybe this was just a one-time thing and it was pointless since he was married. But a couple of months later, when he was traveling through Boston again, his fling heard that his band was coming to town and she showed up at the friend's house where she had met Harlan the last time. "In a way, I hoped she would show up, but at the same time I hoped she wouldn't," he recalled. They talked for hours. At the end of the evening, they admitted they were crazy about each other. He said to her, "You are going to ruin my life." He knew what was ahead. This time, their relationship became more physically intimate, but they did not have intercourse: "I was very Clintonesque about the whole thing. Because there was no penetration, in my mind it wasn't as bad," he explained.

When he returned home from his trip, he struggled for two months over what he should do next. He and Monique began talking on the phone constantly. "I was using a pay phone to call her because I didn't want her number to show up on my cell phone," he recalled. They had already begun talking about a future together. After many restless nights, Harlan decided to tell his wife. He told her flatly, "I fell in love with someone else."

Trish was enraged and dissolved into tears, made one phone call to a friend, packed a few things, and walked out the door. She would pick up the rest of her belongings later when he was out of the house. Harlan described her as devastated; but all he could think about at the time was how much he wanted to be with his girlfriend.

He flew out to Boston. That night, Harlan and Monique had intercourse for the first time. According to Harlan, the sex was amazing: "Being with a new person after seven years, it was totally different. It blew me away. She was a sexual athlete. It was all-over-the-map type of sex." They charged forward emotionally, and both decided that she would move to Chicago so that they could be together.

Almost immediately, things started to fall apart: "When I got into the U-haul truck, we started talking and I had this epiphany that I created the whole thing in my mind. I realized it wasn't going to be the thrilling experience I had built up." But Harlan still wanted to give it a shot; after all, Monique had decided to move and he had already told his wife. Once they got to Chicago, they fought about everything. "She could tell I regretted everything and here she had moved her whole life," Harlan recalled. "She could have been anyone. She provided the fantasy. I thought we had a great connection. It was true we had a lot in common, but we were very incompatible." He realized quickly that although he and his girlfriend seemed to "connect" on many levels, he soon learned they didn't "connect" in many *other* ways that he did with his now-estranged wife.

After living together for two months in Chicago, they decided Monique should move out but they would still date. They were a couple for a year and a half but eventually Monique moved back to Boston. At first they kept in touch, but they quickly decided they had no future. A frustrated Harlan, now with a distinct wrinkle between his brows and a cloud of smoke overhead, explained that he had unfairly blamed his wife: "My relationship wasn't solving every problem in my life. I was in love with my wife, and I realized I was looking for happiness outside myself. It is hard to see the difference between being bored with your life and bored with your partner. But I realized all this a little late."

After Harlan had this revelation, he tried to patch things up with Trish; unsurprisingly, she wouldn't take him back. So, he says he has tried with difficulty to accept that he messed up and needed to move on: "I've been in therapy for two years. I have postdivorce stress syndrome," he joked. "My therapist tells me not to beat myself up."

Many commentators have made the case that the stigma of affairs has begun to fade as the media publicizes, and in some cases glamorizes, these extramarital dalliances. I recently saw a glamorization of infidelity at, of all places, one of my favorite clothing stores. Among the racks of capri pants and microminiskirts I saw a stack of T-shirts that read: MY BOYFRIEND IS OUT OF TOWN and MY WIFE IS OUT OF TOWN. These $17.95 advertisements for infidelity, ironic or not, were the newest trend.

The Gen-X cultural script about affairs is not that you are a faithless jerk if you cheat, but rather that there is a tipping point: that under the right circumstances, anyone is vulnerable to stray. I heard this from some of my unhooked subjects. Take, for example, Adrianna, a thirty-five-year-old career counselor from New Jersey: "When I do get married, I'd like to be able to say I would never have an affair. But you never know. I just would try to keep myself out of a situation where that would happen." It was as if she thought having an affair could happen without her consent.

Today, the cultural message is that affairs are not so much a matter of character, but more a matter of circumstance. This line of thinking puts the blame squarely on the relationship—and the burden often on the noncheating partner.

A couple of years ago, I was forced in one of my own relationships to figure out how I viewed affairs. I learned that my beliefs, in many ways, were in conflict with the attitude I saw around me. I was dating a man who was divorced, whom I will call Tom. I was in love with Tom, and believed that we had a real future together. We were on vacation and had just left a movie theater where we saw the movie *Fatal Attraction,* which led us to discuss extramarital affairs. Tom revealed to me that he had had an affair during his six-year marriage. His news hit me like an avalanche. Before I knew a single detail, I started to cry. Up until that point, I saw marriage as black and white: either you were faithful to your vow or you were not. And I now saw Tom as crossing the great moral divide. Once he revealed this piece of his past, I saw him differently. I viewed him as someone who had different values than I did and I concluded that we could never be together. When Tom saw the look of disappointment on my face, he tried desperately to explain why he had had this affair. He told me about how unhappy he was in his marriage. I responded with a battery of questions. Ultimately, he portrayed himself as a victim locked in a loveless marriage. I struggled with what to do. It was my belief that if indeed his marriage was that unhappy, he should have confronted his wife and addressed the issue of separation before sleeping with someone else. After a tense day and little conversation, we went back to the hotel.

The beautiful room with gold sconces and a lilac bedspread now seemed icy and sterile to me. I crouched in the bathroom tub and called a trusted friend while my boyfriend slept. I whispered as I nervously peeled the ornate wrapper off the soap. I shared with my friend what my boyfriend had told me. I was surprised to find that she was much less disturbed than I. And I was even more stunned to learn that when she was single, she had once had an affair with a married man. My god, I thought—naively—she was a loyal and longtime friend—and she was a kindergarten teacher!

Her advice: "You just never know what is going on in someone's marriage. Sometimes these things happen." As I picked up the pieces of the soap wrapper from the floor of the tub, I began to feel like my black-and-white approach to affairs made me a Martian in my own generation. I slid into the cold sheets next to my sleeping boyfriend. The next morning I opened my eyes to a room-service tray. Tom had ordered all my favorites: an omelet with Swiss cheese and pancakes. When I turned over, I saw that he was staring up at the ceiling. I said, with my mind racing: "Look, Tom, I have never been married. I realize it is unfair of me to pass judgment. Perhaps circumstances would lead me to do such a thing if I were in a bad marriage." At that moment I went against my instincts. I wanted to believe what I was saying so that I could keep seeing this man. But the relationship ended a few weeks later. Tom dumped me without giving a substantial reason. I'll never know if it was because he felt judged by me, or if it was something else. But, in a way, I was relieved, because I was never comfortable with his "bad marriage" defense. I realized that I had allowed my belief system to be shifted, if only temporarily, by the combination of my girlfriend's message, Tom's view of his own innocence, and the surrounding cultural messages I was receiving—that affairs are common and often even justifiable. I, personally, could not get past the affair. I viewed Tom differently after that and I didn't know if I would ever be able to trust him. I got over that breakup, but I wasn't able to get over the fact that Tom had never expressed real regret or taken full responsibility for what he had done. I believe that, regardless of circumstances, having an affair is always a choice.

While only a few women I heard from confessed to either having had an affair with a married man or having had an affair outside their own marriage, I was surprised to note how completely average these women seemed. I met a thirty-two-year-old woman from Minneapolis named Kim, who sells advertising for a newspaper and had been married for three and a half years. She says she is reasonably happily. She told me she thought a **"marriage sabbatical"** would be good for her relationship. She and her husband had actually discussed an arrangement in which each would take a separate vacation and sleep with someone else. At the time of my interview, the idea was still under discussion.

Kim didn't believe that human beings were monogamous by nature; she saw temptation as being inevitable, and thought that an affair would wreak havoc on her marriage. So, to her way of thinking, the "marriage sabbatical" was a problem-solver, not a scandal. She explained, "We have an important connection, and I would not throw it out for a one-night stand. The sabbatical would be about having our own freedom and space, as well as having a sexual component. Part of me would hope our marriage would expand to include that."

Cheryl Jarvis, the author of a book called *The Marriage Sabbatical,* coined this term. In her book, the "sabbatical" involved women who left their families temporarily to follow long-delayed dreams; it had nothing to do with extracurricular sex. But Kim had her own, very Gen-X interpretation of what "a marriage sabbatical" should entail.

This lack of stigma when it comes to extramarital affairs has also trickled down to couples who are "committed" but not yet married. Since the stigma associated with marital infidelity has lessened, the unofficial commitment between a girlfriend and boyfriend today also, to many, may have less meaning. Although the man or woman in the relationship may well expect his or her partner to be faithful, the exclusivity agreement may be taken much less seriously, since singles of our generation cycle through multiple boyfriends or girlfriends before they settle on one partner. For example, my single friend Dorian was recently at a party and approached by a man named Zack, whom she knew had a girlfriend. Zack had been dating his girlfriend for two years. But, after a few drinks and interesting conversation, Zack tried to kiss Dorian. Her shocked response was: "You have a girlfriend." His response was, "So what."

I thought back to Harlan. I followed up with him a year later. He was now out of the music business and working at a more conventional job, as an assistant at an architectural design firm. He said that, after a lot of therapy, he was feeling much better about himself, and he had learned a lot: "For one thing, don't make a commitment you can't keep, because no relationship is going to stay the same."

He explained that he was more realistic about relationships now and was dating again. Now he was doing what he had wanted to do when he was married: going out casually and having a lot of random sex. But, he says, it wasn't the way he imagined it would be: "The first couple months of dating, I thought it was great. You don't get into all the deep stuff and you get to have lots of sex. But now, I'm getting bored of it."

A recent promotion at work made him view commitment in a different light: "I desperately wanted to call someone—and I realized there was no one to call. That is when I realized why I do want a long-term relationship."

A year earlier, Harlan had told me he wasn't sure if he would ever marry again: "I feel dishonest about getting married again because I didn't keep the vows the first time. I mean, does that promise really hold any weight anymore?" But now, he told me, he feels a deep desire to get remarried and this time to "do it right": "There is no substitute for real intimacy. Right now I have sex and friendship," he said, "but everyone needs to love."

All of these strategies from "The Waiting Game," to "Virtual Marriage: Living Together," to "Hedging Our Bets," to "The Policy of Disengagement," to "Starter and Multiple Marriages," and "The Grass Is Greener" Affair are ways Gen-Xers cope with their desire for intimacy, but also their fear of it. While these strategies temporarily satisfy our need to get close without the promise of forever, they can also contribute to keeping us "unhooked."

The Wedding Fantasy vs. the Single Life Glamour

When it comes to marriage, this generation is influenced by two competing fantasies: the image of the glamorous single life competes with that of the fantasy wedding. I have already talked about the sexy image of single life that is created and reinforced by the media. On the other end of the spectrum, the fantasy wedding still looms large for many American women. Perhaps the only thing that seems exciting about marriage in our culture today is the wedding itself.

One of the questions I asked the single women I interviewed was, "Why do you want to get married? What is it about marriage that is important to you?" About one in ten replied that a committed situation would be fine, but that the primary reason to actually get married was the wedding—not the vows, the sanctification of the commitment or the future, but rather a big party with friends, registered gifts, music, flowers, cake, fashion, and formality.

Whitney, the twenty-five-year-old Los Angeles Web developer mentioned earlier, told me, "I don't think it is necessary to get married, but I would, just for the wedding." Another respondent, Isabelle, a thirty-year-old Los Angeles standup comedian, said, "The piece of paper doesn't mean shit. I don't need to get married. I want the relationship and the party. . . . I want my dad to walk me down the aisle and I want my friends around." She wanted what she, like many of the women, seemed to think of as "her day." The interviewees who were focused on the party aspect were not thinking about the importance of vows in front of a judge and a handful of family; they were focused on the extravaganza.

Can the excitement of a spectacular, all-out wedding production, touted by a major industry with big marketing dollars behind it, lure women down the aisle?

Judy, the woman who had become disengaged, admitted that for her, the big wedding fantasy didn't help: "I was really into the idea of getting married, and that included the wedding. Plus, I'm a real planner, so I got really wrapped up in it. I think when you are getting married for the right reasons the festivities aren't as important."

The wedding industry is booming like never before. Now a fifty-five-billion-dollar annual business, it captivates many women. According to the Fairchild Bridal Group, the average American couple spends $26,326 on their wedding day. This figure has gone up by 75 percent over the last fifteen years, according to *Bride* magazine. The average annual income for a newly married couple, according to a 2005 Fairchild Bridal Group Survey, is approximately $73,307. This is the kind of proportion of outlay to income that you see in the developing world, in societies such as India, in which families bankrupt themselves in order to put on a proper wedding-day event.

How is it that in this postmodern, postfeminist, post-nuclear-family America, many young people, especially women, are in some ways even more obsessed with the decorative and display aspects of weddings than they were in the 1950s—when getting married was a young woman's most important goal? The answer: fantasy. We've seen that some of that fantasy element is driven by *Martha Stewart*

Weddings magazine, with its five-foot-high cakes in a trompe l'oeil style, and its dresses festooned with Austrian crystals; we've seen the influence of tabloid paparazzi interest in celebrity weddings—the leaked memos about the salmon *en croute* and the Vera Wang gown.

But why would today's young women—with everything they have going on in their lives—swoon at such a seemingly superficial goal? The average woman has never been treated to the experience that has the become the pinnacle of American society: she is not treated as a celebrity. But on her wedding day, every woman can become not a queen—the 1950s promise—but J. Lo or Carolyn Bessette Kennedy—a star. You may never be a guest at the Oscars or wear an Armani gown, but on your wedding day, in your white silk organza dress, with all eyes upon you and the photographer following you around, you get to feel like Nicole Kidman: pampered by professionals, catered to by family and friends, and showered by hundreds of adoring fans, if only for a few hours. The trip down the aisle can feel like a walk on the red carpet for those of us who won't ever have the opportunity to attend a star-studded event.

Sadly, though, the magazines and wedding planners don't give much attention to the fact that this kind of celebrity lasts a short time, one day—or two, if you count the rehearsal dinner. It's as if you just won an Academy Award, but you wake up the very next day to the reality that your starring days are over. Interestingly, Gwyneth Paltrow said in an interview on *The Oprah Winfrey Show* that she didn't need to have the big special wedding day the way other brides do precisely because she is a celebrity. Oprah and Paltrow agreed that, as celebrities, they "get to be the bride everyday." Clearly, there is a connection in the minds of American women between the fantasy of being a bride and being a celebrity. Evil Influence #6 (The Celebrity Standard) has yet another effect on our relationships.

Many brides attempt to prolong the attention with engagement parties and multiple showers. Therapist Sheryl Nissinen, author of *The Conscious Bride,* estimates that 90 percent of women report "post wedding depression" in the first year of marriage, according to her own nonscientific research. The high is over and their role of bride is forever in the past and a slight depression sets in as they have to resume being a normal person. It is natural, in this state of being uncomfortably out of the spotlight, for many women to look forward to pregnancy and childbirth as their next opportunity to take a starring role. Other women aren't able to so easily forget the dream of romance that the wedding promised—that married life can't possibly live up to—and they get divorced. While these elaborate wedding celebrations and the obligatory gift-giving is often a sign of shallow materialism, I sense there is something deeper here.

The splitup of Hollywood's golden couple, Brad Pitt and Jennifer Aniston, made the cover of practically every entertainment magazine and sparked incessant conversation among many of my generation. Despite the fact that divorce in Hollywood has become a cliché of the rich and famous, this one still seemed to take us by surprise. Why? Brad and Jennifer were this generation's Cinderella story, our Camelot. They had it all: fame, money, and, of course, love. At a time when it is so difficult to believe in love, we hung all our romantic hopes and dreams on their relationship. We wanted to believe that the fantasy of everlasting love and commitment could indeed be real.

Many of us are seduced by the fantasy of a wedding and a seemingly fairy-tale marriage because it helps counter the reality of our pessimistic fears about marriage and bleak divorce rates. Weddings are still a symbol of happily ever after, so it is easy to see why we cling to them in the midst of all our skepticism.

The Marriage-Is-Obsolete Subculture

There is a group of young people who has simply resolved all of these emotional tensions and contradictions by a clear and drastic means: they have stopped believing in marriage altogether. They tend to describe their absolute lack of faith in or connection to the notion of marriage as being a state of liberation or confrontation with an ultimate reality. This subculture is significant because it represents this generation's lack of confidence in the institution of marriage and may well affect the future of matrimony.

Along my journey, I met a twenty-nine-year-old named Jared, from California, with piercing sky blue eyes. He was friendly and soft-spoken. But when he began to speak passionately about relationships, his volume increased considerably. Jared and I became involved in a discussion with a forty-one-year-old married woman, Nina, who sat nearby. The dialogue between them underscored a dramatic difference between two generations when it came to romantic relationships. My conversation with Jared began with a discussion of "the checklist."

Jared began, "It is OK to have a checklist as long as you are fine being alone. I realized my standards were high, but not too high as long as I could accept lifelong bachelorhood. There is no reason to change my standards. I love my life. If I can find someone that enhances the situation I will do it [have a committed relationship], but my life doesn't need enhancing. My cup is full."

"So you don't need an emotionally bonded relationship that usually comes in the form of marriage?" Nina inquired.

Jared shot back, "I don't ever need anyone. I don't want to be codependent. I want to want someone. I don't want to be in a relationship where the world crumbles and falls without that person. My reality isn't based on someone else's reality."

Nina replied, "That is what we [people of her generation] used to call romantic love."

"I am not saying I don't need other people. I am saying that person can ebb and flow—it doesn't have to be one person," he explained to her.

Nina, intrigued or disbelieving, asked, "Have you ever fallen in love?"

"Yes," replied Jared, "and it was not a good feeling. It was an immature place to be and I did not feel fulfilled when I was there."

"You don't value having a lifelong relationship and marriage?" she asked.

Jared replied, "I want to be in a relationship where I am choosing to be with the person everyday. To say I know what I want in thirty years is bullshit. When you get married today, part of your brain knows that [forever] very well might not be true."

Jared was not alone in his belief that marriage is obsolete. He echoed what I heard from a minority of my unhooked singles. Who knows if these people will change their minds if indeed they meet someone and are confronted with the choice between marriage and a lifetime commitment with no contract? Or, what if they are faced with losing the potential partner over the issue? And, if they decide they want children, perhaps their perspective might change. For now, they expressed that, for them, marriage was not necessarily the expected or ultimate path. This subset of people seemed genuinely happy about the deconstruction of marriage; they were not in the camp of singles that were deathly afraid of marriage, nor were they part of the group that wanted that commitment but didn't know how to get there. This subset seems legitimately realistic, from their own undeceived—or supremely cynical—perspective about marriage. They describe their vision of a long-term relationship as being one in which you "choose your partner every day"; a relationship in which commitment, not contracts, dictates the terms. In their eyes, this kind of union transcends marriage and has, indeed, perhaps already made it obsolete.

It is not surprising that many of the people I interviewed were already there, swept away by an infatuation with celebrity-style alternatives: "The couples in Hollywood, like Goldie Hawn and Kurt Russell, that don't marry—that says, I choose this person every day. I want to be in a relationship that feels like a conscious choice. I would not have the mask of 'I'm married, therefore we have a relationship,'" said Mia, the thirty-four-year-old district attorney mentioned earlier, from a conservative Colombian family. The fantasy that a noncontracted union is glamorous by nature seems as strong and groundless a fantasy as the one that maintains that a piece of paper and a gala wedding are all you need for perpetual bliss. As so often is the case in our generation, both of these fantasies focus on the form of the product, not the content of the process.

In fact, Jared—the man who is happy in a world without marriage, the man who sees mutual dependence as "codependence" and vulnerability as immature, may not be a marginal figure at all, but a harbinger of a much bigger change underway.

Some of the men and women in this "marriage is obsolete" subculture shared by Jared described this type of alternative-to-marriage relationship to me as being more romantic than traditional marriage is; this type of relationship is seen as an alternative to what these singles describe as marriage's clear hypocrisy. This type of nonmarriage union also provides the ultimate "freedom" and "choice"—two primary values of this generation.

So will we do away with traditional marriage altogether? We will only know with time.

I'm not saying the answer is to choose to marry or to choose not to marry. I am not saying we should get married young and start families early. What this generation needs to find is a comfort level with making the choices that we do make. This means we have to accept that, with every positive choice, we will have to give many things up. We have to make a commitment to go deeply into one experience, instead of channel surfing and checking out every option and every relationship.

9

Finding True Love

After all I have learned about what isn't working for us in our search for love, at the end of this journey, I feel surprisingly hopeful. We are indeed surrounded by obstacles to love and commitment—but our solution is also waiting for us, in our own hands and hearts.

The approaches to finding love that the dominant culture recommend to us are actually, I have to conclude, guaranteed to frustrate and disappoint us. We can't change the Evil Influences of our culture. But we can change our own inner inclinations—and, by doing so, create an atmosphere in which true love can emerge in and around us.

This means that we have to look first at ourselves.

During the course of my work on this book, I learned that our generation's approach does not work. Even more dramatically, I conclude that in order for our generation to sustain true love, we need to accomplish a complete about-face. Indeed, it requires of us to become different than we are now. It turns out that finding true love is not an external process, but an internal one—it is not about finding a perfect match, but rather deciding to become someone who is both lovable and capable of being open, selfless, optimistic, brave, accepting, patient, and loving.

As I went on this journey, I slowly started to feel hopeful about my own life and my—at first—fragile relationship. As I painfully discovered the more challenging requirements of feeling love and drawing love to me, I found myself growing as a person. I also saw that my relationship was getting stronger.

As each laser of insight from my unhooked singles stripped away my own defenses and assumptions, I slowly abandoned my checklist and I stopped comparing my boyfriend to other men. I began to realize that finding a new partner was not the answer to every disagreement. I found I gradually stopped looking to my boyfriend to fulfill all of my needs all of the time. Eventually, I even stopped expecting to receive love without being loving myself. I took my relationship off autopilot and began working at it. Finally, I consciously looked at my skepticism and deliberately put it aside.

While there is no magic wand that I can wave to bring me true love, I discovered, to my amazement, that my feelings of love and passion were growing stronger. As I changed, my boyfriend, too, seemed to drop his own defenses in relation to me—leading us into a more profound friendship and more intimacy than I had ever imagined could be possible. I felt that at a minimum, I now had a grasp of what *not* to do.

But how do we trust the advice to drop these scripts when, everywhere we look, the culture reinforces them? I felt, on the way, that I needed some practical guidance from those lucky mortals who had learned how to make themselves into soul mates—and had consequently found true love. I sought out people who were able to overcome these inclinations and graduate to commitment. I also spoke to couples who had been joyfully bonded for many years—and asked them to share their secrets.

I realized that this personal evolution has two stages: dropping what sabotages love and then embracing what nurtures it. First, I realized, we all would do better to abandon the following behaviors:

- Focusing on the "I," rather than the "we"
- Setting narrow and even contradictory expectations for our partners to live up to
- Expecting magically to meet our soul mate, instead of being willing to work to create a soul mate out of each other
- Turning our partners into commodities for our own affirmation
- Always expecting, rather than accepting
- Asking constantly what the other person is doing for you, rather than thinking about what you are willing to give
- Expecting to have passion without renewing it
- Holding on to fear, skepticism, and impatience
- And, finally, avoiding fully committing to our relationships

From happily mated people, I learned that the second stage of finding true love involved accepting five "keys":

- Look at yourself first
- Burn your checklist
- Stop speeding
- Go all the way
- Commit and fuel the fire

Look at Yourself First

The one theme that takes precedence over everything else in all the stories of true love that I heard—a theme that, again, is totally at odds with the culture of emotional consumerism around us—is that, when something is wrong in these people's relationships, they consider first what they themselves might be doing to cause the problem.

It is much easier at the first sign of trouble or disagreement to blame the other person and decide he or she is not "the one." A friend of mine, after dating his girlfriend for six months, argued with her about how much time they spent with their respective families. He was more interested in spending time with friends, while she wanted to get to know his family and spend time with her own. After that conversation, he concluded that maybe they were just too different. He decided that he needed to find someone who was more like him and he left her. He thought if only she were different he would fall for her. The passionately in-long-term-love people I heard from would have looked at how they themselves were handling their part of the argument to see if there was more they could do to create an "us" set of values. I found that the people with truly enviable relationships that I encountered all took responsibility for becoming the kind of person who was communicating and caring, rather than fantasizing about ditching the partner when a conflict arose. These people didn't blame the other person when they didn't feel the love they were seeking; rather, they looked at how their own actions got in the way.

My friend Sophia discovered this in her relationship with Clark. I've never seen a couple laugh the way Sophia and Clark do. Sophia is a quirky, easy-going woman from Sioux City, Iowa. She has started her own business making greeting cards that she sells out of her home. Clark, in contrast, grew up in California; he has a rugged, athletic look, a thick head of messy brown hair, and a gap between his two front teeth. In spite of their dissimilarities, together they bring out the best in each other. I've known Sophia for more than ten years, and have known Clark for almost as long.

A decade after we first met in college, we were sitting in the living room of their charming home outside of San Francisco. Hundreds of books lined their bookshelves—an odd collection of science, history, and pop culture. Breakfast was cooking in the kitchen and Ben Harper was playing in the background.

Clark greeted me with a warm hug and asked me what I wanted in my eggs. I pulled up a chair in the kitchen while Clark caught me up on life at Berkeley, where he is getting a graduate degree in engineering. As Clark finished making breakfast, Sophia and I had some time alone together. When I asked Sophia about her relationship with Clark, she reminisced about the day they met: a mutual friend had introduced them their freshman year, in their college dorm.

"I remember seeing him as this quintessential California boy," she said. "He was totally athletic. He played water polo and rode his cruiser bike around campus. He always wore a baseball cap and flip-flops; no matter if it was fifty degrees outside, he always wore flip-flops." She smiled.

Clark and Sophia became fast friends. They did everything together: he tutored her in calculus, they listened to bands play on campus, and they stayed up all night talking in the dorm. "But I had a boyfriend from high school that I was still dating, so I wasn't thinking of Clark in a romantic way," Sophia explained. By Sophia's junior year, though, that relationship had ended. One day, before Christmas break, Clark and Sophia shared their first kiss. "I remember being so excited. I didn't want to part after that." She twirled her hair as she reminisced.

Sophia invited Clark to come home with her for the holidays, but doubted he would, since vacation was only two days away. But Clark surprised her; he changed his airline ticket that very day. "He was so spontaneous. I loved that. And he showed up at my parents' house with his guitar the following day," she recalled. They had a great time with her family. Her parents immediately took to Clark. He played "Blackbird" by the Beatles on his guitar for them.

After that trip, the friendship turned to romance. They enjoyed the ease of a college relationship—late nights with sleepovers, trips together over spring break, and formals. Their collegiate courtship was fun—but not exactly what Sophia had imagined. When her friends' boyfriends would come to pick up their girlfriends for a formal, they arrived with flowers. Clark, on the other hand, she recalled, showed up with a cactus. "I was thinking, What is up with him? My dad was such a chivalrous guy, and Clark would barely open the door for me. I wanted someone that was doting. I wanted a guy who would take care of me. It was a strike against him that he didn't have those chivalrous manners that the good guy was supposed to have."

True, Clark's ways were often unconventional, something Sophia admits she didn't appreciate at the time. But Clark was hardly unromantic, she said, thinking back to those early days together: "He would write songs for me and play them on the guitar. He would paint paintings for me. He would make me cookies."

In spite of these gestures, Sophia still felt resistant; it just wasn't the kind of male courtship she had imagined. She explained she was still stuck on an internal "script": "His approach to romance just wasn't what I had in my head."

Despite her hesitations, she couldn't deny how much fun they were having together: "I had never met anyone like him. He was so funny, so smart, and an amazing engineer." They dated throughout college and when Clark moved to California for a job, they continued to date long distance. After a year, they started to date other people—both because of the distance, and due to the fact that neither was ready to commit. But they remained best friends. A couple of years later, Sophia landed a job in San Francisco. It wasn't long before Sophia and Clark started to date again.

After three years as a couple, Sophia began to seriously evaluate their relationship. She wanted marriage and she loved Clark, but, true to her generation's anxiety, she was deathly afraid. Her model of marriage was a very strong one, she explained, which made making the right choice seem even harder: "My parents had this really wonderful marriage. I saw how great it could be, and it was really hard to live up to this ideal. I had a huge fear of divorce, and of not being able to achieve what they had." Sophia exhaled and crossed her legs on the couch. She recalled: "People kept saying, if you have any doubts, maybe he's not the right one." So whenever any natural hesitations came up, it would shake her to the core. "No one ever said to me, 'Sophia, nobody is perfect, doubts are natural or maybe you should go talk to someone about what is going on with you; maybe *you* are afraid of commitment.'"

Eventually, they began to broach the subject of marriage. But months went by and nothing happened. When she least expected it, Clark popped the question. He got down on one knee, gave her a ring, and proposed. Though they had discussed it over and over, and she had told Clark that she wanted to get engaged, when he finally asked, it still felt somewhat out of the blue. "I had waited for the proposal for so long—and yet, when it came, I panicked," she explained. "The man goes through the fear when he gets the ring, and by the time he proposes he is ready, but for the woman, even if you think it is coming, it hits you like a ton of bricks. I had so much anxiety and fear. Though I said 'Yes,' I was actually freaking out. Inside, I had gotten cold feet. I didn't know if it was right." Sophia called her parents to report the engagement, but she didn't share the news with anyone else. In fact, she asked her parents to keep it a secret.

For the next few weeks, Sophia was a mess. "I was scared shitless. I couldn't sleep or eat," Sophia remembered as her relaxed countenance vanished. Ironically, Sophia and Clark had a wedding to go to a few days later. When they came home after the wedding, Sophia called her parents, crying. Incredibly, Clark stayed in the room to help her, understanding that she was having some kind of meltdown. She recalled painfully, "I was on the phone bawling to my dad, saying, 'I don't know if Clark is "the one."'' I was so out of it. Clark had to undress me while tears were streaming down my face. Here I was ruining this guy's life, and he still loved me so much that he is helping me get undressed so I can go to bed and calm down."

A week after Clark had proposed to Sophia, she was still completely distraught. She decided to go to a therapist. "Here I was with this man I laughed with and loved. I kept asking, 'Am I "in love" with him or do I just "love" him?' I had analysis paralysis," she added. When she arrived at her appointment, she was a nervous wreck and worn out from crying; when she left, she was calm and excited. "I went there to discuss my doubts about Clark and I realized my anxiety had nothing to do with him. It had to do with me," Sophia exclaimed confidently. "I realized that for our whole courtship I had one foot out. I was waiting for Prince Charming to show up. Because Clark hadn't fit my ideal perfectly, I had never really committed to the relationship." As Sophia drove home, she recalled feeling blissful. She started to experience all the feelings of excitement that came with getting engaged to the right person.

When Sophia saw Clark that night, she embraced him passionately and realized she had begun to see him differently. "Once I got over my fear, I looked at Clark through new eyes. I was so grateful for him." She smiled.

"Love doesn't choose you: You choose love. Someone doesn't just show up on your doorstep, whether it is Tom Cruise or Ed Norton or whomever your fantasy man is, and you fall in love. I truly thought when the perfect man showed up, I would just feel all those things. But we do it for ourselves. If you have your walls up—fear and skepticism—you just won't fall head over heels. No one can bring it out if you are not open to it. Once I learned that, everything changed," she confidently declared.

Ten months later, in a beautiful Catholic church in San Francisco, Sophia and Clark married. "When I walked down the aisle, there wasn't a question that I was doing the right thing," she sighed. I was there to watch her walk, beaming down the aisle, in her mother's long-sleeved lace gown. I felt honored to be there as Sophia and

Clark spoke their vows. It was magical the day they wed, precisely because their union wasn't about fantasy, it was real. The wedding symbolized their commitment, but they didn't mistake it for the commitment. True love had endured, despite the obstacles they had faced, and Sophia and Clark took a solemn vow to build a life together.

Now, three years later, I am happy to report that Sophia and Clark seem even more in love and passionate than they were on their wedding day. They actually still keep one of the cacti Clark gave her when they first started dating, as a reminder of their journey together. I realized that, to them, this average day was bliss. "He still totally surprises me and makes me laugh. Going through life with him is a total joy. It feels so new and it keeps getting better and better. I so appreciate what we have because it was a painful road getting here. When I think back, it scares me that I almost threw away the most amazing gift in my life. When I realized that it was me—that I was holding myself back from this relationship—I finally saw what I had. I was ready to accept all the goodness that came with Clark. When you feel gratitude—that is the best practice; when you are thankful for what you have, more great things come to you." She beamed.

In this whole process, Clark hadn't changed a bit. Sophia changed by looking at herself. She didn't try to change Clark or hold her feelings back from him anymore. She let go of fear and she made the choice to let love transform her. When she decided to stop asking herself whether she was "in love" with Clark and started to look at him with an open heart and loving eyes, she fell blissfully in love with him.

The men I spoke to were also surprised at how looking in the mirror could transform their lives and create an atmosphere in which love could grow. At thirty-five, Michael was a successful, single lawyer living in Michigan. After his breakup with an ex-girlfriend, he was convinced that he would never marry. He enjoyed his independence and was focused on his career, making money and traveling with friends. He was content with his life: "I thought I would enjoy my life and marriage wasn't going to be a part of it." Michael admits that at that time he didn't believe in love. His relationship with his ex-girlfriend and the conflict-filled marriage of his parents made him see marriage in a negative light. He thought a relationship would only limit his otherwise full life.

The women in Michael's past were the kinds of women men chase after. He explained with a flat expression: "I was stuck on going after the women who you can't get." Michael's ex-girlfriend Ashley definitely fit the bill. From the first time he met her, he explained, he thought he would marry her: "She fit the mold; beautiful and unattainable." Michael and Ashley dated for two years. Their relationship was full of ups and downs; conflicts followed by great makeup sex. Michael recalled, "In my mind, our relationship was really passionate. We fought and when the fight was over, with all that pent up anger we had great sex." Michael characterized their relationship as a tug of war in which both people were intent on getting their own needs met. After they broke up, Michael avoided relationships altogether.

Six months later he was introduced to Olivia. "She was also attractive but she wasn't all about her looks. She was very approachable, kind and open. She was easy to talk to and be with. She was very even-keeled," Michael remembered with a pensive look on his face. But Michael doubted he would ever have a serious relationship with Olivia. He recalled, "When I first met her I told her I was not interested in a committed relationship. I gave myself an out. I kept it really casual. I had decided I wasn't getting married and it wasn't the right time for me. It had not been that long since my last relationship." He added that in fact he thinks he dated Olivia because he didn't think they had the kind of fiery connection he was used to, so he didn't think he would become attached. Olivia and Michael continued to date casually and see other people. Olivia was skeptical of Michael, since at this point in her life she was looking to meet someone and get married.

They continued to date and were surprised at how much they enjoyed each other's company. Michael thought back to their early dates and his face softened. "I felt so comfortable with her. She let me be myself. She was really relaxed about everything. She had experienced a lot of things I had never experienced so she also brought many new things to my life."

After a couple of months of dating, Michael went away with some friends to a bachelor party weekend in Vegas. He was traveling, spending money, and surrounded by friends; in essence, living the life he thought would fulfill him. But, to his surprise, he found he missed Olivia. He called her on the way home from the airport. "I can't explain what it was, but we had this great conversation." Olivia, however, recalls the conversation vividly. "I remember exactly. He was like a different person. We had this great flirty, interesting conversation. I knew he was into me and into this relationship. Something changed in him."

Michael didn't know it at the time, but he had stopped listening to his head and started listening to his heart. He let go of his cynicism about love. He decided to make a concerted effort to open himself up to this unexpected relationship. "I made a choice to give in to the fact that it was different from my other relationships. I stopped evaluating it and I just let the feeling take over," he sighed.

Michael changed his actions, too. He found that instead of trying to impress Olivia, he wanted to do things for her just for the sake of it: "She made me feel good and I wanted to make her feel good. I wanted to give that feeling back." The more he gave to her, the more his feelings began to grow: "I remember the time I surprised her with a white orchid on Valentine's Day. I used to hate Valentine's Day, but the look on her face, the excitement and appreciation, it was awesome." He smiled.

It wasn't long before Michael decided he didn't want to see anyone else. He and Olivia agreed they would date exclusively. Michael wanted to get to know her and her world better. He met her friends and he brought Olivia to his parents' home in Florida so he could introduce them.

After four months, Michael had fallen for Olivia, he remembered fondly. "Just being around her made me feel so happy. Instead of having a relationship that was so up and down, this one was much more consistent. In the past, I had mistaken the drama for passion. I finally realized it felt so much better this way." To Olivia's surprise, this noncommittal man was already telling her he loved her. In fact, he was the first one to utter the "L" word.

Michael was also thrilled to discover a kind of intimacy with Olivia that was completely new to him. "With Olivia, we can be talking or hugging and I get very physically excited. I am excited by her in a way that I have never been. I never had that feeling with anyone. There isn't a time I don't feel physically close. It isn't that we have sex every night. It is more about the intimacy of hugging and touching, not just the sex—although that is really great, too."

A year into their relationship, despite Michael's declarations that he didn't want a long-term commitment, he asked Olivia to move in with him. He assured her that he did not mean this as a temporary convenience but as a sign of his commitment and a step toward their future together.

From the minute Olivia moved in it felt natural and Michael was surprised at how happy it made him. "At the end of a long day, I love coming home. Every night when I walk through the door and she sees me, she always has a huge smile on her face. That is the best feeling in the world."

Michael found his perspective changed, too. He gesticulated, "I used to see all the benefits of being single: I could be independent, and I didn't have to worry about making the other person happy, but now I enjoy compromising. I love Olivia and nothing feels better than working together and making her happy."

A few months later on an ordinary weekday in July, Olivia got home from work and found Michael in bed. She sat down beside him. He looked at her deeply and took her hand and said, "Olivia, I just don't think things can go on the way they are." She wasn't sure if Michael was breaking up with her or proposing. Michael pulled a ring out of his pocket and smirked at her. "Will you marry me?" She was so shocked that she almost forgot to answer.

"Yes, of course." They both cried and kissed.

Michael smiled and explained the way he asked his fiancée: "I fell in love with Olivia on a regular day and I want to spend all of my regular days with her. That is why I did it on an ordinary day in a simple way."

All of Michael's trepidations about marriage had vanished. He had surrendered himself to his relationship, nurtured the love and let it grow. He explained that he couldn't wait to share the rest of his life with Olivia: "She makes me feel warm, safe, and appreciated. I am so attracted to her emotionally, physically, and sexually."

To Michael's surprise, he no longer cared about the things that were once important to him. "I realized there is more to life than work and acquiring stuff. I don't care about that anymore. I care about sharing time with Olivia and making plans for our future."

"What do you love most about her?" I asked.

"I love her smile. I love that she is a happy person. She is so bright. I love the way we communicate. I love hugging her. I love how excited she is to bake cookies for me. Just sharing the Tuesdays with Olivia is fun. I never knew it was going to be this way with anyone. I never knew how incredible sharing my life with another person would be."

When Michael opened the door to Olivia and gave unselfishly to her and to the relationship, love completely transformed him. He went from looking for a partner as someone to "get," to choosing someone with whom he could form a deep, mutual partnership. His priorities shifted from valuing his career and making money to wanting to share his life with another person. Where he once cherished his independence, he now cherished their connection. By embracing the relationship and allowing this unexpected love into his life, he started to grow as a person. He found his life had become more fulfilling than he had ever imagined.

Through happy couples, I learned that those who had a tremendous capacity to love, loved tremendously. Those who held back from love or were afraid of commitment and were stingy with love never loved intensely despite their loveable partners.

Burn Your Checklist

One of the first things I heard over and over again from happy couples was that when they dropped their expectations they were open to the love that came into their lives. Many couples explained that when they first met their "other half," that person didn't look anything like their vision of an ideal mate. But, when they learned to let go of their preconceived notions, they fell deeply in love.

Take for example, my friend Jennifer, who at thirty was never married. Jennifer, professional and preppie with a warm smile and friendly demeanor, works in corporate sales. She is Jewish, although not religious, and among many things on her checklist, she was seeking an intelligent, successful Jewish man who was also never married. Over the years, she dated many people who fit her checklist, but those relationships never worked out. Then she met Marc.

Marc was Catholic; not her ideal. Worse yet, from her perspective, Marc was divorced. "You always envision getting married to someone and sharing everything with them for the first time. Marc had already done those things with someone else," she explained. So she dated him reluctantly at the beginning: "I tried to blow him off a couple of times. I didn't want to tell people I was dating this divorced guy. My friend Keith said someone was offering to set him up with a divorced woman and he was like, 'No thanks.' It really made me question dating someone divorced."

She explained that she tried to keep her relationship with Marc "casual" because she never expected to end up with him. But by the third date, it was clear that Jennifer and Marc couldn't keep it casual. So they kept dating, but she remained emotionally conflicted. I could hear the tension in her voice as she recalled: "The first month of dating I tried to break it off several times, but Marc kept saying let's give it a chance."

One day he sat her down and said: "Listen, we have an amazing relationship, get over it. This isn't something that should break a relationship apart." Jennifer thought back to former boyfriends who met all of her criteria and recalled all the reasons those relationships didn't work. She explained that other men she dated were not considerate or communicative and they didn't want a commitment the way Marc did. She thought back to one old boyfriend in particular: "He was smart, successful, and was everything I was looking for, but he was emotionally unavailable." At that moment, Jennifer realized she should at least give it a chance with Marc. She started to open herself up to the possibility of a real relationship. They dated for a few months until Jennifer was able let go of her preconceived notions and relax with Marc.

"I finally realized superficial things didn't matter and what did matter is that we were so aligned and we had such a strong connection," she said confidently. The relationship continued to grow. Jennifer and Marc fell deeply in love with one another. At that point, they discussed how their differences in religion could impact their future and they discovered that both of them were willing to compromise when it came to raising children. After just a few months, Jennifer and Marc moved in together.

I have observed their relationship on many occasions. I would say by every account they meet the Gen-X ideal of a happy couple. When I asked Marc about his relationship with Jennifer, his mouth curled. "To me Jennifer is gorgeous and has a great personality. Being around her is addictive. I crave being around her all the time." They are kind and considerate to each other. They are completely at ease when they are together. They laugh together and are each other's best friends. They are very much in love.

"Jennifer, how did things change so fast?" I asked.

"When I got past my 'checklist' and let my guard down, I fell in love." Jennifer glowed.

A few months later, Jennifer and Marc got engaged and less than a year later they married. The actual wedding did not mean much to either one of them, partly because Marc had a blowout wedding for his first marriage. Jennifer spoke fondly about the moment that did matter to them that day: "We had ten minutes after the ceremony. We were alone in the room together. We just looked at each other in such an intense way. For him it was the realization that this time it was different and so right. We both knew we would be together forever. At that moment we just wanted to be alone together. We wished we didn't have to go to the party and through all the festivities of cutting the cake and the first dance. It was a perfect moment, just us."

Two years later, she says their love continues to grow. "Does the divorce thing ever bother you now?" I asked.

"Actually, the divorce was the best thing that ever happened for our relationship. He is a different person because of the trauma of his divorce. He felt like a failure when it ended, there was so much shame. All that made him a great communicator and it makes me a better communicator. One of the things I love most about him is that he has no filter. He talked about all his feelings from the very beginning and he has taught me to do the same." Jennifer sighed.

Ironically, the very reason that Marc did not meet Jennifer's checklist now turned out to be the thing that made their relationship so strong. What she had with Marc was not her picture-perfect package, but a man who communicated with her, was committed to her, created joyful moments with her, supported her, and loved her. Her relationship with Marc brought so many wonderful things that she never could have imagined. The kind of connection they share is not something that could ever have been quantified on a "checklist."

Jennifer looked up at me with a smile and happy, misty eyes. "I can't believe I almost blew it by focusing on the superficial characteristics. He was by no means the guy I envisioned, but he turns out to be the man of my dreams."

Jennifer taught me that love is not about finding someone with the perfect combination of attributes; love is a transformational transaction between two people. True love is not a function of locating the person who satisfies your checklist or fulfills your every expectation. It is an experience that can only happen when you open your heart and let yourself be transformed by love as Jennifer was.

My friend Sadie also found true love when she let go of her preconceived notions of her mate. Sadie and her husband, Dan, have been married for three years and together for six. Sadie is a statuesque, 5'11" brunette. Dan is 5'5". When Sadie first met her husband, she never considered him because she said physically he was not her type. She didn't think she could ever be "in love" with him, she recalled. "I got the best feeling from him, but I knew he was not for me." Sadie had always pictured herself with someone tall, someone who could make her feel feminine and petite. Her last boyfriend, Jessie, while not the best boyfriend, according to Sadie, was quite tall. "He would always stand in front of me and block the wind; that made me feel so feminine and cared for. That made me fall hard for him," she explained.

"When I first started dating my husband, Dan, I kept thinking, he can stand in front of me but he won't block shit." She laughed heartily. She didn't think Dan could make her feel feminine the way her ex-boyfriend did. But although Sadie's skepticism about Dan was nagging away at her, Dan was quite persistent. She tried to give it a chance. They started to date, but they took it slowly: "I wasn't ready to jump in headfirst. It is like going into a cold pool. You dip your feet in first. Then you go in up to your knees. Then you go in a little deeper. Finally you go under. First, we went out in a group. Then we went alone. I wasn't ready to dive in." But Dan was so enamored with Sadie that he was moving the relationship quickly. He introduced her to his parents after a couple weeks and started making references to spending the future together.

It was too fast for Sadie. As her forehead wrinkled, she explained that she was not over her doubts: "Dan was so forthcoming about the future and I was thinking, let's just get through the next date." But Dan kept making plans with her for every weekend and inviting her out with his friends and family.

Sadie couldn't get past her reservations. One day, she broke down in tears. A wave of anxiety came over her. Finally, she confronted Dan: "I thought it was too much too soon and I needed to pull back. I told him to stop calling and he did."

But when Dan stopped calling she found she missed him painfully. Even though that was what she had said she wanted, she certainly didn't expect to feel the way she did. So, Sadie picked up the phone and called him: "I didn't say don't call ever. I just wanted to slow down." So Dan and Sadie started to date again. They took it slowly, at first.

Pretty quickly, Sadie got to know Dan and began to see him differently. She exhaled. "He was incredibly kind, funny, and charismatic." She loved being with him. He made her laugh and they always had great conversation. "He is such a wonderful person and he always treats me with such love and consideration," she grinned. It was not long before Sadie and Dan were inseparable.

A few years later they married.

"What is so special about Dan?" I asked.

"At our wedding, people made speeches about us. I remember someone stood up and said, 'The world is a better place because Dan is in it.' It really is true." Sadie recalled that, at that moment, her friend leaned over to her and laughed. "No one is saying that about you, Sadie." Sadie remembers that she then looked over at Dan and said: "You are so wonderful. I can't believe that you chose me. No one here is saying I make the world a better place." Dan reached over and caressed her hair. He said, "You make my world a better place."

She continued with a look of glee in her eye. "I am crazy about Dan. On my way home from work, I still get excited to see him. He makes me feel cared for and loved every single day. He is so supportive when I am down or going through a rough time."

"So, how do you feel about Dan physically now?" I asked.

"I love the way his eyebrows raise up when I am telling him a story. He is so intent on listening and looks so adorable." She smiled.

"Does he make you feel feminine the way Jessie did?"

"He sends me flowers every week. He calls me beautiful and gorgeous and I believe he really sees me that way. There are girls who have been beautiful and gorgeous their whole lives. I was never that girl," she explained. "When I am at my worst, he always says, 'You look beautiful.' He must be wearing rose-colored glasses when he looks at me. I can't imagine someone who could make me feel more feminine or beautiful."

Now, when Sadie thinks back to her initial hesitation about Dan, she laughs. "When I look at him now, I love everything about him."

Today, Sadie can't imagine being with anyone but Dan. Though Dan did not satisfy her checklist initially, when she dropped those expectations, she found out that he was so much more than she ever expected to find in a mate. When she stopped commodifying Dan, she realized how special he was. Now that she has experienced true love with Dan, she says that no one else could ever take his place.

Philosopher Martin Buber writes: "When two people relate to each other authentically and humanly, God is the electricity that surges between them." It's not just Buber: countless songs and poems have been written about how when you fall truly in love with someone, no one else will do. You know the old Gershwin song "They Can't Take That Away from Me": *"The way you wear your hat, the way you sip your tea . . . The way your smile just beams, the way you sing off key . . ."* All these sources are describing authentic love as being that which loves *uniquely,* the unique irreplaceable qualities of the beloved.

These words are echoed in what I learned from happy couples. When these people talked about their beloved, they did not refer to the sum of that person's parts or mention what the other person offers them, but rather they spoke of his or her uniqueness, that which is indescribable and irreplaceable about that person. One man gushed as he talked about his wife of twelve years: "I love the way she smells. She always smells good to me." Another woman said about her husband of eight years, "No one else may find his jokes funny, but to me, he is hysterical." A man in his thirties smiled when I asked him what was so special about his girlfriend of three years. "I love how soft her cheeks are. I love to kiss them," he said with a grin. I remember sharing this comment with his girlfriend. She sighed happily and looked at me. "That makes me feel so in love and adored. It means more to me than if he had said I am the smartest or prettiest woman he's ever known."

The romantic notion that a person is so unique that he or she is irreplaceable often seems completely lost by my generation. The checklist approach undermines the potential for that kind of connection. *By looking for perfection, we lose the chance to love uniquely.* Jennifer and Sadie eventually felt that kind of unique love for their spouses but only when they dropped the cultural scripts that told them to find a perfect person with each and every quality they were seeking. When they stopped comparing their partners to ex-boyfriends and to their checklists, they fell deeply in love. When they stopped thinking about replacing their mates, their mates became irreplaceable. If they had stuck to their lists they would have been unlikely to have ever experienced the true love that has completely transformed them. What these couples, and others, taught me is that the complete recognition of the other person's uniqueness can't sustain love without work, but love would be a dry formula, doomed from the start, if it wasn't based on appreciation for the uniqueness of the beloved.

Stop Speeding

One of the big mistakes Gen-Xers make is expecting to know in an instant whether we have found our soul mate. This approach to dating ignores the simple fact that it takes time to fall in love.

Elizabeth is an outspoken and intense investigative reporter. When Elizabeth first met Miles, he was extremely quiet. She was quick to assume that he might be boring. At first, she was reluctant to take the time to get to know him. She worked with outgoing men and was surrounded by people who were constantly selling themselves. She was also very busy and didn't want to waste her time. But Elizabeth's best friend, Katrina, who had watched Elizabeth go on dozens of dates over the years and thought Elizabeth was far too critical, suggested that she get to know Miles. Elizabeth continued to see him and tried to keep an open mind. They enjoyed picnics in the park, long bike rides, and romantic dinners. They talked about politics and their shared love of history over bottles of wine. They went for long walks along the river where she lived. And every weekend, their favorite activity was finding a special place to watch the sun set together.

Two months into dating Miles, Elizabeth had lunch with Katrina.

"Elizabeth, you are glowing." Katrina smiled when she saw her friend. Elizabeth told Katrina a joke Miles had just told her and started to twirl her hair.

"Elizabeth, you are smitten, aren't you?" Katrina laughed.

Elizabeth replied, "I guess I am kind of. Miles is so funny. He is so smart and interesting."

"See, you didn't even want to take the time to get to know him," said Katrina.

"I know. You were right about giving it time. He's great. I think I am falling in love with him," she said, smiling.

Elizabeth thanked Katrina. "Thanks for making me hang in there. Miles isn't the kind of guy who 'wows' you on the first date, but I have found that he is so wonderful. Now we have to hope it lasts."

Elizabeth and Miles continued to date. Almost a year into their relationship, Elizabeth's mother was diagnosed with Alzheimer's. Elizabeth was devastated. She was crying every night and began to withdraw emotionally from Miles. She tried to hide that she was an emotional wreck. One night, Miles got into bed next to her, and he could feel that her pillowcase was damp from her tears. He held Elizabeth. "Babe, let's talk about this. What you are going through is real and it's heavy stuff but it's OK. We'll deal with it together."

"I really don't want to bring you or our relationship down with all this stuff. I don't really want to talk, I just want you to let me be. No offense, I just can't right now," she said as she fought back the tears.

The next day Elizabeth sent Miles this e-mail:

I am sorry it has been so difficult to be with me the last couple of weeks. I feel deep sadness about my mother. I have been having awful dreams. Lately I have felt like maybe I should just be by myself because on top of it all I feel guilty that I am not more fun to be with or that I should be a better girlfriend when you have been nothing but loving and supportive.

Miles responded immediately:

Don't be silly—relationships are not about convenience. Besides, circumstances change and I would like to think that I can depend on you when I hit a rough patch. I love you and care about you and I care about your family. Your stress is understandable. Don't worry about being fun; I love you.

That night Elizabeth sat down with Miles and cried for one hour straight. Miles just listened and took her hand. She told Miles that if her mother's condition got worse, she would consider moving back home to North Carolina so that she could help take care of her. She had been afraid to share this news with Miles because their relationship was going so well and obviously a move could complicate or possibly end their relationship. Miles looked deep into Elizabeth's eyes. "So we'll move. If you feel this is something you need to do, you absolutely should do it. I support you. Being there for your family— that is what really matters. I would never stand in the way of that."

"What about your job? You love your life here," she asked.

Miles stroked Elizabeth's hair away from her tears. "I want to be with you. A job, geography—those things work themselves out. What matters to me is being with you. And if being with your mom matters to you, that is what we will do."

Elizabeth felt temporarily consoled about her mom. And at that moment, she decided that Miles was the man she wanted to spend the rest of her life with. Slowly and steadily over months she fell in love with Miles. And when even more time passed, she found that not only was she "in love" with him but she loved and respected him as a person.

Miles and Elizabeth have been happily committed to each other for eight years now. They have a child and have been together through career strains, financial struggles, and even the loss of her mother. Their secret to getting through the tough periods? Time: "When we are going through a tough point in our relationship, I don't bail, or say the heck with it; when I am not feeling particularly loving, I think back to a time when he made my heart flutter. I know and trust that feeling will come back with time. Before I know it, something will happen and he will take my hand when I am in pain or when there is a great accomplishment and I will feel his love."

She looked at a picture of the two of them from the first year they dated: "We have history, so we just get each other. When we are laughing, when we look in each other's eyes, we feel as though we can see each other's soul. We are pretty lucky, but over the years, we have worked really hard at it."

"What do you value the most about your relationship?" I asked. She sighed. "I value the team we have built and the mutual support. I value the roots and entanglements that bring us together. When I look at him, my heart feels very full."

Elizabeth's relationship is a testament to the fact that love can grow deeper with time. Elizabeth could have easily written Miles off without getting to know him, but when she gave him and the relationship time, she found out what a wonderful man Miles is and what a wonderful partner she had to share in life's joys and disappointments. She also found that time was the secret to reconnecting over and over again and making their relationship stronger.

Couples that have been together over the course of decades also tell me that making a concerted effort to make time for each other is important to deepen the love and renew it. Meet Ricky. Ricky is a forty-seven-year-old Puerto Rican man with a toothy smile, a clean-shaven head, and a mustache. Ricky is possibly the happiest man I have ever met. He greets everyone who passes him with a smile and a cheerful, "How are you today?" Ricky met his wife Gina when they were kids. She lived in his building growing up in the Bronx—506 Concord Avenue.

Ricky is always smiling, but when he talks about his wife, his smile grows exponentially: "She is a brilliant, happy person. She is funny and very beautiful." He described her as being petite, with auburn hair, glasses, and sparkling green eyes. Ricky and Gina had played together as children, and had become the best of friends. To solidify their bond, they even became blood brother and sister—a childhood custom that involves poking each other with a needle and mixing their blood.

When she was eleven, Gina's family moved to Chicago. Ricky and Gina promised to keep in touch, but they never did. Six years later, Gina and her family moved back to the neighborhood and she and Ricky were reunited. At that point she was a teenager, and in Ricky's words, "She was a 'hottie.' All the guys in the neighborhood were checking out Gina."

She and Ricky once again became best friends. It wasn't long before Ricky became attracted to her. But, according to Ricky, his friend Leo, a very handsome man, wanted to ask Gina out. Ricky decided to approach Leo before he asked Gina on a date; he said: "I really like her and I want to ask her out." Leo, by Ricky's account, was cocky; he replied, "Sure, go ahead ask her, but she'll say no and then she'll go out with me." Ricky did ask—and, to his delight, Gina said yes. For the next several months, they dated and were inseparable.

They were both gymnasts; when she would compete, Ricky would help her train for competitions. They loved taking trips together to Times Square. They would go out to dinner, see a romantic movie, or go bowling. About six months later, on Valentine's Day, Ricky hauled a three-foot chocolate heart over to her house.

When he arrived, Gina's sister etched in the fogged-up window the word "Quits." Ricky came upstairs, and the sister explained that Gina liked another man and was going to break up with Ricky. He immediately confronted Gina and she said she did in fact want to date another man. Ricky was crushed: "I kissed her and said if it was meant to be, it was meant to be."

Ricky went home and cried—and ate all the chocolate. Two days later, she came back to Ricky. She had changed her mind. They got back together and it was as if it had never happened. Four years later, they married. He was twenty-five. She was twenty-four. "I hit the wife lottery pretty good." He smiled. Today, more than two decades later, Ricky says their relationship is flourishing. They have three grown daughters and a granddaughter, and a couple of years ago, they adopted a young son. Ricky works nights at a restaurant he owns and his wife, a teacher, works days, but over the years, he explained, they always make time for each other: "When we are not working, we are together. During the summer, when she is not working, I take my days off so we can have more time together. We like to go to the beach and the museum. We make an effort to be together." He added, "Every day, no matter what is going on, or how busy we are, she takes the time to say, 'I love you' before I leave the house." Ricky couldn't stop grinning when he talked about his wife: "She is still my honey bun." I asked him how it was that, after having known his wife for so many years, they kept the relationship interesting. He replied, "My friends say to me, 'What do you talk about for all those years?' But we know each other so well that there is so much to talk about."

Martin, who has worked with Ricky for many years, told me un-solicited: "I always admire him for his love of his wife." He recalled years ago when a young woman at the restaurant made a pass at Ricky: "I remember a beautiful woman who always came into the restaurant and asked Ricky to go out with her for a drink. Everyone would say to him, she is beautiful, your wife will never know. Ricky flat out told the woman, 'I love my wife.'" Ricky attested to the fact that his wife trusts him implicitly and that she would never have cause to worry.

He told me about a time his wife had put on a few pounds and said to him, "I've got to go to the gym, I am getting heavy." "I told her, 'Don't worry. I love you. You think it matters to me? It wouldn't matter to me if you blew up; I am in it for the long haul.'" He smiled. I wanted to hug Ricky at that moment. I could hardly imag-ine those words coming from a man of my generation. He contin-ued, "She used to be 105, now she is 160, but she is still the same woman I met when I was a kid. She is still the sexy girl in the leotard I dated when I was a teenager."

Ricky's relationship is a testament to the fact that love and pas-sion can get better over time. He grinned. "We never got into a rut in our love life, we never stopped making love. We always are excited to be together. I'm never bored. It gets better with age—the relation-ship and the sex."

"What is your secret?" I asked.

"You got to have that connection and realize you can't change someone. You have to feel that trust. I trust my wife because I have known her so long. The friendship and trust we have built over all these years together—I know it will be until the very end—until the day I go. I would do it a hundred times over again." He beamed.

"What do you love most about her?" I asked. He pointed to his sparkling grayish eyes: "When my wife looks at me, I know she loves me. I know I love her. She talks about gaining weight, but I've changed, too. That look in her eye when she sees me, she has had that since day one. That look says it all."

At the end of our conversation and the end of Ricky's workday, he started to look at his watch. I asked, "Do you need to go?"

"I want to get home so I can spend time with her before she goes to bed," he said, as his dimples punctuated his smile.

Gina and Ricky had something that was so unlike the relationships I had looked at. Theirs was a relationship built on time carefully spent together. Even though both worked so terribly hard, both put the time spent nurturing the relationship at the top of their set of priorities. I learned that it takes time to fall in love and to build ever-deepening feelings. My generation grew up in the age of microwaves; we can bake a cake in ten minutes—but then we are disappointed when it doesn't taste homemade. Ricky never expected true love to happen in an instant.

While not everyone meets the love of their life in childhood, Ricky's story attests to the fact that love is not an instant reaction; it is something that develops with time. I learned there are no shortcuts to long-term love. For Ricky, love was indeed like fine wine; it got better with age. Elizabeth, too, learned that your soul mate doesn't just appear. It is the struggles, the entanglements, that make two people become each other's soul mate.

Go All the Way

The Gen-X approach of "keeping your options open," or holding back from a complete commitment, is one of the biggest obstacles to finding true love today. Commitment isn't like a high- or low-risk investment. If you don't invest fully, you have no chance of reaping any reward. Many married couples have reminded me that marriage is a leap of faith, even in the best of circumstances. There are no guarantees; there are no money-back returns. By failing to fully commit, many of us cheat ourselves out of the kind of depth we long for in a relationship. Over and over, the couples with successful relationships told me how their unions transformed them, once they fully committed.

When I was visiting a friend in the Cascade Mountains of Oregon in late September, and puzzling over how to find true love, I happened to start chatting with a fifty-five-year-old nurse with wispy grayish hair and skin the color of rose petals, who sat peacefully on a wooden bench under a tree heavy with yellow foliage. She saw me scribbling notes in my black-and-white composition book, and asked me what I was writing. I replied politely, "A book about relationships," and hoped that she would let me go back into my mental cocoon. She repeatedly asked, like a bird tapping on my shoulder, "What about relationships?" I tried to tune out her lyrical voice so I could get back to my own internal cogitation; where, I kept asking myself, could I find the answer to how to make love grow? Then the woman—who introduced herself as Elaine—began to tell me the most incredible love story I had ever heard.

She told me about her relationship with a man named Kirk. Kirk was twelve years older than Elaine, but quite active and fit. Elaine smiled. "He had the most beautiful, muscular legs. He was a runner." Kirk was outgoing; he loved to tell corny jokes: "His friends called him 'Colonel Corny.'" He was tall, lean, and balding, with a bit of red hair left. They had met at a social club for single parents. Both of them had been married before, and had grown children.

Elaine was immediately taken by him: "I had this strong draw to him that had nothing to do with the outside stuff." The draw was his gregarious personality and his spiritual side. They were instantly comfortable with each other. They would dance all night without ever sitting down, or they would go running together. "He would slow down his pace to run with me," she reminisced. "It was unquestionable, we had a strong commitment to each other." They had considered marrying, but they did not wish to fall into traditional roles; for Elaine and Kirk, getting married was not "the end all." She explained that their potent connection and permanent commitment to each other seemed certain. The form of the relationship—a wedded union or an unofficial bond—was immaterial. They decided they were better off not tying the knot: "It didn't matter whether we had a piece of paper," she explained.

Elaine and Kirk had been blissfully together for five years. They enjoyed traveling together, camping, and hiking. Then one day, Kirk was diagnosed with a rare and terminal form of liver disease. But this tragedy wasn't the end of their happiness together; on the contrary, Elaine recalled with a serene voice, "It was at that moment that our commitment to one another grew stronger. We decided to laugh through his illness." I listened intently, like a pupil in the front row of a class. I felt Elaine had something incredibly important to share.

The next few years of their relationship would have tested even the strongest of couples, but Elaine and Kirk felt closer with each day of being tested. Together they waited anxiously for a liver transplant that they hoped would save Kirk's life. As he was failing, "Kirk told me 'You don't have to do this' [stay with him]. I told him I was staying and there was nothing that he could say to make me do otherwise." Her voice grew louder.

Unfortunately, the two found out that the transplant could not help him. Elaine remained calm and even joyful as she recounted these painful events: "After he saw my dedication to him, the relationship became even deeper." Through the hospital visits, his painful bouts of physical distress, and their tears, they knew they were in it together. She never for one minute doubted that she would remain by his side. "There were flaws in him that could have broken us up without a real commitment," she recalled, gazing at the foliage.

"What kind of flaws?" I asked.

"I am a very positive person and he was very negative sometimes, but I loved him and he adored me," she explained as her eyebrows seemed to smile along with her. The commitment helped them through not only their own personality frictions, but something far more threatening.

No matter how tough it got, it seemed their love was indestructible. Theirs had been a sexually passionate union; but when Kirk's condition worsened, they could not engage in sexual activity for two years. Elaine explained that the loss of their sexual life did not affect them so very deeply: "It wasn't so important. His illness didn't weaken our love at all." I could hardly imagine myself going through such an experience with unwavering commitment. Elaine leaned toward me. "You know, I would wash his bottom in the hospital and I still felt attracted to him. He would protest; I told him I would happily do it for ten more years . . . as long as he didn't go away.

"Unfortunately, it didn't happen that way." Her voice began to tremble. After eight years together, Kirk died and Elaine was there when he did so. A flood of emotion came over me. I tried to hold back my tears because I didn't want to upset Elaine, but she could see I was moved by her story.

When she finished, I turned to her and said, "What did you have that other couples don't? Why were you able to sustain a relationship that would have broken up other people?"

She didn't hesitate for a moment: "Personal commitment got us through. We had that initial draw that was not based only on physical attraction—though the attraction was certainly there. After that it was about commitment—and a spiritual connection," she said intently.

"What has having this kind of love done for your life?" I had to know.

"I am so at peace with myself. I don't need anything more, or for it to happen again. At the time, I felt like part of myself was cut off. Now I cherish the relationship I had." Elaine smiled. "I feel like he is a part of me. I've incorporated him into my life. I was only with him for eight years, but he had such a big impact on my life. To be able to be loved by someone like that—whom I loved—is worth everything we went through. It was very reciprocal. He helped me be a better person," she explained, her voice now shaky.

A woman who stood by listening to this conversation started to well up with tears.

"You are so lucky," she uttered, wiping her swollen red eyes.

"Yes I am." Elaine nodded. "Every time Kirk saw me, he had this beautiful smile."

Elaine showed no sadness or anger as she spoke about losing Kirk. I realized that she felt so lucky to have had him in her life and in a way she felt like she was still with him. That was all she needed. She explained some of the reasons her relationship was so strong: The words she used were "acceptance" and "dedication." What she was describing was the opposite of the picture-perfect package, the soul-mate delivery that to Gen-Xers is supposed to confer true bliss. What she had—that gave her such joy—was devotion and struggle, acceptance and loss, and gaining things she did not know she would gain. "It was a journey with this man," she smiled.

Elaine had given herself completely over to this man. She was not selfish or self-protective. Elaine never held back from her commitment to him; on the contrary, her commitment went all the way to "death do us part." Because she had totally committed to this man, even through to his death, she was able to have the kind of deep, unconditional, all-consuming true love that most of us hope to be lucky enough to ever experience.

Commit and Fuel the Fire

Contrary to all the messages in popular culture, committed couples actually experience greater passion than singles having one-night stands. The conventional wisdom is that passion dies with time. But happy couples in relationships for many years say that it is the commitment, not the initial chemistry, that actually fuels the eros long-term. In other words, it is not about just feeling the spark. In making a commitment, you have the choice to tend to the spark. Romantic love and chemistry cannot substitute for commitment, but commitment can actually fuel romantic and physical love. While it was at first hard for me to readjust my brain to this way of thinking, these couples convinced me that their passion grew much deeper with commitment.

My friend Janie and her husband had a romantic courtship. They met, they fell in love, and within two years they were married. She got pregnant right away. She told me something that at first I could not believe: "Since having a baby, we actually have the most incredible sex."

"Why?" I asked. "I thought when you have kids it becomes all about the kids and the romance and sex goes out the door."

"Not at all," she replied. "It is exactly the opposite. Since having the baby, the true passion is seeing my husband with my child. Our sex life is better than ever because we feel more connected. We have a child that is part of him and part of me and we will be raising this child together."

"Really? That is wonderful," I said with admiration.

"When I look at him, I have a newfound respect for him as I see him in a new role—as a husband and a father. I see someone who rises to the occasion. He is up with the baby when he is sleep deprived. That makes my heart leap in a way that it never has before," she said as her mouth curled up.

I was surprised by what she said and thought that what they have must be exceptional. But when I talked to other happy couples, they affirmed that the passion in their relationships got more intense with the commitment.

I was recently seated next to an older couple, Linda and Bill, on an airplane. The flight was overbooked and the cabin was extremely warm. While other couples that boarded the plane were bickering, I noticed that Linda and Bill were smiling, and remaining kind to one other. Bill lent a hand not only to his wife, but to others around him, lifting luggage and passing blankets. Once they were seated, they held hands and spoke lovingly to one another. I overheard them say they had just celebrated their fortieth anniversary. I inquired about how they met.

Linda confided their secrets of long-term devotion as her husband watched the movie. Linda had met her husband when she was a teenager. They had dated for seven years before they married. "I wanted to wait until I was old enough to get married," she explained in a quiet voice. But after having waited so long to get married, the infatuation and initial euphoria of the early stages of their relationship had settled down. Linda had asked herself whether she and her husband had enough passion to last a lifetime. But, Linda said, shrugging, "I loved him. He is a wonderful man, so I took a risk as to whether we had enough passion." She continued to tell me about all the fantastic qualities her husband possesses. She said he is intelligent, supportive, interesting, fun, and a wonderful parent. She told me how he made sacrifices for her and she for him. She said they were best friends. But what I really wanted to know was how the passion was in their relationship now.

"So, how would you describe your relationship today?" I asked.

Without hesitation she replied, "Very passionate. As I said, when we married, I took a chance on the passion. It not only rekindled to where it was in the early years, but it grew tremendously. A deep pas-

sionate love grew over the years because of the depth of the relationship. He was there when I got sick. I was there when he got sick. We
have children together. We laugh together."

She continued, "In a good marriage, the passion is not there
every single moment, it flows; but the passion gets deeper and deeper
through the years. Over time, it is friendship and attentiveness to each
other that creates the passion, which is not the blind euphoria that
you have when you first meet someone. That kind of superficial passion feels good, but it isn't based on anything deep, so it doesn't sustain. The kind of passion I have now with my husband is the most
intense passion I have ever experienced in my life."

At that moment, she put her hand on her husband's knee. "I have
such a special man. When I kiss him, it is the most delicious kiss in
the world. I adore looking at his face. I could look at this face forever.
To me he is Robert Redford." She gestured with her hands as if she
were touching his cheeks. I glanced over and felt a quiet amusement.
Bill was a lovely man, but he was far from Robert Redford.

"Wow, that is beautiful, that you feel that way about him after
forty years." I smiled.

"We are comfortable together. We love each other and respect
each other. We would do anything for each other. Out of the depth
of the relationship comes incredible intimacy and, of course, passion,"
she explained gleefully.

I was so surprised by the message of both Janie's story and Linda's
that I shared it with a friend of mine who has been married for four
years, but has been with her husband for over a decade.

"Both of these people told me that not only was it untrue that
passion died with time, they said the commitment actually made the
passion much stronger. Is that what you've experienced in your marriage?" I inquired.

Her answer: "Oh my God, yes. We had been together for so long
before we got married, but after we committed to each other, the passion went through the roof. People think of commitment and they

think of it as a burden. But for me, that is when I had the real fire-works."

She explained that their initial romantic connection was like the seed of the relationship. She described the commitment as the stem, and the passion as the flower that blooms out of the commitment they make to each other every day

I learned from these couples that when we drop the cultural script, which tells us that the initial euphoria of the relationship is the best part, we can experience an even deeper fulfillment with our partners. Again, I am not saying initial chemistry doesn't matter. It is rare and important, but it isn't enough. Marriage expert John Gottman, PhD, writes that "friendship fuels the flames of romance." These couples tell me the feelings they have with their long-term partners is more like a shock wave through the body than an actual spark. Rabbi Shmuley Boteach, author of *Kosher Sex,* says physical at-traction is the beginning of every relationship, and remains a pivotal component even long after a deep love has grown. But it is the com-mitment and our emotions that dress up our beloved so that to us they always appear beautiful, even as they grow older. He writes: "Physical attraction is the bait of the relationship, whereas love is the hook."

All of these couples found love at every step of the way because they made different choices than most of my Gen-X singles did. While my generation can't change the world around us overnight, we can drop the inclinations and adopt approaches that attempt to counter the cultural messages around us—and apply them to our own longing for true love.

It turns out that instead of demanding answers from potential partners, in order to get true love, we have to be willing to ask our-selves questions.

In other words, we need to ask: Am I willing to become *the kind of person* who is capable of experiencing true love?

If you are still not sure, I urge you to ask yourself the following questions:

Do I fully believe life is better with someone than alone, on my terms?

This is the very first thing you must ask yourself before you begin a relationship with anyone. If you don't believe in your core that your life will be better with a partner, then you will not have the incentive to become the kind of person who can create true love. A lifelong commitment requires, among other things, a lot of fortitude; without the true desire for a partner, it will be impossible to go the distance. If you don't believe this statement, then stop entering relationships right now, wait, and ask yourself this question again.

Am I willing to think of a relationship in terms of what I can give instead of what I can get?

A happily married woman once told me that the more you give, the more you will love. She explained, "If you are constantly waiting for the other person to give to you, it will never be enough."

Rabbi Boteach writes: "Love is not measured by the beating of a heart, but by the actions of the hands. The best way, therefore, to gauge the authenticity of the affections of lovers is to see what they do about their love." To say you are "in love" means nothing, but to act out of love means everything.

Am I willing to stop asking whether I am in love with the other person and start asking if I have been loving with this person?

As I learned from these couples, love is a conscious choice. Over time, you can't expect to be "in love" with someone without doing the work to make love grow. When you are loving, you look at your partner with loving eyes. When you are angry, you look at your partner with angry eyes. If you are not being loving, you cannot love.

Am I willing to drop my skepticism and believe in the power of love?

Rabbi Boteach also writes: "People who marry and remain successfully married believe love conquers all. They go into marriage believing that there will be far more joyous occasions than painful ones." Marriage is a leap of faith. If you are afraid, self-oriented, or cynical you can keep yourself from falling in love. It is only when you are open, optimistic, and trust love that you can actually fall in love.

Do I believe that love is not just one part of my life but that it *is* my life?

When my father looks at my mother he often says, "I have the best life. I wouldn't trade places with anyone." My father does not mean that his life has been particularly rosy. What he means is that his life *is* his love. To him, love is at the center of life and, since he loves my mother profoundly, he views his whole life positively through this lens. His belief that love is not just a part of one's life has created a relationship with my mother that is rich, fulfilling, and all-consuming. Whether or not you choose to marry or decide to be part of a lifelong committed relationship, of all the choices you make in your life, the choice to commit to someone will likely take the most effort and have the most impact, and it can potentially bring you the most joy. It is only when we shift our paradigm and begin to realize that love— for most human beings—ultimately defines our happiness that we can experience the kind of all-consuming love that we crave.

Before I wrote this book, when I would see young couples holding hands, I would think: how romantic; they found each other. Now, it is when I see older couples holding hands that I have real admiration, for they have chosen each other over and over again. Ultimately, I learned that true love is not a chemical reaction, or a wish list.

True love is a daily practice—the daily practice of being open to it.

Love, it seems, demands a daily openness to transforming yourself and being transformed by love.

Listening to all these people taught me to approach every day with the man in my own life with more care and kindness than I had been concerned about before I took this journey. Because of Sophia and Clark, Olivia and Michael, Jennifer and Marc, Sadie and Dan, Elizabeth and Bill, Ricky and Gina, Elaine and Kirk, and Linda and Bill, as well as all the others who were gracious enough to open their hearts to me—I now look at myself, and at what I am bringing to my own relationship every day, differently. I think a lot more carefully than I used to about how *my* actions either build or undermine the "sand castles."

What "sand castles"? I was recently at a wedding in a glorious church in New York City, listening to the words of the "Ave Maria." The reverend looked at the beautiful young couple, prayed for their union—and then offered some advice. He spoke about children who build sand castles on the beach near the shore where he lives. He described the elaborate structures' high walls and protective moats, and how the tide comes in and damages or destroys the sand castles at the end of every day. "But the beauty of it all is that love's labor is never lost for these children. The next day they're back at it again, repairing what has been damaged, rebuilding what is destroyed.

"A lifelong marriage requires the persistence of children at the seashore. Each partner must resolve to revive the dreams, to resurrect the hopes, to rebuild the love, every day," he said. "Every day," he continued, "as the tides of the world wash away your love, you must rebuild it with the fierce determination of children."

I hope this book helps you build and rebuild your own sand castles.

UNHOOKED DICTIONARY

Bling Ultimatum: The most intense kind of pressure a woman puts on her boyfriend to get engaged.

> "Jane gave John the *bling ultimatum*: If they weren't engaged in six months, she was moving out."

Booty Call: Someone you call up just for sex. *See also: Hookup.*

> "He text messaged me from bars but never asked me out on a real date. I was just his *booty call*."

Booty Call with a Twist: Someone you call for a hookup who turns out to bring more than just sex to the table.

> "At first he thought it was just a one-night thing, but it turned out to be a *booty call with a twist*."

Buzz: The euphoria someone gives you when you are in love, usually associated with the early stages of romance.

> "I drove all night to see her because she gives me the *buzz*."

Celebrity Standard: The glorification of celebrity life that causes us to compare ourselves to stars and creates unrealistic expectations about single life and luxury.

Checklist: The list of requirements we feel someone must fulfill before we can enter into a committed relationship with them. *See also: Résumé.*

> "He's kind, funny, and loyal, but he's certainly not everything on my *checklist*."

Close the Deal: Having intercourse after hot pursuit.

> "The day after Dean saw his friend Evan leave the bar with a woman, Dean asked him if he had *closed the deal*."

Connection: An instant bond beyond physical attraction that we, as Gen-Xers, strive for but can't always sustain. Can occur along with or separately from the *buzz*.

> "We had this unbelievable *connection*. I knew I had to see her again."

Consumer Sex: Sex that has been taken to a whole new level of casualness for this generation, thereby turning intercourse into yet another mode of currency.

Cult of I: Our self-oriented goals, values, and lifestyles that encourage us to prioritize the satisfaction of our needs and desires over a relationship. Gen-Xers are often hesitant to trade the freedoms of single life—spending what they want, living how and where they want—for the restrictions of relationships that necessitate certain compromises. *See also: The Fallout from the Marriage Delay, The Waiting Game.*

Cyber Courting: When someone uses e-mail, IM, or text messaging in the beginning stages of a relationship to test the romantic waters without committing to a phone call or face-to-face meeting.

Deal Breaker: The quality or behavior that can eliminate someone as a potential romantic or sexual partner.

"Jared didn't go out with her again because she slept with him on the first date, and he considered that a *deal breaker*."

Disposable Love: When love becomes a commodity that Gen-Xers dispose of, usually in pursuit of something newer or better. *See also: Upgrade, Upgrade Mode, Keeping Your Options Open.*

Divorce Effect: The profound impact of divorce (and fear of divorcing) on this entire generation, regardless of what the marital status of one's parents might be.

Double Booking: Scheduling two dates for the same evening. *See also: Express Dating.*

"He kept looking at his watch on our date; it was clear he had *double booked* me."

DTR Talk: The "Defining the Relationship" conversation initiated by one member of a couple to determine the other's level of commitment. These talks can seem as stressful to a couple as the Middle-East Peace Talks.

"Jennifer thought after four months it was time for the *DTR*, since she had no idea if Ted was dating other people."

Express Dating: The Gen-X approach to dating in which singles speed through dates, schedule quick dates, or double book so they can maximize their time and go on dates with several people. *See also: Double Booking.*

Fallout from the Marriage Delay: The negative effects of Gen-Xers' tendency to put off marriage. Fallout includes the ticking biological clock or fear of aging out of the dating market.

First Date Interview: When a man or woman quizzes their date as if conducting a job interview to assess whether that person is prepared for and appropriate for marriage. *See also: MAB Agenda.*

Friends with Benefits (Fuck Buddies): Common Gen-X terms for hooking up with a friend.

> "Sarah was feeling lonely so she called her *fuck buddy*. It was good while it lasted, but she regretted it in the morning."

Grass Is Greener Affair: Infidelity caused by a need to see what else is out there, often occurring in relatively happy marriages.

Hedging Our Bets: Entering into a marriage or a commitment thinking that you can always get out of it. Some Gen-Xers go a step further by creating actual safety nets such as keeping a separate apartment "just in case." *See also: Marriage Lite.*

Hookup: Refers to the gamut of physical intimacy from kissing to sex and is part of every Gen-Xer's vernacular. As singles of this generation know, hookups can refer to casual one-night encounters, ongoing physical trysts, or they may precede or punctuate a date. Sometimes they can even turn into a relationship. *See also: Booty Call.*

> "Tina went out that night, dressed up in a sexy outfit, looking for a *hookup*."

Inadvertent Effects of Feminism: The unintended consequences of feminism, such as confused expectations for courtship and gender roles that can wreak havoc on our relationships. An example is when a man or woman in a relationship expects a partner to play both a traditional role and a more egalitarian role at the same time.

Keeping Your Options Open: Never committing to one person because you always think someone better is going to come along. *See also: Upgrade, Upgrade Mode, Disposable Love.*

MAB Agenda: The "Marriage And Baby" agenda, is when someone is dating with the specific intention of getting married quickly and starting a family. This term is often used to describe women with a ticking biological clock. *See also: The First Date Interview.*

> "Even though James says he wants to get married, nothing turns him off more than a woman with the *MAB agenda.*"

Marriage Heavy: A full commitment to marriage that includes compromise, tolerance, forgiveness, and also risk. Many Gen-Xers avoid this kind of deeply committed intimacy to minimize the loss of independence. *See also: Marriage Lite.*

Marriage Is Obsolete Subculture: Gen-Xers who don't believe in the formal commitment of marriage.

Marriage Lite: The Gen-X version of commitment—intimacy without risk and without traps. The common Marriage Lite strategies among Gen-Xers include: *The Waiting Game, Virtual Marriage, Hedging Our Bets, Policy of Disengagement, The Starter Marriage,* and *"The Grass Is Greener" Affair.*

Marriage Sabbatical: Taking a break from marriage, usually undertaken by members of the unhooked generation who are married but not fully committed. This can refer to something as dramatic as a temporary physical separation or an understanding between two people to have an open marriage. The term was first coined by Cheryl Jarvis, author of *The Marriage Sabbatical,* for women who took time away from their families to follow their personal and professional dreams. *See also: Marriage Lite.*

Multiple Choice Culture: Refers to the dizzying choices provided by current consumer culture, multiplied by technology that convinces us that more choice is always better, even in our romantic relationships. An example is when singles have difficulty committing to one person because they think there may always be a better choice out there.

Pessimism Paradox: The common Gen-X sentiment about lifelong commitment: we want it but we have doubts about whether marriage can ever supply it.

Phase One: The more noncommittal phase of life for Gen-Xers that revolves around self-oriented pursuits such as work and sex and focuses on living in the present. *See also: Play Mode.*

Phase Two: The more committal phase of life that focuses on building a future with a partner. If two people are in different "phases," it can keep them from becoming a couple.

Play Mode: The Gen-X state of having fun in the form of casual dating and casual sex: in other words, not ready for commitment. *See also: Phase One.*

> "Stacy wasn't ready for a steady boyfriend—she was still in *play mode.*"

Policy of Disengagement: When engagement doesn't necessarily mean a full commitment by both halves of the couple and can result in a broken engagement.

Readiness Factor: An individual's level of preparedness to commit. *See also: Phase One, Phase Two, Play Mode.*

Recycling: Having sex with an ex because either you still have feelings or physical attraction or because you want sex and it is easy, safe, and comfortable.

> "Even though she hadn't had sex in a while she vowed not to *recycle,* because that only leads to trouble."

Résumé: Items on the checklist that are practical, such as having a good job or coming from a nice family, but have nothing to do with chemistry or attraction. *See also: Checklist.*

"She is the kind of girl you marry. She had the *résumé,* but we didn't have that spark."

Settling: A Gen-Xer's worst nightmare: ending up with a partner who is lacking something on his or her checklist. *See also: Keeping Your Options Open, The Total Package.*

"I am not going to *settle;* I'd rather be alone."

Seven Evil Influences: The cultural influences unique to Generation X that converge, undermine relationships, and can keep us unhooked. They are: *The Cult of I, Multiple Choice Culture, The Divorce Effect, The Inadvertent Effects of Feminism, The "Why Suffer?" Mentality, The Celebrity Standard,* and *The Fallout from the Marriage Delay.*

Soul Mate: The ultimate find to Gen-Xers—someone you share a romantic connection with, who is your best friend, and in many cases someone you seemed destined to meet.

"When I find my *soul mate* I will get married."

Starter Marriage: A term coined by Pamela Paul, author of *The Starter Marriage and the Future of Matrimony,* for a marriage that lasts five years or less and does not produce children. Paul cites several reasons for what she calls a "growing trend" among this generation such as longer engagements, the vogue for mega-weddings, and the fear of divorce.

Three Categories of Sex: Refers to the common media depiction of sex as falling into three different types: **Hot sex**—casual sex that often happens outdoors or in public places and is portrayed as the best kind. **Romantic sex**—sex within a relationship that often happens after an elegant meal or in a dreamy venue and is depicted as more sweet than hot. **Married sex**—sex that is almost nonexistent, is depicted as a chore, and is considered the sex at the bottom of the food chain.

Total Package: A combination of good looks, brains, and personality; someone who has everything. *See also: Settling.*

> "I won't settle for anyone who is less than the *total package*."

Unhooked: Unattached, single. Also refers to members of this generation who are in a relationship but aren't fully committed.

Upgrade: The seemingly better partner some consider replacing their current partner with. *See also: Keeping Your Options Open, Disposable Love.*

> "He says he's committed to his girlfriend, but he's always looking for the *upgrade*."

Upgrade Mode: When we actively keep an eye out for a partner who might be "better" than our current partner. *See also: Keeping Your Options Open, Disposable Love.*

Virtual Marriage: Living together as either a substitute for marriage, or as a way to try marriage out without having to fully commit.

Waiting Game: Putting off marriage for as long as possible in order to avoid having to grow up, compromise, or settle.

"Why Suffer?" Mentality: The dangerous belief system enforced by the culture that we should be happy all the time and that our partners should be responsible for making us happy all the time.

Wilma Flintstone Effect: The modern woman's longing for a symbol of a traditional female role. An example would be when a woman, even a feminist, desires a big diamond engagement ring or flowers as proof that she, as a woman, is adored.

NOTES

1 INTRODUCTION: UNHOOKED GENERATION

Pg. 7   U.S. Bureau of the Census, *Current Population Survey,* Series P20-553, "America's Families and Living Arrangements" (Washington, D.C.: US Government Printing Office), March 2003.

All references to this statistic come from: U.S. Bureau of the Census, *Current Population Survey,* Historical Table "America's Families and Living Arrangements" (Washington, D.C.: US Government Printing Office), 2003.

Pg. 10   Shmuley Boteach, *Kosher Sex* (New York: Broadway Books, 1999), p. 148.

Maggie Gallagher, *The Abolition of Marriage: How We Destroy Lasting Love* (Washington D.C.: Regnery Publishing Inc, 1996), p. 87.

2 HOW DID WE GET HERE?

Pg. 16   Barbara Dafoe Whitehead and David Popenoe, "The State of Our Unions 2004," The National Marriage Project, 2004.

Pg. 18   All discussions of marriage in the 1950s come from this book by
            Elaine Tyler May, *Homeward Bound: American Families in the Cold
            War Era* (New York: Basic Books, Inc., 1988), p. 183–186.

Pg. 21   On divorce: Kendall Hamilton and Pat Wingert, "Down the
            Aisle?" *Newsweek,* July 20, 1998.

Pgs. 21–22 E. Mavis Hetherington and John Kelly, *For Better or for Worse:
            Divorce Reconsidered* (New York: W.W. Norton & Company, 2002),
            p. 253.

            Elaine Tyler May, *Homeward Bound,* p. 202, 203. (See note for
            Chapter 2, p. 18)

Pg. 23   Betty Friedan, *The Feminine Mystique,* 5th edition, with a new in-
            troduction by Anna Quindlen (New York: W.W. Norton & Com-
            pany, 2001), p. 62.

Pg. 25   Keith Valone, quoted in Sarah Bernard, "Playing Doctor," *Elle,*
            May 2004, p. 197.

Pg. 26   Marketer quoted in Nina Munk, "Money Trails; My Generation:
            Hope I Shop Before I Get Old," *New York Times,* August 14, 2005.

            Karen Ritchie, *Marketing to Generation X* (New York: Lexington
            Books, 1995), p. 45.

3 OUTRAGEOUS EXPECTATIONS: THE SEARCH FOR "THE CHECKLIST,"
"THE UPGRADE," "THE SOUL MATE"

Pg. 32   Marilyn Graman, *There Is No Prince and Other Truths Your Mother
            Never Told You* (New York: Lifeworks Books, 2003).

Pg. 37   Elaine Tyler May, *Homeward Bound,* p. 29. (See note for Chapter
            2, p. 18)

            Elaine Tyler May, *Homeward Bound,* p. 193–194.

Pg. 38   Elaine Tyler May, *Homeward Bound,* p. 201–203. (See note for
            Chapter 2, p. 18)

            E. Mavis Hetherington and John Kelly, *For Better or for Worse,*
            p. 272–273. (See note for Chapter 2, p. 22)

Pg. 39   Steven Johnson, *Mind Wide Open: Your Brain and the Neuroscience of
            Everyday Life* (New York: Scribner, 2004), p. 152.

Pgs. 39–40 Florence Falk, telephone interview, May 2004.

Pg. 40   Helen Fisher, *Why We Love: The Nature and Chemistry of Romantic
            Love* (New York: Henry Holt, 2004), p. 121.

Pg. 41   U.S. Bureau of the Census, *Current Population Survey,* Historical
            Table "America's Families and Living Arrangements" (Washing-
            ton, D.C.: US Government Printing Office), 2003.

            On education levels: Ellis Close, "The Black Gender Gap,"
            Newsweek, March 3, 2003, p. 46.

Pg. 42   Tucker quoted in Ellis Close, "The Black Gender Gap."
            Belinda Tucker, phone interview, June 2005.

Pg. 52   Barry Schwartz, *The Paradox of Choice: Why More Is Less* (New
            York: HarperCollins, 2004), p. 3.

Pgs. 52–55 Sheena S. Iyengar and Mark Lepper, "When Choice Is Demo-
            tivating: Can One Desire Too Much of a Good Thing?", *Journal of
            Personality and Social Psychology,* 2000, 79, 995–1006.

Pg. 56   On romantic love: Helen Fisher, *Why We Love,* p. 3. (See note for
            Chapter 3, p. 40)

            F. R. P. Akenhurst and Judith M. Davis, ed., *A Handbook of the
            Troubadours* (Berkeley: University of California Press, 1995).

            For a discussion of romantic love see Diane Ackerman, *A Natural
            History of Love* (New York: Vintage Books, 1994).

Pg. 57   Helen Fisher, *Why We Love,* p. 183. (See note for Chapter 3, p. 40)
            Discussion of neuroscientists' findings on p. 24.

Pgs. 58–59 Barbara Dafoe Whitehead and David Popenoe, "The State of
            Our Unions: Who Wants to Marry a Soul Mate?" The National
            Marriage Project, 2001.

Pg. 59   Barbara Dafoe Whitehead and David Popenoe, "The State of Our
            Unions: The Social Health of Marriage in America 2000," The
            National Marriage Project, 2000.

            Plato, *The Symposium: The Dialogues of Plato,* trans. by R. E. Allen,
            The Speech of Aristophanes 189c–193e, Volume 2 (New Haven:
            Yale University Press, 1991), p. 31.

Pg. 61   Maggie Gallagher, "The Soulmate Generation," Townhall.com,
            June 20, 2001.

            Maggie Gallagher, telephone interview, April 2004.

4 CONTRADICTORY NEEDS, CONFLICTING AGENDAS

Pg. 71   David M. Buss, *The Evolution of Desire: Strategies of Human Mat-
            ing,* (New York: Basic Books, 2003 revised edition), p. 46.

5 THE MEDIA: WEDDED DIS

Pg. 80   Nielsen Media Research, 1995–1996 Primetime Television Season.

Pg. 83   Nielsen Media Research, "Selected Series Finales," 2004.

Pg. 86   Associated Press, "U.S. Marriage Is Weakening, Study Reports" *New York Times,* July 4, 1999, section 1, p. 15.

Pg. 88   Nielsen Media Research, 1996–2005 Primetime Television Seasons.

Pg. 96   Robert T. Michael et al., *Sex in America: A Definitive Survey* (Boston: Little Brown, 1995), Table 8, p. 116.

Pg. 98   Schoenborn, CA, "Martial Status and Health United States 1999–2002," No. 351, advance data, December 15, 2004, National Center for Health Statistics.

6 THE COLLAPSE OF COURTSHIP AND THE DEATH OF ROMANCE

Pg. 102   Graham Mudd of comScore Networks, e-mail to the author, June 20, 2005.

Pg. 103   Andrew Cherlin, quoted in Karen S. Peterson, "Wooing the Past: Courtship Flirts with a Comeback," *USA Today,* September 27, 2000, p. 9D.

Pg. 108   Ellen Fein and Sherrie Schneider, *The Rules: Time-Tested Secrets for Capturing the Heart of Mr. Right* (New York: Warner Books, 1995).

Pgs. 108–109   Greg Behrendt and Liz Tuccillo, *He's Just Not That Into You: The No-Excuses Truth to Understanding Guys* (New York: Simon Spotlight Entertainment, 2004).

Pg. 112   Edward Hallowell, "Why Smart People Underperform" *Harvard Business Review,* January 2005, p. 55.

Pg. 116   Barbara Dafoe Whitehead, *Why There Are No Good Men Left: The Romantic Plight of the New Single Woman* (New York: Broadway Books, 2003), p. 107.

Pg. 121   Barbara DaFoe Whitehead, *Why There Are No Good Men Left,* p. 129. (See note for this chapter, p. 116)

Pg. 127   Norval Glenn and Elizabeth Marquardt, "Hooking Up, Hanging Out, and Hoping for Mr. Right: College Women on Dating and Mating Today," The Institute for American Values, 2001.

Pgs. 127–128   Elizabeth Paul, "Hookups'": Characteristics and Correlates of College Students' Spontaneous and Anonymous Sexual Experiences" *The Journal of Sex Research,* February 2000, Volume 37, No. 1, p. 76–88.

Pg. 128   Tom Wolfe, *Hooking Up* (New York: Picador, 2000), p. 7.

Pg. 132   Vanessa Grigoriadis, "The New Position on Casual Sex," *New York Magazine,* January 13, 2003.

Benoit Denizet-Lewis, "Friends, Friends with Benefits of the Local Mall," *New York Times Magazine,* May 30, 2004, p. 30.

Bowling Green State University survey as referenced in Benoit Denizet-Lewis, "Friends, Friends with Benefits of the Local Mall."

Pg. 133   "The Playboy Casual Sex Survey," *Playboy,* August 2003, p. 76.

Pg. 134   Nepal quote as referenced in Helen Fisher, *Why We Love,* p. 86. (See note for Chapter 3, p. 90)

7 GEN-X SEX

Pg. 137   Eli Coleman, phone interview, September 2004.

Pg. 141   David Amsden, "Not Tonight Honey, I'm Logging On," *New York Magazine,* October 20, 2003, p. 30.

Pg. 145   Lynn Harris, "Sexual Aptitude Test," *Glamour,* November 2004, p. 140.

Warren St. John, "In an Oversexed Age, More Guys Take a Pill," *New York Times,* December 14, 2003.

RC Rosen et al., "Evaluation of Safety, pharmacokinectis and pharmacodynamic effects of subcutaneously administered PT-141, a melanocortin receptor agonist, in healthy male subjects and in patients with inadequate response to Viagra," *International Journal of Impotence Research,* Vol. 16, April 1, 2004, p. 135–142.

Pgs. 145–146   Warren St. John, "In an Oversexed Age, More Guys Take a Pill." (See note for this chapter, p. 145)

Pg. 152   "Guy Spy: Male Mind Reading," *Cosmopolitan Magazine,* July 2001, Vol. 231, p. 98.

Pgs. 154–155   Erica Jong, *Fear of Flying* (New York: Signet, 1988), p. 11.

Pg. 155   Nancy Friday, *My Secret Garden* (New York: Pocket Books, 1973).
           Robert T. Michael et al., *Sex in America,* p. 146–7, Table 12.

Pg. 159   Wendy Shalit, *A Return to Modesty: Discovering the Lost Virtue* (New
           York: Touchstone, 1999), p. 181.

           Robert S. McElvaine, *Eve's Seed: Biology, the Sexes, and the Course
           of History* (New York: McGraw-Hill, 2001), p. 339.

8 MARRIAGE LITE

Pg. 162   Barbara Dafoe Whitehead and David Popenoe, "The State of Our
           Unions 2001," The National Marriage Project, 2001.

Pg. 163   U.S. Bureau of the Census, "Number, Timing and Duration of
           Marriages and Divorces; 1996, Table 11 (Washington, D.C.: US
           Government Printing Office, Feb. 2002).

           "National Vital Statistics Report," Vol. 54, No. 5, March 2005,
           National Center for Health Statistics.

           Marline Pearson, "Can Kids Get Smart About Marriage?" Na-
           tional Marriage Project, 2000.

           Maggie Gallagher, telephone interview, April 2004.

Pgs. 165–166   John Gottman, *The Seven Principles for Making Marriage Work*
           (New York: Three Rivers Press, 1999), p. 2.

Pg. 170   Barbara Dafoe Whitehead and David Popenoe, "The State of Our
           Unions 2004," The National Marriage Project, 2004.

           Norval Glenn, telephone interview, April, 2004.

Pg. 171   "Married Too Fast, Too Young," *The Dr. Phil Show,* September 3,
           2003.

Pg. 172   Ethan Watters, *Urban Tribes: Are Friends the New Family?* (New
           York: Bloomsbury, 2003).

           Barbara Dafoe Whitehead and David Popenoe, "The State of Our
           Unions 2001," The National Marriage Project, 2001.

Pg. 173   Jennifer Steinhauer, "When the Joneses Wear Jeans," *New York
           Times,* May 29, 2005.

Pg. 174   Vital and Health Statistics, "Cohabitation, Marriage, Divorce and
           Remarriage in the United States," Series 23, No. 22, July, Na-
           tional Center for Health Statistics.

Pg. 175   Barbara Dafoe Whitehead and David Popenoe, "The State of Our Unions 2002," The National Marriage Project, 2002.

Linda J. Waite and Maggie Gallagher, *The Case for Marriage: Why Married People Are Happier, Healthier and Better Off Financially* (New York: Doubleday, 2000), p. 46.

Pgs. 175– 176   Vital and Health Statistics, "Cohabitation, Marriage, Divorce and Remarriage in the United States." (See note for this Chapter, p. 174)

Pgs. 178–179   Paul R. Amato and Stacy Rogers, "Do Attitudes Toward Divorce Affect Marital Quality?", *Journal of Family Issues,* January 1999, Vol. 20, No. 1, p. 69.

Pg. 182   Pamela Paul, "Calling It Off," *Time,* October 2003.

Pg. 183   Rachel Safier, e-mail to the author, October 7, 2005.

Pamela Paul, "Calling It Off." (See note for this Chapter, p. 182)

Pg. 186   On 1950s curricula: Jeffrey P. Moran, *Teaching Sex: The Shaping of Adolescence in the 20th Century* (Cambridge: Harvard University Press, 2000), p. 131-133.

On UK curriculum: BBC World Service, "Children to Get Marriage Lesson," September 9, 1999.

Pg. 187   Pamela Paul, *The Starter Marriage and the Future of Matrimony* (New York: Random House, 2003), p. xv.

Walter Kirn and Wendy Cole, "Twice as Nice," *Time,* June 19, 2000, p. 53.

ABC News.com, "Starter Marriages," January 24, 2003.

Pg. 188   Barbara Graham, "The Future of Love: Kiss Romance Good-bye— It's Time for the Real Thing," *Utne Reader,* November 1, 1996.

Judith Wallerstein, Julia Lewis, and Sandra Blakeslee *The Unexpected Legacy of Divorce: A 25 Year Landmark Study* (New York: Hyperion, 2000), p. 295.

Pg. 189   Alfred C. Kinsey, *Sexual Behavior in the Human Female* (Philadelphia: W.B. Saunders Co., 1948, p. 585.

Alfred C. Kinsey, *Sexual Behavior in the Human Male* (Philadelphia: W.B. Saunders Co., 1953), p. 416.

Cynthia and Samuel Janus, *The Janus Report on Sexual Behavior* (New York: Wiley, 1993), p. 196.

Edward O. Laumann et al., *The Social Organization of Sexuality: Sexual Practices in the United States* (Chicago: The University of Chicago Press, 1994), p. 210 Table 5.10.

Pgs. 189–190　Tom W. Smith, "American Sexual Behavior: Trends, Socio-Demographic Differences, and Risk Behavior," General Social Survey of the National Opinion Research Center, April 2003, GSS Topical Report No. 25.

Pg. 190　Tom W. Smith quoted in Lorraine Ali and Lisa Miller, "The Secret Lives of Wives," *Newsweek,* July 12, 2003, p. 47.

Lorraine Ali and Lisa Miller, "The Secret Lives of Wives," p. 47.

Pgs. 190–191　Shirley P. Glass, PhD with Jean Coppock Staeheli, *Not "Just-Friends": Rebuilding Trust and Recovering Your Sanity After Infidelity* (New York: Free Press, 2003), p. 220–221.

Pg. 192　Shirley P. Glass, PhD with Jean Coppock Staeheli, *Not "Just Friends,"* p. 221. (See note for this chapter, p. 190–191)

Pgs. 198–199　Cheryl Jarvis, *The Marriage Sabbatical* (New York: Broadway Books, 2002).

Pg. 201　All wedding data comes from: Cathy Hornblower of the Fairchild Bridal Group, phone interview, October 2005.

Pg. 202　"New Mom Gwyneth's First Interview & Jude Law," *The Oprah Winfrey Show,* August 26, 2004.

Pgs. 202–203　Sheryl Nissinen, e-mail to the author, June 2005.

9　FINDING TRUE LOVE

Pg. 225　Martin Buber Homepage, www.buber.de

Pg. 241　John Gottman, *The Seven Principles for Making Marriage Work,* p. 20. (See note for Chapter 8, p. 165–166)

Shmuley Boteach, *Kosher Sex,* p. 41. (See note for Chapter 1, p. 10)

Shmuley Boteach, *Kosher Sex,* p. 184.

Pg. 243　Shmuley Boteach, *Kosher Sex,* p. 148–149. (See note for Chapter 1, p. 10)

Pg. 244　Reverend William Brettmann, Fifth Avenue Presbyterian Church, November 13, 2004.

ACKNOWLEDGMENTS

I owe this book first and foremost to the support of my parents. Their belief in me has led me to this project and to every important endeavor in my life. They are wonderfully inspiring role models of enduring passion and commitment.

Brian Sampson, this book belongs to you on many levels; your input, encouragement, and commitment to the book and to me have shaped these pages and my life in ways I can't even express. Thank you.

My deepest gratitude to Naomi Wolf, a wonderful mentor and loyal friend. Without your support this would not have been possible. My life is truly enriched by your presence.

I am especially grateful for the personal influence and inspiration of Oprah Winfrey, with whom I was privileged to spend the majority of my professional career. My experience at *The Oprah Winfrey Show* not only gave me the skills to execute this book but the conviction to make my own mark on the world. In many ways Oprah helped pave the way for this journey.

I would like to thank my friends Rachel Hanfling, Jill Leiderman, Tera Small Muellerleile, Eve Roth, and Sibby Ross Thomsen, who shared this relationship angst and without whom I would not have been moved to write such a book. They provided stories and subjects, and housed me during the interviewing process. I am particularly grateful to my friend, marketing extraordinaire Suzanne Saltzman Ginestro, who provided invaluable contributions on the design and marketing front and read every word. Thanks to Jill Barancik, who provided endless enthusiasm, support, and insights on this project. I am indebted to my childhood friend, Tamara Miller, who has been my rock and my cousin, Debbie Dreyfuss, who supported me and this book in every way she could. Above all I am grateful for the friendship and support of all these women.

My deep appreciation for my agents, John Brockman and Katinka Matson, who believed in this book from the very beginning. Their thoughtful insights and those of Russell Weinberger are much appreciated. I feel blessed to have them all in my corner.

I am especially grateful to my editor, Peternelle van Arsdale, for her enthusiasm and her invaluable editorial contributions at every single stage. Her insights and encouragement raised the bar over and over again. Thanks to Kiera Hepford for pursuing permissions and for tending to the details. Thanks to Beth Dickey, who took such a personal interest in this topic and made sure that it could reach the widest possible audience and to Katie Wainwright, who relentlessly pitched the book to producers and editors. I am grateful to Bob Miller, Ellen Archer, and Will Schwalbe for believing in this book and for welcoming my input at every stage of production.

My appreciation to Kristen Kemp, my coffeeshop writing companion, who sustained me on a daily basis through this process and offered astute editorial guidance. I am grateful for my friend and media guru, Lisa Cohen, who prepared me to speak as articulately as possible on behalf of the book. Thanks also to the Woodhull Institute and its community for their vision and their heartfelt support.

Above all, I am grateful to the men and women who agreed to narrate their experiences to me. I thank them for their time, their candor, and their trust. I hope they gain as much from these pages as I did from talking with them.

Finally, I am indebted to all women writers who came before me, who bravely paved the way.